OBJECTIVE

IELTS

Michael Black
Wendy Sharp

Self-study Student's Book

Intermediate

CAMBRIDGE
UNIVERSITY PRESS

CAMBRIDGE UNIVERSITY PRESS
Cambridge, New York, Melbourne, Madrid, Cape Town, Singapore, São Paulo

Cambridge University Press
The Edinburgh Building, Cambridge CB2 2RU, UK

www.cambridge.org
Information on this title: www.cambridge.org/9780521608855

First published 2006

Printed in Italy by Eurografica (part of the LEGO group)

A catalogue record for this publication is available from the British Library

ISBN-13 978-0-521-60885-5 Self-study Student's Book
ISBN-10 0-521-60885-6 Self-study Student's Book

ISBN-13 978-0-521-60882-4 Student's Book
ISBN-10 0-521-60882-1 Student's Book

ISBN-13 978-0-521-60873-2 Workbook
ISBN-10 0-521-60873-2 Workbook

ISBN-13 978-0-521-60874-9 Workbook with Answers
ISBN-10 0-521-60874-0 Workbook with Answers

ISBN-13 978-0-521-60872-5 Teacher's Book
ISBN-10 0-521-60872-4 Teacher's Book

ISBN-13 978-0-521-60881-7 Cassette Set
ISBN-10 0-521-60881-3 Cassette Set

ISBN-13 978-0-521-60880-0 Audio CD Set
ISBN-10 0-521-60880-5 Audio CD Set

Designed and produced by Kamae Design, Oxford

Map of Objective IELTS Intermediate Student's Book

TOPIC		TEST SKILL **AC** = Academic **GT** = General Training	TASK TYPE	LANGUAGE FOCUS **V** = Vocabulary, **G** = Grammar, **P** = Pronunciation
Unit 1 **Communicate!** 8–11 Communication	1.1	**Reading** (AC / GT) **Speaking**	True / False / Not given Short-answer questions Part 1	**V** Paraphrase **V** Ways of communicating
	1.2	**Writing extra** (AC / GT) **Listening**	Spelling errors Note completion	**G** The passive **P** Spelling and numbers
Test folder 1 12–13		Reading	**Yes / No / Not given**	
Unit 2 **A healthy diet** 14–17 Food and drink	2.1	**Listening** **Speaking**	Note completion Part 1	**P** Weak and strong forms **V** Adjectives describing food
	2.2	**Writing extra** (AC / GT) **Speaking**	Using appropriate language Part 3	**G** Comparing things or talking about similarities and differences **G** Adverbs of degree
Writing folder 1 18–19		Academic Writing Task 1	**Describing processes**	
Unit 3 **City attractions** 20–23 Leisure in the city	3.1	**Speaking** **Reading** (GT)	Part 1 Multiple matching	**G** Cause, purpose and result
	3.2	**Listening**	Note completion	**V** Descriptive adjectives **V** Adjectives ending in *-ing* and *-ed* **P** Word stress in related words
Test folder 2 24–25		Listening Reading	**Matching**	
Unit 4 **Ways of learning** 26–29 Education	4.1	**Speaking** **Listening** **Reading** (GT)	Part 3 Multiple choice Multiple choice with multiple answers Reading effectively	**V** Words used in academic writing
	4.2			**G** Review of present tenses **P** Word stress
Writing folder 2 30–31		Academic Writing Task 1	**Handling data 1 – line graphs**	
Revision Units 1–4 32–33				
Unit 5 **Discovering the past** 34–37 History	5.1	**Reading** (AC / GT) **Speaking**	True / False / Not given Multiple choice Note completion Part 3	**V** Types of building **V** Collocations related to research
	5.2	**Listening** **Writing extra** (AC)	Labelling Task 1: A description of a place	**G** Review of past tenses
Test folder 3 38–39		Listening Reading	**Sentence and note completion**	
Unit 6 **What is job satisfaction?** 40–43 Work	6.1	**Listening**	Flow-chart completion Sentence completion Labelling a diagram Table completion Multiple choice	**V** Work **V** Collocations with *money*
	6.2	**Writing extra** (GT) **Speaking**	Task 1: Letter of application Part 2	**G** Past simple or present perfect?
Writing folder 3 44–45		Academic and General Training Writing Task 2	**Understanding the question and planning your writing**	

TOPIC		TEST SKILL AC = Academic GT = General Training	TASK TYPE	LANGUAGE FOCUS V = Vocabulary, G = Grammar, P = Pronunciation
Unit 7 Selling dreams? 46–49 Advertising	7.1	Speaking Reading (AC / GT)	Parts 1 and 3 Multiple choice Headings	V Word formation
	7.2	Listening	Sentence completion Matching	P Sentence stress G Relative clauses V Advertising
Test folder 4 50–51		Reading	Headings	
Unit 8 Time to waste? 52–55 Leisure activities	8.1	Reading (GT) Speaking	Table completion Part 1	G Talking about the future
	8.2	Listening Speaking	Short-answer questions (lists) Short-answer questions Part 3	P Vowel length V Leisure activities
Writing folder 4 56–57		General Training Task 1	Writing a letter	
Revision Units 5–8 58–59				
Unit 9 Climate change 60–63 The environment	9.1 9.2	Reading (AC) Speaking Listening Writing extra (AC)	Summary completion Part 3 Note and table completion Task 1: A diagram	G Countable and uncountable nouns V Collocations related to the environment
Test folder 5 64–65		Reading Listening	Summary completion	
Unit 10 A place to work or live in 66–69 Buildings	10.1 10.2	Speaking Listening Writing extra (GT) Speaking	Part 1 Note completion Task 1: A letter of complaint Part 2	P Polite intonation V Phrasal verbs and collocations with *house* and *home* G *-ing* forms and infinitives 1
Writing folder 5 70–71		Academic Writing Task 1	Handling data 2 – bar and pie charts and tables	
Unit 11 Animal life 72–75 Animals	11.1 11.2	Reading (AC) Listening	Multiple choice Multiple choice with multiple answers Sentence completion	V Definitions relating to social organisation G Articles V Compound nouns P Diphthongs
Test folder 6 76–77		Listening Reading	Multiple choice with multiple answers Multiple choice	
Unit 12 Sport: just for fun? 78–81 Sport	12.1 12.2	Speaking Listening Speaking Reading (AC / GT)	Part 1 Table completion Part 3 Matching	V Sport V Word formation G *Should, had better, ought to*
Writing folder 6 82–83		Academic and General Training Task 2	Connecting ideas 1	
Revision Units 9–12 84–85				
Unit 13 Choices 86–89 Making decisions	13.1 13.2 	Reading (AC) Listening Speaking	Locating information Multiple choice Multiple choice Note completion Part 3	V Collocations with adverbs G Conditionals
Test folder 7 90–91		Reading	Locating information	
Unit 14 The importance of colour 92–95 Colour	14.1 14.2	Listening Writing extra (AC) Speaking Listening	Matching Listening for specific information Task 1: Describing changes Part 3 Short-answer questions	V Words and phrases related to change P Linking words V Colours V Adjectives describing personality G *-ing* forms and infinitives 2 V Confused words V Comment adverbs
Writing folder 7 96–97		Academic and General Training Task 2	Making a general statement, giving examples and using comment adverbs	

MAP OF OBJECTIVE IELTS INTERMEDIATE STUDENT'S BOOK 5

Content of the IELTS Test

Each candidate takes four IELTS test modules, one in each of the four skills, Listening, Reading, Writing and Speaking. All candidates take the same Listening and Speaking Modules. There is a choice between Academic and General Training in the Reading and Writing Modules.

Listening 40 questions approximately 30 minutes

There are four sections to this part of the test and they are always in the same order. Each section is heard **ONCE** only. During the test, time is given for you to read the questions and write down and check your answers. Ten minutes is allowed at the end of the test for you to transfer your answers from the question paper to an answer sheet.

Section	Format	Task types	Objective Test folder
1 and 2	The first two sections are concerned with social needs. There is a conversation between two speakers, followed by a monologue.	Questions are chosen from the following types: • multiple choice • short-answer questions • sentence completion	TF 6 TF 3
3 and 4	Sections 3 and 4 are concerned with situations related to educational or training contexts. There is a conversation between up to four people and then a further monologue.	• note completion • summary completion • labelling a diagram • table/flow-chart completion • classification • matching	TF 3 TF 5 TF 10 TF 8 TF 2

Reading 40 questions 60 minutes

There are three reading passages in the Reading Module with a total of 2,000 to 2,750 words (Academic) or 2,000 to 2,500 words (General Training). All answers must be entered on an answer sheet during the test. No extra time is allowed to transfer answers.

Academic	General Training	Task types	Objective Test folder
Texts are taken from magazines, journals, books and newspapers, which have been written for a non-specialist audience. They deal with issues which are interesting and accessible to candidates entering undergraduate or postgraduate courses or seeking professional registration. At least one text contains detailed logical argument. One text may contain non-verbal materials such as diagrams, graphs or illustrations.	Tests are taken from notices, advertisements, official documents, booklets, newspapers, instruction manuals, leaflets, timetables, books and magazines. The first section, 'social survival', contains texts relevant to basic linguistic survival in English. The second section, 'training survival', focuses on the training context – either training itself or welfare needs. This section involves a text or texts of more complex language. The third section 'general reading', involves reading longer, more complex texts.	Questions are chosen from the following types: • multiple choice • short-answer questions • sentence completion • note completion • summary completion • labelling a diagram • table/flow-chart completion • headings • Yes/No/Not given • True/False/Not given • locating information • classification • matching	TF 6 TF 3 TF 3 TF 5 TF 10 TF 4 TF 1 TF 1 TF 7 TF 8 TF 2

Writing 2 tasks 60 minutes

Task	Academic	General Training	Objective Writing folder
Task 1 allow about 20 minutes for this	Describing graphic data / a diagram You will be assessed on your ability to: • organise, present and compare data • describe a process • describe an object, event or sequence of events • explain how something works You must write at least 150 words.	Writing a letter You will be assessed on your ability to: • write a personal or formal letter • ask for and provide factual information • express needs, wants, likes and dislikes • express opinions, complaints You must write at least 150 words.	**Academic** WF 1 WF 2 WF 5 WF 10 **General Training** WF 4 WF 10
Task 2 allow about 40 minutes for this	Writing an essay You will be assessed on your ability to: • present the solution to a problem • present and justify an opinion • compare and contrast evidence • evaluate and challenge ideas You must write at least 250 words.	Writing an essay You will be assessed on your ability to: • provide general factual information • outline a problem and present a solution • present, evaluate and challenge ideas You must write at least 250 words.	**Academic and General Training** WF 3 WF 6 WF 7 WF 8 WF 9 WF 10

Speaking approximately 11–14 minutes

The Speaking Module consists of an oral interview between you and an examiner.

Part	Format	Timing	Objective Test folder
Part 1 Introduction and interview	The examiner introduces him/herself and asks questions about familiar topics, for example, your home, family, job and interests.	4–5 minutes	TF9
Part 2 Individual long turn	The examiner gives you a card, which contains a topic and some prompts, and asks you to speak for 1–2 minutes on the topic. The examiner asks one or two questions to round off the long turn.	3–4 minutes (including 1 minute preparation time)	TF9
Part 3 Two-way discussion	The examiner invites you to take part in a discussion of a more abstract nature, based on questions thematically linked to the Part 2 topic.	4–5 minutes	TF9

Communicate!

1 **The pictures show different methods of communication. With a partner:**

- put them in order of how often you use them
- say what you last used them for.

EXAMPLE: *I use text messaging most. I last sent a text message to tell my friend where to meet me.*

Reading

Test spot

There is a lot to read in both the General Training and Academic Reading Modules (between 2,000 and 2,750 words) and you only have one hour, so you may need to improve your reading speed. By the end of this course, you should be able to read up to 300 words per minute. Time yourself and use the approximate word count given with this symbol ⏱ to work out your reading speed, dividing the number of words by the time taken. Keep a record, so you can see what progress you are making.

2 **Read the text opposite as quickly as you can and say where you would find this text. This type of reading is called 'skimming'. We skim a text in order to get a general idea of what it is about. Don't worry too much about words you don't know.**

⏱ about 500 words

3 **Read the text again to find the following information. This is called 'scanning'. We 'scan' a text to search for specific information.**

1 the year schoolchildren started learning Silbo Gomero
2 the countries Gomerans went to live in
3 where Silbo Gomero came from originally

Whistling in La Gomera

An ancient language of whistles that enabled long-distance communication long before the invention of the mobile phone will be saved from extinction on a volcanic island off the west coast of Africa. The island is part of the Canary
5 Islands and is called La Gomera. The language, Silbo Gomero, which sounds like birdsong, was used by the people on the island to communicate up to three kilometres across the deep valleys that radiate from La Gomera's central volcanic peak.

With the opening of the island to tourism and the arrival
10 of the telephone, Silbo Gomero had started to die out. Luckily, the island authorities realised what they were losing before it was too late and, since 1999, Silbo Gomero has been part of the school curriculum for children up to the age of 14. About 3,000 students spend 25 minutes a week
15 learning it, which is enough to understand the basics. The name, Silbo Gomero, comes from the Spanish verb 'silbar' meaning to whistle and 'Gomero' meaning 'coming from the island of La Gomera'.

The language is made up of four vowels and four
20 consonants, which can be whistled to make more than 4,000 words. In the past, children learnt it from their parents but as fewer and fewer adults were teaching their children, it became necessary for the government to take over. According to Eugenio Darias, a teacher of Silbo Gomero
25 and director of the island's Silbo programme, 'There are few really good silbadores, fluent whistlers of the language, so far, but lots of students are learning to use it and understand it. We've been very pleased with the results.'

An important step towards saving the language was the First International Congress of Whistled Languages, which was held in La Gomera in 2003. Silbo-like whistling has been found in parts of Greece, Turkey, China and Mexico, but none is as developed as Silbo Gomero. Research will now be carried out in Venezuela, Cuba and Texas – all places to which Gomerans have traditionally emigrated and where traces of the language still survive.

Dr Francisco Rivero is a researcher at La Laguna University in Santa Cruz de Tenerife. 'Historically, from the earliest settlers up until quite recently, the Silbo Gomero language was the mobile phone of the period. It allowed people to communicate across great distances because its frequency allowed the sound to be transmitted.' Although Silbo probably originated in the Atlas Mountains of North Africa 2,500 years ago, it was adapted to La Gomera by adopting Spanish speech patterns. 'It relies on vowels rather than consonants,' explains Dr Rivero. 'These are whistled at different frequencies, using Spanish grammar. If we spoke English, we'd use an English structure for whistling. It's not just disjointed words – it flows, and you can quite easily have a proper conversation with someone.'

'Silbo Gomero is the most important pre-Hispanic cultural heritage we have. It is unique and has many values – historical, linguistic, anthropological and aesthetic,' says Moises Plasencia, Director of the Canary Islands' Historical Heritage department. Señor Plasencia has begun working to persuade UNESCO to support La Gomera's efforts to save the island's language.

Test spot

True / False / Not given tasks test understanding of factual information, and the questions are always in the order in which the answers occur in the reading passage. It's a good idea to underline the part of the text where you find the answer. This will help you to see if an answer is *Not given*. ⋯⟩ **TF 1** (This means: Look at Test folder 1 for more information.)

4 Scan the text to do the following task.

Read the article about Silbo Gomero. Do the following statements agree with the information in the reading passage? Write
TRUE   *if the statement agrees with the information*
FALSE   *if the statement contradicts the information*
NOT GIVEN *if there is no information on this*

Example:
0 Silbo Gomero was only used face to face.
Answer: False (The information giving the answer is underlined in the text.)

1 Silbo Gomero began to disappear with the introduction of more modern technology.
2 Schoolchildren in La Gomera enjoy learning Silbo Gomero.
3 Schoolchildren on the island have a 25-minute lesson in Silbo Gomero once a day.
4 Eugenio Darias is the best teacher of Silbo Gomero on the island.
5 Having an international conference on the island is believed to be a good thing for the future of Silbo Gomero.
6 It would be impossible to adapt Silbo to English.

5 In the IELTS Test, the questions often do not repeat words from the text, but say the same thing using different words. This is called *paraphrasing*. It is important to be able to recognise and understand paraphrasing.

Find words or phrases in the text which have the same or similar meaning to the words or phrases below. Use an English–English dictionary to check your answers. The relevant paragraph number is given in brackets.

1 the summit or top (1)
2 to begin to disappear (2)
3 the essentials or fundamentals (2)
4 consists of (3)
5 some evidence of (4)
6 immigrants (5)
7 came from (5)
8 was changed to suit different conditions (5)
9 depends on (5)
10 not well connected (5)

Speaking *Part 1*

Test spot

The first part of the Speaking Module takes about four to five minutes. It is the same whether you do the General Training or the Academic Module. You will be asked general questions about yourself, your home and family, your job or studies or your interests. ⋯⟩ **TF 9**

6 With a partner, ask and answer these questions. Make sure you don't just say *Yes* or *No*. Always expand your answer.

  1 Do you have a large or small family?
  2 Who do you talk to most in your family? Why?
  3 What problems do you have when you talk to someone in a second language?

Grammar The passive

1 The passive is very important in academic writing. It is often used in newspaper reports, in formal notices and in technical writing about processes in science and engineering. (See **WF1** for how the passive is used in Academic Writing Task 1.)

   Look at the sentences below. Which do you think is more impersonal and formal?

   a The Congress was held in La Gomera in 2003. (passive)

   b Some people held the Congress in La Gomera in 2003.   (active)

2 The passive is formed by using tenses of *be* + past participle, or modal verb + *be* + past participle. Look at these examples from the reading passage in 1.1.

   (Silbo Gomero) ... **will be saved** from extinction
   future simple passive

   (The island) ... **is called** La Gomera
   present simple passive

   (Silbo Gomero) ... **was used** by the people on the island
   past simple passive

   (Silbo Gomero) ... **can be whistled**
   modal passive

   Silbo-like whistling **has been found** in parts of Greece
   present perfect simple passive

   Underline the other examples of the passive in the reading passage.

   G ⋯⋗ **page 138** (This means: Look in the Grammar folder on page 138 for more information.)

3 The passive is often used when the person responsible for the action (the agent) is either not known or is not important. If we *do* want to mention a person, then we use *by*.

   With a partner, talk about the following inventions, which are all to do with communication.

   EXAMPLE: *I think the telephone was invented in ... by ...*

1	The telephone	1966	Henry Mill
2	The World Wide Web	1951	Chester Carlson
3	The photocopier	1876	Tim Berners-Lee
4	The fax machine	1714	Xerox
5	The typewriter	1994	Alexander Graham Bell

4 Read this article about the history of the mobile phone. Decide if the verbs need to be active or passive and put them in the right form.

Motorola designer Rudy ▶ Krolopp with DynaTAC portable cellular phone prototypes, 1983

The first public telephone call on a portable radiotelephone **1** (make) .... on April 3rd, 1973 by Martin Cooper, one of a team of engineers in Motorola's Communications Systems Division. Previously, people could only phone someone from a building or a car. Martin Cooper says, 'As I **2** (walk) .... down the street talking on the phone, New Yorkers **3** (look) .... amazed at the sight of someone actually moving around while making a phone call.'

The phone that Cooper **4** (use) .... looked like a large brick. In 1983 the 28-ounce 'DynaTAC' phone, the world's first commercial handheld cellular phone, **5** (introduce) .... by Motorola. Each phone **6** (cost) .... the consumer $3,500. Today there **7** (be) .... more mobile subscribers than landline phone subscribers in the world, and mobiles **8** (weigh) .... very little and **9** (can buy) .... for as little as $35.

Mobile phones today **10** (use) .... to send photos and receive e-mails as well as for making phone calls and text messaging. In the future, who knows what else mobile phones **11** (use) .... for? Certainly, most people **12** (not seem) .... able to leave home without one.

5 Complete these sentences using the verb in brackets in the right form of the passive.

   EXAMPLE: My phone (make) .....*was made*..... in the USA.

   1 It (think) .... that more text messages (send) .... by girls than boys.

   2 Bill Gates (say) .... to be the richest man in the world today.

3 One mobile phone (steal) .... every three minutes in the UK.

4 Mobile phones (should / switch off) .... in the cinema.

5 Yesterday, Helen (tell) .... to switch her phone off during lectures.

6 When mobile phones (first design) .... , security was a big issue.

7 Text messaging (often use) .... because it is cheaper than phoning.

8 I (just call) .... by an old friend I haven't seen for ages.

9 Mobiles (carry) .... by virtually everyone in the near future.

10 The photos (take) .... at the party last night using Alex's mobile.

Writing extra

6 The *Cambridge Learner Corpus* shows that the following are common spelling errors made by IELTS candidates. Correct each word.

1 goverment
2 contries
3 becose
4 advertisment
5 acheive
6 wich
7 shoud
8 enviroment
9 thrugh
10 begining

Pronunciation *Spelling and numbers*

7 🎧 You may be asked to write letters or numbers in the IELTS Test. Spell out the names of the people below. Then listen to the recording to check your pronunciation.

1 JOHANNES GUTENBERG (inventor of the Gutenberg printing press)
2 THOMAS EDISON (inventor of the phonograph)
3 VLADIMIR KOSMA ZWORYKIN (inventor, television camera)
4 WILLIAM CAXTON (printer of the first book in English)
5 PHILO T. FARNSWORTH (inventor, television)
6 Q (inventor in James Bond films)

8 🎧 Now listen and write down the numbers you hear – they will be dates, telephone numbers, amounts of money, etc.

9 Work with a partner. You should each write down ten dates or numbers which are important to you. They could be birthdays, house numbers, telephone numbers, etc. Tell your partner why they are important to you.

EXAMPLE: *29th December. This date is important to me because it's my birthday.*

Listening

10 Look at the task below. There are some notes with some information missing. Before you listen, decide, with a partner, what sort of information is missing.

Example: Name of shop:	Answer: Computer Solutions

Printers available to use in: **1** .... and ....

Price range: from **2** £........... to £..........

Name of printer recommended: **3** TRION ....

Shop open: until **4** .... on Saturdays

Address of shop: 15 **5** .... , Hollowridge.

Location of shop: **6** ....

Nearest car park: behind the **7** ....

Method of payment: **8** ....

Ask to see: Jack **9** ....

Location of printers: **10** .... floor

🎧 Now, listen to the conversation between a student and someone who sells computers and complete the notes. Write **NO MORE THAN THREE WORDS AND/OR A NUMBER** for each answer.

Test folder 1

Yes / No / Not given and True / False / Not given

(Academic Reading and General Training Reading Modules only)

You will be given some sentences which relate to the reading passage. The sentences follow the order of the passage.

You must decide whether each sentence agrees with the text or contradicts it, or whether there is not enough information in the passage for you to decide.

Yes / No / Not given is used to test your understanding of the writer's opinions. *True / False / Not given* is used to test your understanding of factual information.

Advice

- Skim the whole passage before you start working on any of the tasks. Then read the instructions, so that you know what you need to do. They are not always phrased in the same way.
- Read the first statement. It may help to underline key words.
- Look through the passage to find the relevant information, and think carefully about what it means. Underline the part of the text that contains the answer. Decide if the statement agrees with or contradicts the passage or is *Not given*. Remember you must base your answer on what is in the passage, not on your own knowledge or what you think is likely to be true. *Not given* means that there isn't enough information in the passage to decide if the statement is *True* or *False* (or *Yes* or *No*).
- Continue with the other statements in turn. If you can't find the relevant part of the passage, it probably means that the statement is *Not given*.
- Always give an answer – you won't lose any marks if it's wrong. If you're not sure, choose *Not given*.

This passage is similar to those in the Academic Reading Module and Section 3 of the General Training Reading Module, but it is only about 600 words. (See *Content of the IELTS Test* on pages 6–7 for the length of reading passages in the Test.)

The Functions of Language

The question 'Why do we use language?' hardly seems to need an answer. But our everyday familiarity with speech and writing can make it difficult to realise how complex the skills are that we have learned. This is particularly so when we try to define the range of functions to which language can be put.

'To communicate our ideas' is the answer that most of us would give to the question – and, indeed, this must surely be the most widely recognized function of language. Whenever we tell people about ourselves or our circumstances, or ask for information about other people and their circumstances, we are using language in order to exchange facts and opinions. It is the kind of language which is found in any spoken or written interaction where people wish to learn from each other. But it would be wrong to think of it as the *only* way in which we use language. There are several other functions where the communication of ideas is irrelevant.

Emotional expression

Mr X carefully leans his walking stick against a wall, but it falls over. He tries again, and it falls a second time. He shouts at the walking stick. How should we classify this function of language? It cannot be 'communication of ideas', for there is no one else in the room.

Here we have one of the commonest uses of language – a means of getting rid of our nervous energy when we are under stress. This type of language can be used whether or not we are alone. Swear words are probably the commonest signals to be used in this way, especially when we are angry. But there are also many words that we use to express positive feelings, such as affection, or a reaction to beautiful art or scenery.

The most common linguistic expressions of emotion consist of conventional words or phrases (such as 'Gosh', 'My') and the semi-linguistic noises often called interjections (such as 'Wow' and 'Ouch').

Social interaction

Mrs P sneezes violently. Mrs Q says, 'Bless you!' Mrs P says, 'Thank you.' Again, this hardly seems to be a case of language being used to communicate ideas, but rather to maintain a comfortable relationship between people. No factual content is involved. Similarly, the use of such phrases as 'Good morning' or 'Pleased to meet you', and conventional exchanges about health or the weather, do not 'communicate ideas' in the usual sense.

Phrases of this type often state the obvious (e.g. 'It's a lovely day') or have no content at all (e.g. 'Hello'). They are used to maintain a friendly relationship between people, arising out of the basic human need to signal such an attitude. If someone does not say these sentences when they are expected to, their absence may be interpreted as a sign of distance or even danger.

These illustrations apply to English and to many European languages. But cultures vary greatly in the topics which they permit in this type of social interaction. The weather is not as universal a conversation-filler as English people might like to think! Other topics are used to serve the same purpose, and some cultures avoid this type of language and prefer silence.

The power of sound

In many situations the only apparent reason for a use of language is the enjoyment that the users or listeners gain from the sounds, and this applies to all age groups. Many children's rhymes are of this type, as are the lyrics of popular songs, and the voices of individuals singing in the kitchen or the bath.

Do the following statements reflect the claims of the writer in the reading passage?
Write
YES if the statement reflects the claims of the writer
NO if the statement contradicts the claims of the writer
NOT GIVEN if it is impossible to say what the writer thinks about this

Example: Answer:
Using a language involves complicated skills.   YES
(But our everyday familiarity with speech and writing can make it difficult to realise how complex the skills are that we have learned)

1   Most people are aware that a major function of language is to communicate ideas.
2   We communicate ideas every time we use language.
3   The communication of ideas involves at least two people.
4   We are becoming more aware of how language is used for emotional expression.
5   Interjections are similar in all languages.
6   Phrases like *Good morning* can be used to express a range of feelings.
7   The weather is used as a standard topic of social communication in all languages.
8   Some types of sounds can give pleasure to both adults and children.

A healthy diet

1 Compare the two diets below.

- What are the staple foods of each diet?
- What differences and similarities are there between the two diets?
- Are there some foods which are better for you than others?
- Which foods contain mainly
  a carbohydrate? b protein? c fat?

THE TRADITIONAL HEALTHY ASIAN DIET PYRAMID

THE TRADITIONAL HEALTHY LATIN AMERICAN DIET PYRAMID

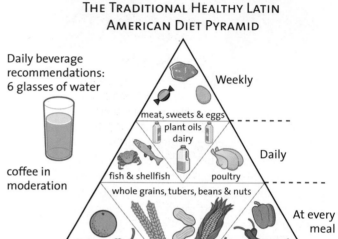

Listening

Test spot

In Part 2 of the Listening Module you will hear one person talking about something of general interest. There is usually more than one type of question. You will often need to listen for specific information – that is dates, times, names, important words.

Always read through the questions very carefully before you listen, to get an idea of what you are listening for.

You will hear a lot of information, but you don't need to understand it all. You should always look ahead to the next question so that you don't miss hearing the answer to a question.

Write the exact words that you hear, but don't write more than the maximum number of words. You will only hear each section once in the IELTS Test. ⋯▸ TF 3

2 You are going to listen to someone talking about two websites. Look at the questions below and, with a partner, decide what type of information you are going to listen for.

Websites about Food	
The History of Rice	
Rice first grown:	**1** .... years ago
Amount of rice produced every year:	**2** over .... tonnes
Number of calories in one serving of rice:	**3** .... calories
Three things you can make from rice:	drinks, glue and
	4 ....
Yokohama Noodle Museum	
Date museum opened: **5**	
Day museum closed: **6**	
Souvenir shop: on **7** .... floor	
old **8** .... shown on TV	
Number of noodle shops in the theme park: **9**	
Journey time by train from Tokyo: **10**	

🎧 Listen to the recording and complete the notes. Write **NO MORE THAN TWO WORDS AND/OR A NUMBER** for each answer.

Pronunciation *Weak and strong forms*

Short words like *a*, *and*, *some*, *to*, *at*, etc., are usually not stressed in spoken English.

MENU

Starters
Soup of the day
Melon

Main courses
Steak
Salmon
Chicken
(served with chips and salad
or vegetables)

Desserts
Raspberries and cream
Ice cream (chocolate,
vanilla, or strawberry)
Cheese and biscuits

Drinks
Tea
Coffee
Soft drinks
Mineral water

3 🎧 **Listen to the conversation. What types of words are stressed?**

Man: I'll have soup to start with, please.
Waiter: And for the main course?
Man: Steak, please.
Waiter: With chips and salad or with vegetables?
Man: I'll have some vegetables, please.
Waiter: And to drink?
Man: Just a glass of water.
Waiter: OK, right away, sir.

Waiter: Would you like a dessert?
Man: Yes, some raspberries and cream, please. And a cup of coffee.

Now, with a partner, order a meal from the menu.

4 🎧 **Sometimes we stress the short words. Listen to this example:**

*I ordered raspberries and cream **and** ice cream.*

Look at the conversations below. Are the underlined words weak (W) or strong (S)? Write W or S and then listen to the recording to check your answers.

1 A: <u>Do</u> you like chocolate?
   B: Yes, I <u>do</u>.
2 A: Where's <u>the</u> waiter?
   B: <u>That's</u> him, by the bar.
3 A: What <u>do you</u> want with the raspberries, cream or ice cream?
   B: I'd like cream <u>and</u> ice cream – they're lovely together!
4 A: I'm eating <u>at the</u> Savoy Hotel tonight.
   B: Not <u>the</u> Savoy Hotel in London?

Vocabulary Adjectives describing food

5 **Match the food to the appropriate adjective.**

1 meat which is beginning to smell	ripe
2 a hot curry	rotten
3 a perfect apple	fresh
4 yesterday's milk	spicy
5 three-day-old bread	bland
6 unsalted food	burnt
7 black toast	sour
8 newly laid eggs	stale

Speaking *Part 1*

6 **Answer the questions with a partner.**

1 What kinds of food do you like best?
2 Are there any things that you dislike?
3 What is your idea of a perfect meal?
4 What do you eat on special occasions?
5 How well do you cook?

Useful language

Likes, dislikes, preferences
I *love* bananas.
I really like ice cream.
My favourite is …
I'm not keen on (eating) green vegetables.
I can't *stand/bear* (eating) meat.
I hate tomatoes.

I prefer rice to potatoes.
I'd rather drink tea than coffee.
I think chocolate is nicer than anything else.
I'm good at …
I can only cook …
My speciality (= the thing I'm best at cooking) is …

Grammar

Comparing things or talking about similarities and differences

1 In both the Speaking and Writing Modules of the IELTS Test you are often asked to compare and contrast. Look at the table of comparative and superlative adjectives and complete the rules below.

adjective	comparative	superlative
quick	quicker	(the) quickest
happy	happier	(the) happiest
modern	more modern	(the) most modern
expensive	more expensive	(the) most expensive

EXAMPLE: *A dish of noodles is one of **the quickest meals** you can make – it's much **quicker than** making a rice dish, for example.*

To form the comparative
- with one-syllable words, we add **1** ....
- with two-syllable words ending in *-y*, we change the *-y* to **2** .... and add **3** ....
- with most other two-syllable words and words with three or more syllables, we add the word **4** ....

To form the superlative
- with one-syllable words, we add **5** ....
- with two-syllable words ending in *-y*, we change the *-y* to **6** .... and add **7** ....
- with most other two-syllable words and words with three or more syllables, we add the word(s) **8** ....

Negative comparatives and superlatives

EXAMPLES: *Interestingly, although rice **isn't as rich** in Vitamin C **as** the potato, it is **less fattening than** the potato.*

*The museum is open every day except for Tuesday, with Sunday being the busiest day and Thursday being **the least busy**.*

To make negative comparisons we use *not as* + adjective + **9** .... or *less* + adjective + **10** ....
To make negative superlative statements we use **11** ....

G ⋯⟩ page 138

2 Complete the sentences using the comparative or superlative form of the word in brackets.

EXAMPLE: My mother is a (good) .....*better*..... cook than my father.

1 This is (good) .... hamburger I've ever eaten!
2 The old chef was (bad) .... than the new one.
3 This restaurant is (expensive) .... in London. It costs a fortune.
4 This is one of the (easy) .... recipes I know – a child could make it.
5 These apples are (sweet) .... than those.
6 José's mother always finds (cheap) .... vegetables in the market than in the supermarket.
7 People say small vegetables are (nice) .... than large ones.
8 I think salad is (healthy) .... than chips.
9 Chips are (not expensive) .... as caviar.
10 Our college canteen is (expensive) .... place to eat in town – three courses for only £5!

Using adverbs of degree

To talk about similarities and differences more precisely we can use the following adverbs of degree in front of comparative structures. We can also use them to compare quantities. You will need to use adverbs of degree in the Academic Writing Module for Task 1.

a bit	a good deal	considerably	a lot
much	a great deal	a little	slightly

With superlative structures we can use *by far*.

G ⋯⟩ page 138

3 Look at the chart below and the examples that follow. Then write six sentences about the consumption of sugar and tea.

	rice ('ooo tonnes)	sugar ('ooo tonnes)	tea ('ooo tonnes)
China	134,800	10,000	495
India	83,680	17,900	693
Indonesia	36,500	3,700	-
Japan	8,790	2,400	136
Brazil	8,100	10,500	-

EXAMPLES:

(almost) the same   *Brazil consumes almost/nearly as much rice as Japan.*

not the same   *Japan doesn't consume (nearly) as much rice as India.*

more/less   *India consumes a great deal more / much more rice than Indonesia.*

superlative   *China consumes by far the most rice.*

4 Write a list of what you eat and drink in a day and compare it with others in the class. Write five sentences using the information you find out and report back orally to the class.

EXAMPLES: *I drink considerably more coffee than most people. Leila eats slightly more chocolate than I do.* (= written, more formal register)

I drink a lot more coffee than most people. Leila eats a bit more chocolate than I do. (= spoken, informal register)

Writing extra

In the IELTS Writing and Speaking Modules you will be marked on how well you use vocabulary. It is important not to confuse informal and more academic language, or use words which are inappropriate. It's also better not to use abbreviations (*etc.*, *e.g.*) or contractions (*I'm, we've*) in formal writing.

Look at these examples from the Grammar section.

less formal language	more formal language
a lot more/less	considerably / a good deal more/less
a bit more/less	slightly / a little more/less by far the most

5 The following sentences all contain words that IELTS candidates have used inappropriately. Underline all the inappropriate words and replace them with a suitable word or phrase from the box. One word is used twice.

a great deal	angry	because	become
children	friends	goods	manager
men	people	regarding	women

1 Some people get mad when they find that they do not have enough water to grow their crops.
2 Kids are the ones who suffer most during food shortages.
3 Many children eat junk food cos they see their mates buying it.
4 The boss of the supermarket told us to put the stuff on the shelves.
5 There were some guys planting rice in the field.
6 Men eat a lot more meat than ladies.
7 About the food you ordered for your party, could you please confirm the date on which it is required?
8 Many persons in the world do not have enough to eat.

Speaking *Part 3*

Test spot

In Part 3 of the Speaking Module, which lasts between four and five minutes, the examiner and the candidate will talk about more abstract issues and ideas linked to the topic of Part 2. ⋯⟫TF 9

6 With a partner, discuss the following questions.
1 What do you think about the way food is produced nowadays (factory farming, GM food, organic food)?
2 Do you think all children should learn to cook at school?
3 What role do fast food and junk food play in your country?

Useful language

Expressing and justifying an opinion
I think/believe that ... because ...
In my opinion, ... This is because ...
Well, first of all, ...
The first point I'd like to make is (that) ...
Let me explain.

Writing folder 1

Academic Writing Task 1: Describing processes

In Task 1 of the Academic Writing Module you may be given a diagram or other graphic data and asked to describe a process or explain how something works. You should spend 20 minutes on this task and you should write at least 150 words.

Advice

- Look carefully at the diagram or graphic data and make sure you understand what it is about.
- Use your answer sheet to make notes on, but remember to cross them out when you have finished your answer.
- Begin your answer by writing a summary sentence to introduce what the diagram or flow chart is about.
- Note that the passive is often used in this task.
  ···❖ Unit 1
- Count approximately how many words you write. You should try not to write too much.

1 Look at the diagram below and decide which of the following summary sentences is best.

  a The diagram shows the human digestive process.
  b The diagram shows how food is taken to the stomach.
  c Human digestion takes a long time.

mouth – teeth and enzymes break down the food

oesophagus – muscles move the food down the tube

stomach – gastric acid helps digest the food

small intestine – the food mixes with bile (a chemical produced in the liver)

large intestine – water is removed; bacteria digest the food

Waste products are excreted

2 The following is a description of the process of food digestion. When you write about a process it is important to make sure you give the information in the right order. Put the sentences a–g in order and then use the best sequencing word in each space.

first of all	then	next	finally	after

  a The resulting mass is .... swallowed and is passed through the throat into the oesophagus. The oesophagus is a long tube which connects the throat with the stomach. It uses muscle action to send the food mass to the stomach.
  b .... passing through the small intestine, the food enters the large intestine, where water is removed and there are bacteria to help in the digestion process.
  c ...., food in the mouth is broken down by the process of chewing with the back teeth and then by the action of enzymes.
  d ...., waste material is excreted.
  e Here it is mixed with a chemical called bile, which is produced in the liver.
  f ...., the food mass mixes in the stomach with gastric acid, which breaks down the food further and helps digestion.
  g From the stomach, the partly digested food goes into the small intestine.

3 Underline the verbs in sentences a–g in exercise 2. Which verbs are passive and which are active? Which tense is used? Why?

4 You will get marks for organisation. Try to avoid paragraphs which have only one sentence, except possibly for the introductory paragraph. Your answer needs an introductory paragraph followed by two to three more paragraphs, each consisting of several sentences.

How would you ~~describe~~ c/a /f.ge/b,d ~~~~ human digestive system ~~~~

5 Look at the pictures below. With a partner, talk about the process.

1 cacao tree   ripe red pods

grown in S. America, Africa, Indonesia

2 pods harvested   white cocoa beans

3 beans fermented

4 spread in sun to dry

5 put in large sacks

6 transported by train or lorry

7 taken to factory

8 beans roasted

9 beans crushed   outer shell removed

10 inner part pressed
liquid chocolate produced

6 Now complete the following Task 1.

You should spend about 20 minutes on this task.

The illustrations above show how chocolate is produced. Summarise the information by selecting and reporting the main features.
Write at least 150 words.

Planning your answer

1 Think about what your opening sentence will be.
2 Select what you think are the main points of the process and do not add anything irrelevant – for example the fact that you personally love chocolate!
3 Join some of the sentences together using sequencing words and relative pronouns (*which, that, where, when*). You will lose marks if you use too many or not enough sequencing words, or if you use them incorrectly.
4 Is there unnecessary repetition? Avoid this by using pronouns – *it, they*, etc.
5 Organise the sentences into paragraphs – two or three, possibly four.
6 Check your spelling (especially of the words which you are given) and grammar.
7 Check that you have written enough.

City attractions

Speaking *Part 1*

1 Discuss these questions with a partner.

If you were given a free holiday in any city in the world …

1 Which city would you like to visit, and why?

2 What would you enjoy doing during the day?

3 How would you spend your evenings there?

4 Where would you prefer to stay, and why?

5 Think about your last holiday. What do you remember most?

Reading

2 Here is some information about four of the attractions in Edinburgh, the capital of Scotland. Read about one attraction at a time, and discuss with a partner why it is popular. These phrases may be useful.

It appeals to people who …
It attracts people who …
It's a good place to go if …

A **EDINBURGH CASTLE** is well known throughout the world. It used to be the home of Scotland's kings and queens and it has some impressive buildings from the 15th and 16th centuries. <u>It stands on Castle Rock, a massive volcanic rock in the heart of the city</u>, with a magnificent view of the surrounding countryside and of the Firth of Forth, an inlet of the sea. There have been settlements on Castle Rock for nearly 3,000 years because of its good position. The Military Tattoo, a floodlit spectacle of military drum and bagpipe music, takes place at Edinburgh Castle every August, as part of the Edinburgh Festival.

B **OUR DYNAMIC EARTH** is the most exciting attraction to have opened in Edinburgh in recent times. Inside a striking, purpose-built tented structure, there is plenty of interactive entertainment on offer for both children and adults alike. Our Dynamic Earth explores the extremes of our planet Earth. Travel back in time to witness the Big Bang, feel the earth shaken by an erupting volcano, fly over glaciers, feel the chill of polar ice, and get caught in a tropical rainstorm. It's pre-historic, volcanic, antarctic, dynamic, fantastic! Out of this world … but about this planet!

C In the 19th century, people travelling by train between Edinburgh and places north of the Firth of Forth had to change to a ferry to cross the water, then transfer to another train. This was very time-consuming. The solution was to construct the **FORTH RAILWAY BRIDGE** a few kilometres west of Edinburgh. It was opened in 1890, and has been in continuous use ever since.

D Situated under one end of the Forth Bridge, **DEEP SEA WORLD** brings you face to face with the creatures of the deep. From 112 metres of underwater tunnels you can enjoy a spectacular view of the piranhas and other tropical fish in the aquarium surrounding you. Or you can go scuba diving among the sharks. You must be at least 16 and in reasonably good health for this, because swimming with sharks can be pretty terrifying! Teachers – contact Deep Sea World about how we can help the children in your class to improve their scientific skills.

Edinburgh Castle

Edinburgh Tattoo

Our Dynamic Earth

Forth Railway Bridge

Deep Sea World

3 For which attraction is each of the following statements true?
*Write the correct letter **A–D**.*

Example: *Answer:*
This attraction is located in the city centre.   *A*
(The relevant phrase in the passage is underlined.)

1 This was built to save people time.
2 An unusual building was designed to house this attraction.
3 There is an age limit on one of the activities at this attraction.
4 This attraction is used in the same way as it was over 100 years ago.
5 A performance is given here once a year.
6 Educational activities can be arranged here on request.
7 In this attraction visitors can learn about different regions of the world.

Grammar Cause, purpose and result

4 Complete each sentence 1–6 with the correct ending a–g from the box below. Think about both the grammar and the meaning. There is one extra ending which you will not need to use.

1 Castle Rock has been inhabited for nearly 3,000 years because of
2 The Forth Bridge was constructed so
3 You must be reasonably healthy to swim with sharks, because
4 The Forth Bridge was made particularly strong because
5 A lot of interactive exhibits were used in Our Dynamic Earth so that
6 Our Dynamic Earth is popular with children because of

> **a** it seems more like entertainment than education.
> **b** trains could cross the river.
> **c** it would appeal to children.
> **d** its good position.
> **e** the interactive exhibits.
> **f** it can be pretty terrifying!
> **g** many people were afraid it would collapse.

5 Now complete these rules by choosing the correct alternatives.

EXAMPLE: *Because* is used to introduce a ⟨cause⟩ / *purpose*. It is followed by a ⟨clause⟩ / *infinitive* / *noun phrase*.

1 *Because of* is used to introduce a *cause* / *purpose*. It is followed by a *clause* / *noun phrase*.
2 *So (that)* is used to introduce a *cause* / *purpose*. It is followed by a *clause* / *noun phrase*.

6 What is the difference between the meanings of *so* in these two sentences?

1 The underwater tunnels at Deep Sea World were designed so visitors could get close to the fish.
2 Tickets for the Military Tattoo sell very quickly, so it's worth booking as early as possible.

Decide if *so* in each of these sentences introduces a purpose (when *so that* is also possible, particularly in writing) or a result (when *so that* isn't possible). In two sentences, both meanings are possible.

3 Our Dynamic Earth was constructed on a former industrial site so it would help to improve that district of Edinburgh.
4 The Forth Bridge is a striking structure so it is well known around the world.
5 The water in Deep Sea World is heated so tropical fish can survive there.
6 Castle Rock is an extinct volcano so there is no danger of an eruption.
7 Our Dynamic Earth offers plenty of exciting activities so visitors have the experience of a lifetime.

G ···⟩ page 138

7 Talk to a partner about living in a city. Use *because*, *because of* and *so (that)* to expand your answers. This will help you with Part 3 of the Speaking Module. Here are some suggestions of ways to begin:

Living in a city is good/bad for young people because of …
A lot of people move to cities so that …
Cities can be exciting because …

3·2

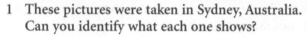

1   These pictures were taken in Sydney, Australia. Can you identify what each one shows?

Listening

2   🎧 You are going to hear a conversation that is similar to those in Part 1 of the Listening Module. In this task you need to listen for specific information in order to complete the notes.

You will hear Jerry, an Englishman, asking an Australian friend, Robin, for advice about his trip to Sydney.

First read the notes and discuss what kind of information you need to listen for.

Complete the notes below.
*Write **NO MORE THAN THREE WORDS AND/OR A NUMBER** for each answer.*

Information from Robin about Sydney

Example:	Answer:
Temperature: will probably be about ....25............ degrees	

Pylon Lookout:
access from the **1** ....
go up to the **2** .... for a view of the harbour

Opera House:
tours last about **3** ....
tickets sold in the **4** .... at the Opera House

The Rocks:
the **5** .... district of Sydney
has popular **6** .... and ....

The Dragon Festival:
more than **7** .... competitors
first event includes **8** .... and ....

Vocabulary Adjectives

3   Here are some adjectives that are often used in guide books.

beautiful	crowded	famous
fascinating	massive	
spectacular	striking	
terrifying	thrilling	

Choose the word from the box that is closest in meaning to the words in *italics* in the sentences below. There is one extra word which you will not need.

1   Edinburgh Castle stands on a *very big* rock in the centre of the city.
2   The Military Tattoo can be a *very exciting* experience.
3   The Sydney Opera House is very *unusual in appearance*.
4   The Dragon Festival is a *magnificent* event that attracts thousands of spectators.
5   Sydney Harbour Bridge is *well known* around the world.
6   Sydney is a *very attractive* city.
7   There are some *very interesting* museums to visit in Sydney.
8   Sharks can be *frightening* if you get too close to them.

22   UNIT 3

Adjectives ending in -ing and -ed

Some verbs have two related adjectives, one ending in -ing and the other in -ed.

Adjectives ending in -ing have an active meaning, for example, *an interesting city* is one that interests someone, such as the speaker.

Adjectives ending in -ed have a passive meaning, for example, *I'm interested in architecture* describes the effect that architecture has on me. These -ed adjectives are related to verbs used in the passive (see Unit 1).

4 Complete this table. Be careful with the spelling.

verb	'active' adjective, -ing	'passive' adjective, -ed
to amaze	amazing	
to astonish		astonished
to excite		excited
to fascinate		fascinated
to frighten	frightening	
to interest		interested
to surprise		surprised
to terrify	terrifying	
to thrill	thrilling	

5 Circle the correct alternative.

1 A *fascinating / fascinated* book was published recently about the history of Sydney.
2 Edinburgh is really *interesting / interested*, because a great deal has happened there over the centuries.
3 I was *astonishing / astonished* to discover that Sydney has a large Chinese population.
4 Many people are *fascinating / fascinated* by foreign cities that are very different from ones in their own country.
5 I'm very *interesting / interested* in the way that Sydney has developed.
6 An *amazed / amazing* number of people watch the Dragon Boat Races.

6 Now complete these sentences by telling a partner about cities you have visited or lived in.

1 I think … is a very exciting city, because …
2 Some visitors to … are amazed that …
3 It's surprising that … doesn't have …
4 Most people who visit … for the first time are thrilled when they see …
5 It's astonishing that … is …

Pronunciation *Word stress in related words*

7 In the word *spec'tacular*, the second syllable, *ta*, is stressed (shown by ' in front of the syllable). Most words have one stressed syllable, but it is not easy to work out which one it is, so whenever you learn a new word, make sure you also learn which syllable is stressed.

Make sure you know the meanings of the words below. Many of them are used in this unit. The two words in each pair have different stressed syllables. Mark the stressed syllable in each word.

EXAMPLE: 'spec.ta.cle (n)   spec'ta.cu.lar (adj)

1 in.form (v)   in.for.ma.tion (n)
2 ob.serve (v)   ob.ser.va.tion (n)
3 solve (v)   so.lu.tion (n)
4 ac.tive (adj)   ac.ti.vi.ty (n)
5 lo.cal (adj)   lo.ca.li.ty (n)
6 na.tion (n)   na.tion.al.i.ty (n)
7 a.ca.de.my (n)   a.ca.de.mic (adj)
8 sci.ence (n)   sci.en.ti.fic (adj)

🎧 Listen and check your answers.

8 Now complete this rule about the position of stressed syllables.

When a word ends in …………… , …………… or …………… , the stressed syllable is always the one immediately before that ending.

Try and think of other words that follow the rule in the box above.

9 This is how the pronunciation of *activity* is shown in the *Cambridge Advanced Learner's Dictionary*: /æk'tɪv.ɪ.ti/.

With a partner, try and read the words below. They were all used in this unit.

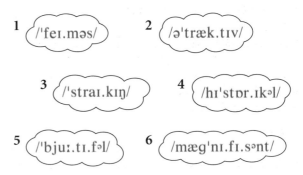

1 /'feɪ.məs/   2 /ə'træk.tɪv/

3 /'straɪ.kɪŋ/   4 /hɪ'stɒr.ɪk.əl/

5 /'bjuː.tɪ.f.əl/   6 /mæg'nɪ.fɪ.sənt/

Test folder 2

Matching

(Academic Reading, General Training Reading and Listening Modules)

You may be asked to match questions with options from a box in all three modules. In the General Training Reading Module *only*, you may need to match questions with parts of the passage.

In the Listening Module, the questions follow the order of the passage. In the Reading Modules they don't.

Sometimes there are more options than questions, and you must choose a different option each time.

Sometimes there are more questions than options, and you will see the instruction **NB You may use any letter more than once.**

Listening

1 🎧 You might find a task like this in Section 2 of the Listening Module. In the test the listening passage would be longer than this.

What is the focus of each day's activity?
*Choose your answers from the box and write the letters **A–J** next to questions **1–5**.*

1	Monday	....
2	Tuesday	....
3	Wednesday	....
4	Thursday	....
5	Friday	....

A	art
B	shipping
C	famous people
D	former amusements
E	geography of the city
F	old homes
G	the range of museums
H	transportation
I	visiting local people
J	wildlife

Advice

Reading Modules
- Skim the whole passage before you start working on any of the tasks. Then read the instructions and the task carefully. It may help to underline the key words.

Matching questions with options in a box
- Read the first option in the box and then find the part of the passage that mentions it. Read what is written about it. Look through the questions. If you find one that matches what is in the passage, write your answer. If nothing matches, it may be one that you don't need to use, so go on to the next option.
- You might find it helpful to underline the part of the text that contains the answer.
- Remember that the words in the questions or in the box may be paraphrases of words in the passage.

Matching questions with parts of the reading passage (GT only)
- Read each part of the passage in turn, and see which of the questions match it before going on to the next part of the passage.

Listening Module
- Read the task before you listen.
- If you miss an answer, stop thinking about it when you hear the speaker going on to talk about the next question, or you'll miss that one.

All modules
- Check that all your answers are different, unless you read the instruction 'NB You may use any letter more than once'.
- Always give an answer – you won't lose any marks if it's wrong.

Reading

Guided London walking tours

A Dickens's London

Follow in the footsteps of Charles Dickens, the nineteenth century writer, and listen as we recite parts of his novels and bring characters like Oliver Twist vividly to life. Stand by the remains of the Marshalsea, where Dickens's own father was imprisoned, and which is the scene of much of his novel 'Little Dorrit'.

B Mayfair

For more than 250 years Mayfair has been the most upmarket district in London, and many well-known books have been written here. We explore streets with familiar names like Savile Row, famous for its men's suits, and Piccadilly, home of the Royal Academy.

C Clerkenwell to the Angel

We walk along St John Street, where animals used to be driven on their way to Smithfield Market, and see a 1504 gateway. We pass the historic Sadler's Wells Theatre and the original termination of the New River, constructed to bring water to London from springs over 30 km away.

D South Bank

We walk along the River Thames to Bankside, where the former power generating station has been transformed into Tate Modern art gallery. Close by we see the new Globe, a replica of Shakespeare's theatre of four hundred years ago, then continue to Borough Market, where you'll find it hard to choose among all the fine food and other goods on sale.

E London's oldest buildings

In a secret city of ancient buildings, courtyards and narrow streets, you'll discover how Stinking Lane and Turnagain Lane got their names, and go inside some of London's oldest and most fascinating buildings, some of which can only be visited by special arrangement.

2 This passage is about 300 words long and is similar to a Section 1 text in General Training Reading. Here you need to match the questions to parts of the text.

Look at the five descriptions of guided walks A–E.
For which walk is each of the following statements true?
Write the correct letter A–E.
NB *You may use any letter more than once.*

Example: *Answer:*
This tour includes the site of a former prison.   A
(the remains of the Marshalsea, where Dickens's own father was imprisoned)

1 This tour includes a street well known for its clothes shops.
2 On this tour excerpts from books are read aloud.
3 On this tour you can see a building that has been converted to a new use.
4 On this tour you can see where an artificial watercourse used to end.
5 This tour includes going inside places that are normally closed to the public.
6 This tour includes a functioning market.
7 This tour is of an area that has high status.
8 This tour takes you to a modern theatre.
9 On this tour you will learn the meanings of some street names.

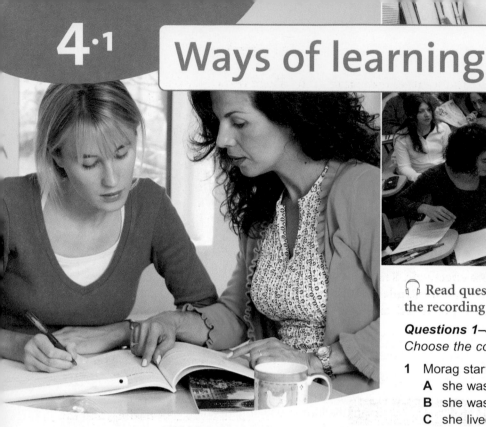

4·1 Ways of learning

Speaking *Part 3*

1 In small groups, discuss these questions.

- Do you think it is better to have one-to-one lessons or to study in a class?
- What are the advantages or disadvantages of one-to-one lessons?

Listening

Test spot

Multiple-choice tasks are used in the Listening and Reading Modules. First read the questions and the options. As you listen, consider *all* the options. Only one of them is right, unless you are told to choose more than one (as in questions 5 and 6 below). ⋯⟶ TF 6

2 🎧 You are going to listen to a radio interview with Morag, who is 16. She is talking about her experience of having lessons at home instead of going to school.

Read the example question.

0 How old was Morag when she started having lessons at home?

   A 4   **B** 7   **C** 8

Now listen to the example on the recording and notice that Morag talks about all three ages, but the answer to the question is C – she says *I left when I was eight, and my mother's been teaching me at home ever since.*

🎧 Read questions 1–4, then listen to the next part of the recording and answer them.

Questions 1–4
*Choose the correct letter, **A**, **B** or **C**.*

1 Morag started having lessons at home because
   A she was unhappy at school.
   B she was not learning much at school.
   C she lived a long way from the nearest school.

2 What does she dislike about learning at home?
   A Her mother always knows what she is doing.
   B She has to study for most of the day.
   C She is unable to spend time with friends.

3 She thinks that working on projects
   A takes too much time.
   B helps her to understand the subject.
   C teaches her how to use the Internet effectively.

4 What does she find most difficult about working on projects?
   A writing reports
   B finding information
   C planning the project

🎧 Now read questions 5 and 6. Here you have to choose more than one of the options. Listen, and as Morag mentions each of the options, find it in the list, and put a tick (✓) if it is a right answer, and a cross (✗) if it is wrong.

Questions 5 and 6
5 Which **THREE** subjects does Morag enjoy studying?
   A history   **D** biology
   B geography   **E** economics
   C English   **F** foreign languages

6 Which **TWO** careers is Morag interested in?
   A sport   **D** teaching
   B cinema   **E** medicine
   C music

3 Do you think it's a good idea for Morag to be taught by her mother? Would you like to have been taught at home?

Reading

4 What advice would be useful for someone who wants to read more effectively? In small groups, discuss which of these pieces of advice you would give.

1 First decide why you're reading the text.
2 Always read a text in full.
3 Read the title to find out what the text is about.
4 Ask other people questions about the subject.
5 Look for the main information in the last sentence of each paragraph.
6 Copy the most important parts of the text.

5 The following advice was given by a university, to help students to read books and academic papers more effectively. Read it, and decide which of the above six pieces of advice it includes. Put a tick (✓) beside the advice in exercise 4 if it's included, and a cross (✗) if it isn't.

⏱ about 250 words

READING FOR COMPREHENSION

As a student you'll need to read a great many articles, books and texts on the Internet, so make sure you can do it effectively. Before you start reading, decide what your purpose is. Then you should choose the most suitable
5 reading method. For instance, if you need to find something specific, such as information about a particular person or topic, scan the text until you find the person's name or a mention of the topic, then read just the relevant section. Scanning is the most rapid form of reading.

10 If you need to find out the main theme and ideas of the text, you'll need to read more of it. First spend two or three minutes looking at the title, subheadings, introduction and summary, if there is one. Write down the questions that you want answers to, for example, *Why did such-and-such*
15 *happen?* or *What was the result of such-and-such an event?* Then read the first sentence of each paragraph: if it's relevant, read the rest of the paragraph. Otherwise go on to the next. Also use the writer's linking phrases as a guide, words like *the first point, however, to sum up*, and so on.

20 Above all, interact with what you're reading. Work out how it relates to what you already know. Make sure you can follow the writer's thought processes. Make notes about the topic, using your own words rather than copying what you have read.

Reading effectively means using your brain – simply moving
25 your eyes across the words is a waste of time!

Which of these is your brain?

Vocabulary

6 These words and phrases paraphrase words in the passage which are more suitable for academic writing. Find the words in the passage. They appear in the same order.

1 understanding   ....
2 the reason for doing something
....
3 a way of doing something
....
4 particular   ....
5 connected with what you are interested in   ....
6 the name of a book, article, etc.
....
7 is connected   ....

7 Complete each sentence with a word from exercise 6.

1 There is more than one .... of reading, and the best one depends on what you intend to gain from that book or article.
2 The .... usually indicates what a book is about.
3 If you need .... information, it may help to scan the text for it.
4 The .... of reading a textbook is usually to get information.
5 ...., particularly when reading in a foreign language, requires mental effort by the reader.

8 In small groups, discuss what's important for effective learning at school or college, for example:

• the number of students
• the ability of the teachers
• activities during lessons
• equipment and facilities
• whether all the students have a similar knowledge of the subject.

4·2

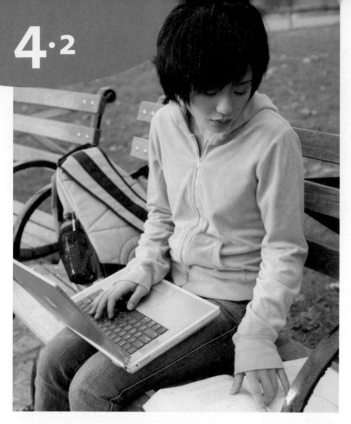

1 Talk to a partner about how you study or work.

- Do you usually study or work on your own, or with friends?
- Do you do anything while you're studying or working, for example, eat, talk, or listen to music?
- How often do you take a break?
- What are you studying or working on at the moment?

Grammar Review of present tenses

Present simple and continuous

2 These sentences come from the recording in 4.1. Choose the meaning (a, b or c) from the box that best suits the verb in *italics* in each sentence.

> **a** a temporary activity around the time of speaking
> **b** how often an action is carried out
> **c** something that is true in general, or permanently

1 We *start* around 9 o'clock, five days a week.
2 At the moment I'*m doing* research into the island where we *live*.
3 I *spend* most weekends with other people.
4 I *enjoy* doing things on my own.
5 I'*m thinking* seriously about becoming a doctor.
6 Some people *think* I must be lonely.

Now write *present simple* or *present continuous* beside each of the meanings (a, b and c) in the box.

3 Choose the correct alternative, and decide whether the meaning is a, b or c from the box in exercise 2.

1 We *study / are studying* South America in our geography lessons this month.
2 I *understand / am understanding* why some people find photography interesting.
3 I can't talk to you now – I *have / am having* lunch.
4 How often *do you work / are you working* on the computer?
5 Morag *thinks / is thinking* about her project.
6 I *think / am thinking* it's more fun to study with other people than on my own.
7 I *never spend / am never spending* much time studying in the evening.

> Some verbs are rarely used in the continuous tense. Many of them describe
> - a state of mind, e.g. *believe, understand*
> - a feeling, e.g. *like, love, want*
> - a relationship, e.g. *belong, cost, include.*

4 The following sentences show common errors that IELTS candidates have made in the use of tenses. Correct the errors.

1 How much time I spend doing homework is depending on what else I want to do.
2 Please stop talking – I listen to the teacher.
3 Most people are feeling tired when they've worked hard all day.
4 This week we have lessons in the library because our classroom is being decorated.

Present perfect simple

5 These are the three main meanings of the present perfect tense. Choose the most suitable meaning, a, b or c, for each sentence below.

> **a** an action or situation that started in the past and continues to the present
> **b** an action or situation that finished at an unspecified time in the past
> **c** a past action or situation, with the emphasis on its result in the present

1 Morag *has lived* on a remote island for the last few years.
2 We can't use the Internet because the computer *has crashed*.
3 Most people *have had* lessons that were boring.
4 I'*ve read* some interesting books about biology.
5 The school *has bought* some new equipment which will help the students studying physics.
6 I'*ve known* since I was a child that I want to go to university.

Present perfect continuous

6 The present perfect continuous is used to describe:

a actions which have lasted for some time and are likely to continue
b actions which lasted for some time and have just stopped

Look at these examples. Which use, a or b, matches each one?

1 In this programme we*'ve been looking* at different forms of education, and now we'll leave that and turn to health.
2 In this series we*'ve been looking* at different forms of education, and today we're going to talk about having lessons at home.
3 Joanne *has been revising* for her maths exam, and now she's starting business studies.
4 Many young people *have been using* computers since they were children.

G ···❖ page 139

7 Talk to a partner. Imagine that you haven't seen each other for two or three weeks. Tell each other what you've done since you last met, using the present perfect simple and continuous.

EXAMPLE: *I've been to the cinema twice.*
I've been studying for exams (and I haven't finished yet).

Here are some verbs for you to use:

be	eat	go	read
see	study	talk	visit
walk	practise		

Pronunciation *Word stress*

8 With a partner, put a mark (') in front of the stressed syllable in each of the words in *italics*.

EXAMPLE: Now in this programme we've been looking at different forms of *e.du.'ca.tion* for children up to the age of 16.

1 But now I *pre.fer* it.
2 The only *di.ffi.cul.ty* is that I'm the centre of attention.
3 After that I have to write a *re.port* on what I've found out.
4 What subjects do you *stu.dy*?
5 I do a lot of projects on *par.ti.cu.lar* topics.
6 We learn how the *cli.mate* affects the way we live.
7 I find the *pro.nun.ci.a.tion* of foreign languages quite difficult.
8 I can't seem to remember the *vo.ca.bu.la.ry*!
9 I think *pho.to.gra.phy* is fascinating.
10 There are so many things you can do when you take *pho.to.graphs*.

🎧 Now listen and check that you have marked the right syllables.

9 Write the words from exercise 8 in the right boxes below. The most useful clue to the pattern is whether the word ends in one of a number of suffixes. If it doesn't, it's often a question of how many syllables follow the stressed syllable. It will be helpful to complete the boxes for pattern 1 first.

This symbol • means that a syllable is stressed.
– means a syllable is unstressed.
(–) means any number of unstressed syllables (including none)

1 Pattern: stress on the syllable before certain suffixes, including:
-cian, -graphy, -ial, -ian, -ic, -ical, -ics, -ious, -ience, -ity, -logy, -sion, -tion,
e.g. *ex'per.ience*

a ⬚   b ⬚

2 Pattern: (–) • e.g. *be'cause*

a ⬚   b ⬚

3 Pattern: • – e.g. *'some.thing*
This is the main pattern for words of two syllables.

a ⬚   b ⬚

4 Pattern (–) • – – e.g. *'In.ter.net*
This is the main pattern for words of three or more syllables.

a ⬚   b ⬚

5 Pattern (–) • – – – e.g. *'ne.ce.ssa.ry*

a ⬚   b ⬚

Does your name have any of these stress patterns? If so, write it by the appropriate pattern.

Read the words to a partner, so they can check that you say the words with the stress on the right syllable. Then they should read the words to you.

When you learn a new word, use an English–English dictionary to find out which syllable is stressed. Mark that syllable in your notes.

10 Tell a partner how you feel about studying. What are you interested in? What are you good / less good at? What are you looking forward to?

Writing folder 2

Academic Writing Task I: Handling data 1 – line graphs

In Task 1 of the Academic Writing Module you may be given one or more line graphs and asked to explain what they show. You should spend 20 minutes on this task and you should write at least 150 words.

Advice

- You will need to compare the information as well as describe it. For language of comparison/similarities/differences see Unit 2.2.
- It is important not to offer your opinion on the graph or to try to give reasons for the figures mentioned.

1 A line graph is a way to summarise how two pieces of information are related. Look at chart 1. Which sentence, a or b, is a better summary of the chart?

a The graph shows how much money was spent on students in California from the end of the 70s to the beginning of the 21st century.

b The graph shows how many dollars were spent on each student's education in the state of California in selected years between 1977 and 2002.

Chart 1

State spending per student in California

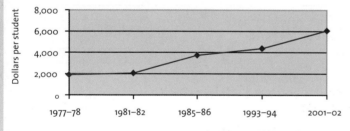

Chart 2

**Redbridge University
Spending on books and computers 1989–2000**

2 Look at chart 2. Use appropriate vocabulary from the Useful language box on the opposite page to complete the following sentences:

Noun + adjective

EXAMPLE: There was a ....*sharp rise*........ in the amount spent on books in 1993, compared with the previous year.

1 There was a .... in the amount spent on computers between 1992 and 1994.

2 There was a .... in spending on computers from 1998.

3 There was a .... in spending on computers in 1992 and then again in 1998.

4 There was a .... in spending on books from 1997.

Verb + adverb/adjective/noun

EXAMPLE: Spending on computers ....*fluctuated slightly*........ between 1992 and 1994.

5 Spending on books .... from 1992 to 1993.

6 Spending on books .... in 1993.

7 Spending on books .... from 1994 to 1996.

8 Spending on computers .... in 1996.

9 Spending on computers .... in 1998.

10 Spending on computers .... in 1999 and 2000.

Useful language

Expressing changes
to rise / a rise
to increase / an increase
to go up
to double

to reach a peak

to hold/remain steady
to be stable
to be constant
to level off

to fluctuate
a fluctuation

to decrease / an decrease
to decline / a decline
to fall / a fall

slight / slightly
gradual / gradually
steady / steadily

dramatic / dramatically
steep / steeply
sharp / sharply

Time expressions
for the period
since 1999
for five years
between 1990 and 2001
in 1987

3 Complete the report below, which describes the chart showing school enrolment in the USA. Each space has a clue to the type of word needed, to help you.

School enrolment in the USA (student numbers in millions)

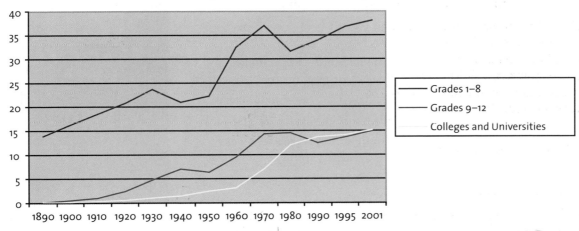

The chart shows the increase **0** (preposition) ....*in*........ the number of people who received an education in the USA **1** (preposition) .... 1890 and 2001.

2 (preposition) .... the beginning of the twentieth century numbers of those who were enrolled in grades 1–8 and in grades 9–12 (high school) began to **3** (verb) .... By the end of the twentieth century figures for the former **4** (verb + preposition) .... around 38 million, compared to 15 million for high school. Only two periods showed a **5** (noun) .... – starting in the 1930s and 1970s for grades 1–8, and in the 1940s and 1980s for grades 9–12.

The number of students in colleges and universities was much lower than those enrolled in grades 1–8, and was generally below those in grades 9–12. The number of students going on to further education **6** (verb and adverb) .... until the end of the 1960s, when there was a **7** (adjective and noun) .... This **8** (noun) .... continued until the 1990s, when numbers were level with those leaving high school – around 15 million.

Overall, during the twentieth century there was a **9** (noun) .... in the number of Americans receiving an education at all levels.

Units 1–4 Revision

Topic review

1 Read these sentences and say which are true for you, giving more details. Try to expand your answers.

  1 I was sent over 50 text messages last week.
  2 I wouldn't want the latest mobile phone as a present.
  3 In my opinion, the computer will never take the place of books.
  4 I like to think my diet is healthier than that of my friends.
  5 I would never buy fast food.
  6 I am the best cook in my family.
  7 I prefer city to beach holidays as there is more to do there.
  8 I need to study abroad so I can get a better job.
  9 Sydney would be a great city to visit.
  10 I get stressed in the city because of the traffic.

Grammar

Passive/active

2 Read this description of how glass bottles are made. Put the verb into an appropriate form – passive or active, simple present or past, or present perfect.

No one knows exactly when or where glass **0** (first make) __was first made__ . It probably **1** (originate) .... in Mesopotamia, where pieces of well-made glass **2** (find) .... In those days, glass **3** (always make) .... by hand. A glassblower **4** (blow) .... through a hollow tube and **5** (make) .... a bottle shape out of the hot glass.

In the thirteenth century, Venice **6** (become) .... an important centre for glass making. Venetian glass **7** (praise) .... for its imaginative forms and, in fact, glass makers in Murano, an island near Venice, **8** (forbid) .... to leave the island in case they **9** (give) .... away their secrets to others.

Today, bottles and jars **10** (usually make) .... by machine. In the factory, sand, soda, lime and crushed glass **11** (mix) .... together. This mixture **12** (heat) .... in a huge oven called a furnace to 1,560 degrees C. It **13** (melt) .... and **14** (become) .... red-hot liquid glass. Next, a lump of the hot, soft glass **15** (remove) .... from the furnace and dropped into a metal mould. Finally, air **16** (blow) .... into the glass in the mould to make a bottle.

Present tenses

3 Correct the following sentences, if necessary. Some sentences are correct.

1 I live in England for six months.
2 Our principal is believing in democracy in the classroom.
3 That briefcase belongs to Paula.
4 I am enjoying studying mathematics this term.
5 Elsa is never understanding which are the healthiest things to eat.
6 Franco has waited outside the gallery since four o'clock.
7 I've been going to the college twice this week.
8 I'm seeing Lisa tonight.
9 I've been knowing how to drive since I was eight.
10 Water is freezing at 0 degrees centigrade.
11 Dr Scott knows my father since 1960.
12 What do you do? – I read a book.
13 How are you feeling now?
14 Paul is working hard on his thesis at the moment.

Comparatives and superlatives

4 Look at the 2005 statistics for the cities below and write six sentences comparing the cities.

	population	area (km²)	number of high-rise buildings
Beijing	7,746,519	16,808	289
Durban	847,324	2,291	173
Hong Kong	6,787,000	1,001	7,422
Las Vegas	517,017	294	98
New York	8,115,135	800	5,444
Osaka	2,598,589	290	740
São Paulo	10,600,060	1,525	3,014

© Emporis 5/2005

EXAMPLES: *Hong Kong has by far the largest number of high-rise buildings of the seven cities mentioned here.*

Durban has a larger number of high-rise buildings than Las Vegas, and has a much greater area.

Prepositions

5 Complete these sentences using a preposition.

1 My class consists .... students from all over the world.
2 Sue depended .... her mobile to keep in touch with her family.
3 The tour guide in the coach got .... very well with the driver.
4 How did you get to the restaurant – .... foot or .... taxi?
5 Marco was very good .... whistling.
6 I'm looking forward .... finishing the term.
7 The courier was very quick .... counting out the change.
8 My brother is keen .... cooking Chinese food.

Vocabulary

6 Circle the correct alternative.

1 This city tour is really *bored / boring*.
2 I was very *surprised / surprising* to get a fax from the college.
3 It was really *excited / exciting* to have lessons by radio.
4 Tom was *astonished / astonishing* to read that a quarter of Americans are overweight.
5 This book I'm reading on further education is very *interested / interesting*.

7 Which word is different?

1	attractive	crowded	fascinating	impressive
2	terrifying	frightening	worrying	spectacular
3	bland	fresh	sour	burnt
4	sour	rotten	stale	spicy

Discovering the past

1 Match places 1–4 with photographs A–D and then say which type of structure each is.

1 The Great Wall, China	a temple
2 The Moai, Easter Island	a system of defence
3 The Parthenon, Greece	tombs or burial chambers
4 The Pyramids, Egypt	sculptures

Reading

2 Read the article and answer the following questions. Don't worry about the spaces in the article for now.

1 Where is Easter Island?
2 Who built the Moai and why were they built?

3 Words a–e are taken from the article. Match them with their meanings, 1–5, then decide where they fit in the article.

a	clan	1	an area or type of work or study
b	sites	2	no longer active
c	remains	3	places that are being dug up to find information
d	field	4	ruins, what's left behind
e	extinct	5	a family group or tribe

⏱ about 700 words

The Moai of Easter Island

Easter Island was named by a Dutchman, Jacob Roggeveen, who arrived there on Easter Day, 6 April 1722, but its native name is Rapa Nui, sometimes translated as 'centre of the Earth'. Nearly 4,025 km from the coast of Chile and 4,185 km
5 from Tahiti, this island is a triangular volcanic rock of just 17 square kilometres, and is one of the most isolated places on Earth. The top of the highest of its three volcanoes, which are now (1) ...... , is 511m above sea level. Currently, the island has 3,000 inhabitants and a single town, Hanga Roa. Easter Island
10 or Rapa Nui is now a nature reserve and is governed by Chile. The island is particularly known for the large statues or sculptures, called Moai, which are found there.

In 1989, the Chilean government invited Giuseppe Orifici, an Italian archaeologist, to visit the island. Impressed by the
15 wealth of archaeological (2) ...... , Orifici arranged to begin digging the following year. He co-ordinated a team of experts, each a specialist in their own (3) ...... , who visited the island for several weeks over the next ten years. These specialists ranged from archaeologists and anthropologists to botanists
20 and sculpture experts.

Scientists once believed that the Rapa Nui people had originally come from South America around the 7th century.
However, a few surviving traditions, as well as the shapes of some of the sculptures, show that the people are from Polynesia and probably arrived on the island in the 5th century. Recent
25 research on bones and teeth strongly supports this theory. While anthropologists Dr Andrea Drusini and Professor Daris Swindler were carrying out research on teeth from various (4) ...... on the island, they found that something known as a 'genetic bottleneck' had occurred. On a small island, where people never
30 marry outside their own (5) ...... , inbreeding is inevitable, and as a result, the gene pool for each group is narrow. A particular feature, such as large or missing teeth, then shows up within family members with much more regularity than would otherwise be expected and this enabled the scientists to prove where the
35 people had originally come from.

Bones were found mostly in burial chambers beneath the Moai. It is thought that the social and economic power of a clan chief was measured by the size and number of Moai he had, so there was fierce competition between clan chiefs to build the biggest
40 and best. Usually, each chief had between one and 15 Moai on his family's tomb, all of which were between 3m and 8m tall. More were constantly being built – in total, nearly 12,000 are thought to have been made, using rock from the Rano Rarku volcano. The largest of the Moai found by Orifici's team was 33m
45 tall and weighed nearly 300 tonnes. Sometimes the sculptures were engraved – one has carvings of a boat – while others have large or small ears, depending on the clan that built them.

Test spot

Each section of the Reading Module has a text (or, in sections 1 and 2 of GT, texts) followed by a set of questions. There will be a variety of question types on each text – for example, multiple choice, sentence completion or a matching task.

You will need to go back to the beginning of the text each time you begin a new section of questions.

4 Questions 1–6

Do the following statements agree with the information in the article? Write

TRUE   *if the statement agrees with the information*
FALSE   *if the statement contradicts the information*
NOT GIVEN *if there is no information on this*

1 Orifici organised the experts who came to Easter Island.
2 Experts believe the Rapa Nui people came from South America.
3 Burial chambers varied from clan to clan.
4 Each of the Moai took many months to construct.
5 No Moai were made after the sixteenth century.
6 The Rapa Nui people were hungry because they refused to eat fish.

Question 7

*Choose **TWO** letters **A–E**.*

In which **TWO** centuries did a number of new people come to Easter Island?

A 5th   **B** 7th   **C** 16th   **D** 17th   **E** 18th

Most have a pukao – a kind of hat made of red volcanic rock.
50 Completed Moai were arranged to face in towards the island, and played an important part in the religion of the island. Islanders worshipped them as ancestors who had become gods.
The building of Moai and the religion associated with it lasted until the 16th century. A number of factors led to its collapse and
55 the near collapse of the Rapu Nui people, including population growth and the destruction of the forest. But it seems that the main reason was that the religion had simply got too big for the island. More and more people were building ever larger Moai and they weren't spending enough time growing food or fishing. The
60 fish close to the shore were hunted to extinction and increasing numbers of trees were destroyed to use as rollers to transport the Moai. When there were no more trees, the land lost its fertility, people starved and there was no wood to build boats to escape. Luckily, a new, less demanding, religion grew up during the 17th
65 century, which saved the islanders and enabled limited resources to be shared out more fairly.
Europeans arrived in the 18th century and destroyed much of what remained by introducing foreign diseases and importing a few species which destroyed the native plants
70 and animals. It was also at this time that the key to the Rapa Nui written language was lost.
The history of Rapa Nui and its people should be a warning to us all in the 21st century – to take care of our natural resources before it is too late.

Questions 8–10

Complete the notes below.
*Choose **NO MORE THAN THREE WORDS AND/OR A NUMBER** from the reading passage for each answer.*

The Moai sculptures
8 were made from rock taken from the ....
9 could be as high as ....
10 were moved about the island on wooden ....

Vocabulary

Collocations related to research

5 Which verb in each group (1–4) doesn't collocate with the noun on the right?

1 to get, to do, to perform, to carry out   an experiment

2 to make, to find, to lead to   a discovery

3 to draw, to arrive at, to do, to reach   a conclusion

4 to get, to make, to analyse, to evaluate   results/statistics

Speaking   *Part 3*

6 Look at this question and responses a–c below. Which response would gain more marks? Why?

Can history teach us anything or is it a waste of time?

a No, it's a waste of time.
b I consider that society could learn a great deal from the study of history because history has a habit of repeating itself.
c Well, history is very interesting. My favourite historical person is Captain Cook because he discovered many places.

With a partner, ask and answer the following questions. Remember to expand your answers.

1 Do you think history is taught well?
2 What could be done to make students want to study history?
3 Do you think students should have more choice in which area of history they study? What would you choose?

Useful language

Suggesting and giving answers
Let me give you an example.
A case in point is …
Let me explain why I think that.
For one thing, they could …, and for another, …
Personally, I think that … / I would choose …

5·2

Grammar   Review of past tenses

1   Look at the three tenses below and match each with the correct explanation **a–c**. Then match the examples 1–4, which are taken from the reading passage in 5.1, with the right tense and explanation.

past simple PS
past continuous PC
past perfect simple PPS

> **a** to talk about something which is unfinished at a particular time in the past
> **b** to talk about something that happened before a particular time in the past
> **c** to talk about something which began and ended in the past

1   In 1989, the Chilean government *invited* Guiseppe Orifici to visit the island.
2   Scientists once *believed* that the Rapa Nui people *had* originally *come* from South America.
3   More and more people *were building* ever larger Moai and they *weren't spending* enough time growing food or fishing.
4   While anthropologists *were carrying out* research on teeth ... they *found* that something known as a 'genetic bottleneck' *had occurred*.

G ···⟩ page 139

Past simple

2   With a partner, take it in turns to ask and answer questions based on the prompts and the answers in the box.

EXAMPLE: *When did the Space Age start?*
It started in the 1950s.

0 The Space Age / start
1 The Berlin Wall / fall
2 The Pharaohs / build the Pyramids
3 Cavemen / do the wall paintings at Lascaux
4 Mao Zedong / govern China
5 The USA / become independent

> around 2600 BC   in the late 1700s
> from 1949 to 1976   in 1989   in the 1950s
> approximately 15,000 years ago

Past continuous and past simple

3   Complete the sentences with either a past simple or past continuous form of the verb in brackets.

EXAMPLE: Archimedes (have) *was having* a bath when he suddenly (shout) *shouted.* Eureka!

1 I (dig) .... a hole when I suddenly (see) .... the gold coin.
2 Dr Smith (give) .... a lecture this morning when the fire alarm (go off) ....
3 While we (look) .... round the gallery, we (hear) .... a loud noise outside.
4 The museum director accidentally (drop) .... an ancient vase when he (put) .... it back on the shelf.

Past perfect simple

4   Before Europeans arrived on Easter Island, a number of things had happened. With a partner, say what those things were, based on the prompts below.

EXAMPLE: Some people / arrive there from Polynesia in the 5th century.

Some people had arrived there from Polynesia in the 5th century.

1 The people / build large sculptures called Moai.
2 They / use volcanic rock to build them.
3 They / carve pictures on some of the Moai.
4 They / cut down the forest.
5 They / stop fishing.

5   Complete the passage using the verbs in brackets in either the past simple, past continuous or past perfect simple tense.

TUTANKHAMEN'S TOMB

The British archaeologist Howard Carter **(1)** (work) .... for Lord Carnarvon when he **(2)** (discover) .... the tomb of King Tutankhamen. Carnarvon was keen to be the first person to find the tomb and the treasure it **(3)** (contain) .... Before this Carter **(4)** (spend) .... many years looking for the burial place but **(5)** (not have) .... any success. However, in 1922, Carter **(6)** (be) .... very lucky. His team **(7)** (begin) .... digging on November 1, 1922. On November 4, while they **(8)** (dig) .... in the Valley of the Kings, they **(9)** (find) .... a staircase and this **(10)** (lead) .... them to a sealed door. Luckily, no one **(11)** (break into) .... the tomb before them and the contents **(12)** (be) .... still untouched.

Listening

Test spot

There are different types of diagram in the Listening Module. There may be a map, a plan, a process, a chart or a picture of an object. Study the diagram very carefully before you listen.
···⟶ TF 10

6 You are going to listen to a guide talking about a museum. Before you listen, talk about a museum you have visited. Where was it? What was it like? What did you like best in the museum? Can you remember where everything was?

Useful language

Directions
on your left, on your right
straight ahead
the ground/first/second floor
in the corner/middle
at the side/back
behind / in front of / opposite

7 🎧 Look at the floor plan of the museum below and listen to a guide talking about the museum.

Label the rooms on the map of the museum. Choose your answers from the box below and write them against numbers 1–5 on the map.

A	African paintings
AA	Australian art
B	Bookshop
ER	Egyptian room
GS	Greek sculpture
L	Lift
NAC	Native American clothing
R	Restaurant

Main entrance

Writing extra

8 Write a description of your first school, explaining where it was and saying where the main rooms were. Mention any changes which were made to the building or grounds. You must write at least 150 words.

Test folder 3

Sentence and note completion

(Academic Reading, General Training Reading and Listening Modules)

Notes usually focus on one part of the passage. *Sentences* in the Reading Modules may relate to different parts of the passage.

The questions always follow the order of information in the Listening Module, and usually do in the Reading Modules.

The sentences or notes normally use different words from the words in the passage to express the same ideas.

If you have to choose words from the passage, you will be told the maximum number of words to use for each answer.

If you have to choose words from a box, there will be more words than spaces, and they are usually different from the words in the passage. In the Reading Modules a box may contain the endings of sentences.

Words must be spelt correctly to gain marks.

Listening

1 🎧 This passage is similar to Section 4 of the Listening Module.

Complete the sentences below.
*Write **NO MORE THAN THREE WORDS** for each answer.*

Example: *Answer:*
Most people lived in homes made of ....mud.......... .

1 The city probably functioned as the .... of the region.
2 The name 'Zimbabwe' may mean ....
3 Construction is thought to have started in the .... century.
4 The Great Enclosure was probably a .... home.
5 .... was probably held back by the relatively poor soil.
6 .... is no longer believed to be the reason for founding the city here.
7 The city was rich because it was a ....
8 A shortage of .... and other resources probably contributed to the city's decline.
9 Nobody lived in the city after approximately ....

2 🎧 This passage is similar to Section 3 of the Listening Module.

Complete the notes using words or phrases from the box.

aim	books	catalogue	cross-references
daily life	district	questions	record
society	software	source documents	

Researching family history
- first find relevant **1** ....
- decide on **2** ....
- make a **3** ...., starting with self
- plan **4** ....
- try to find **5** ....
- study details of **6** ....
- choose suitable **7** ....
- include **8** ....
- join a **9** ....

Reading

3 This passage is similar to those in the Academic Reading Module, but it is only about 300 words long.

Why Study History?

Happiness in life could be defined as successfully acting as the chief character in a story one has written oneself. While individuals create a meaningful personal story through action, experience, behaviour and memory, so too the history of a nation (or other group) is a story that gives meaning to the members of that nation living today.

Historians try to combine an understanding of social, economic, political and cultural activity into a general story, explaining how these have affected each other to shape the general course of human events.

Historians use rational scientific methods like the study of statistics and data, but their goal is to tell stories that make sense and have a plot. Many facts are, or seem, certain. But the meaning of those facts, or even the full story of what happened, is less obvious than one might think. To understand and explain the past, the historian must develop a theory and test it against the evidence he or she has collected. In a nutshell, the more evidence it can satisfactorily account for, the better the theory.

Much of the evidence that historians use was not available to people of the time, and much material that existed then has been lost. Relatively little new evidence comes to light, so historians largely rely on developing new methods of analysis, asking new questions, or following new story lines that show the relevance of evidence that was previously ignored.

No historical theory can be proved beyond all doubt, because there is room for interpretation in any human activity. Every time one tries to understand the past, one gains insight into the uncertainty of any knowledge: history is sometimes more like a detective story than an experiment in a laboratory.

*Complete each sentence with the correct ending **A–G** from the box below.*
*Write the correct letter **A–G** next to each sentence.*

1 Nations use history to understand ....
2 Historians show the interaction between ....
3 Historians try to explain ....,
4 Historians often need to work out ....
5 We can never be certain about ....

A	alternative ways of interpreting existing material.
B	scientific and non-scientific approaches.
C	various influences on our lives.
D	new sources of evidence.
E	as much as possible of what is known.
F	explanations of the past.
G	the present situation.

What is job satisfaction?

1 Average hours worked per week in UK

Chart: Hours (y-axis, 40–46) vs Years (x-axis: 1980, 1985, 1990, 1995, 2000, 2005)
Legend: ☐ Full-time workers

2 UK employees inspired by their bosses

Chart: Percentage (y-axis, 60–75) vs Hours worked per week (x-axis: 18-28, 28-35, 35-40, 40-50, 50-60, 60-70)

For example: 65% of people who work 18–28 hours per week feel inspired by their boss.

1 Talk about charts 1 and 2 above. What do the charts tell you about working life today?

2 What makes a good job? Rank the following 1 to 8, with 1 being the most motivating for you, and discuss your decisions with your partner.

- flexible working hours
- being part of a team
- an excellent salary
- good holidays
- promotion prospects
- staff facilities, e.g. a sports centre
- responsibility
- an inspirational boss

Listening

Test spot

Section 4 of the Listening Module is always a talk or short lecture related to academic work or study. There will be a mixture of task types and you will be told which questions to read, and be given time to read them, before you hear the recording.

3 You are going to hear a woman giving a lecture to a group of business students on the subject of motivation at work. In the test the recording may pause, but it won't be stopped. For this exercise, however, you should stop after each group of questions so you can look carefully at the next set of questions before you listen to the next part of the recording.

The questions are in the order in which you will hear the answers in the recording. Write **NO MORE THAN TWO WORDS AND / OR A NUMBER** for each answer.

🎧 *Questions 1 and 2*
Complete the diagram below.

Motivation model

Needs or expectations → influence/affect people's 1 .... → achievement of goals → 2 .... → (back to Needs or expectations)

Complete the sentences below.

Taylor wrote his theory in the **3** .... century.

Taylor's theory was that people only worked for **4** ....

Later research concluded that some people preferred to work **5** ....

🎧 **Questions 6 and 7**

Complete the diagram below.

Look carefully at the diagram and check you understand where to write your first answer.

Maslow's theory

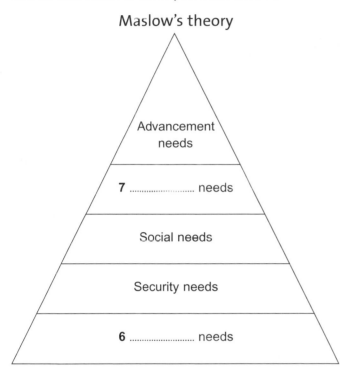

Advancement needs

7 .... needs

Social needs

Security needs

6 .... needs

🎧 **Questions 8 and 9**

Complete the table below.

Look at the table and notice that in this section you need to listen for percentages.

Source of job satisfaction	% of employees
Inspirational leader	72%
Type of work	**8** ....
Good pay	50%
Flexible working hours	**9** ....

🎧 **Question 10**

Choose the correct letter, A–D.

What does the speaker say about workers in the UK?

A They want to have a good lifestyle.

B Socialising at work is not a priority for them.

C They want to earn a lot of money.

D Having a job title is a priority for them.

Vocabulary

Collocations with *money*

4 Complete the sentences with a verb from the box in the right form.

change	give	invest	leave	lend
make	pay	save	spend	waste

1 Don't .... your money on buying a cheap office desk – it won't last very long.

2 My grandmother .... me £10,000 when she died.

3 Claudia .... all her money on presents for the family.

4 Don't .... your money at the airport – they don't give a very good rate.

5 Every month I .... a certain percentage of my salary into my pension scheme.

6 Can you .... me £20 until the weekend?

7 The woman .... £10 to the man playing the guitar in the market square.

8 If you .... your money in stocks and shares, you might lose it.

9 Jon .... over £100 by buying his books second hand.

10 Steve Rogers .... his money selling insurance.

5 How do you handle money? Ask and answer these questions with a partner.

1 Do you spend more than you have?

2 What's the best way to make money?

3 Would you ever buy anything second hand?

4 Would you lend or borrow money?

5 What do you think about investing on the stock exchange?

The Shanghai stock exchange

Grammar Past simple or present perfect?

> **Present perfect** *There **have been** many theories which **have attempted** to explain the nature of motivation.*
>
> **Past simple** *In 1943, Maslow **identified** five important needs which he **placed** in a triangle.*

1 IELTS students often confuse the past simple and the present perfect. Look at some facts about each tense. Which fact is true for the past simple (PS) and which is true for the present perfect (PP)? Write PS or PP next to each statement 1–4.

　1 This tense is used to talk about events and situations that occurred at a specific time. The time is either stated or is clear from the context.
　2 This tense is used to talk about events and situations that occurred in the past (and may be continuing), but we don't know when, or the time isn't important.
　3 We use it with words like *ago, in 2001, at the weekend, on Monday, in March, in the morning*, etc.
　4 We use it with words like *for, since, often, just, already, yet, three times*, etc.

G ···⟩ page 139

2 Read this article about the British entrepreneur Richard Branson. Circle the correct tense.

Richard Branson was born in 1950 and **1** *grew up / has grown up* in Britain. He **2** *went / has been* to public school, where, at the age of sixteen, he **3** *started / has started* a national magazine called *Student*. After **4** he *left / has left* school, he **5** *went / has been* to Oxford University but **6** *didn't graduate / hasn't graduated*. At the age of 20, he **7** *founded / has founded* Virgin Records and **8** *opened / has opened* a shop in London's Oxford Street.

Since then, the interests of Branson's Virgin Group **9** *expanded / have expanded* into publishing, transport and hotels. Virgin Atlantic Airways, which Branson **10** *started / has started* in 1984, is now the second largest British long-haul international airline. Branson **11** *founded / has founded* the airline with the idea of offering competitive and high quality first-class and economy services. In 1993, the combined sales of Virgin Group companies **12** *exceeded / has exceeded* US$1 billion.

3 With a partner, ask and answer questions 1–8 using either *Have you ever …?* or *Did you …?* Use each of the verbs in the box once, in the right form. Give full answers.

have	have	learn	see
spend	take	think	want

　1 .... a job?
　2 .... computing when you were at school?
　3 .... of being a doctor?
　4 .... any time doing work experience?
　5 .... to be a train driver/nurse when you were young?
　6 .... an inspirational boss or teacher?
　7 .... your parents' advice about jobs when you were at school?
　8 .... an advisor about your career?

Branson **13** *spent / has spent* most of his life living in London and Oxfordshire, but he **14** *didn't only spend / hasn't only spent* his time working. Since 1985, he **15** *tried / has tried* to break a number of land and air speed records. His boat **16** *crossed / has crossed* the Atlantic in 1986 in a record time, and in 1991 Branson **17** *broke / has broken* all records in his balloon flight across the pacific.

What type of person do you think Richard Branson is? Would you like him as your boss? Do you think he sounds inspirational? Why, or why not?

Writing extra

4   In the GT Writing Module you may be asked to write a letter of application for a job.
    (···▸WF 4) You will need to use a range of vocabulary, some quite specialised, in your letter.

Complete the letter with words from the box.

closing
CV
Department
experience
interview
manager
post
qualified
salary
skills

> Dear Sir,
>
> I am writing to apply for the **1** .... of Sales Manager
> advertised on 3rd March in *The Times* newspaper. I have worked for the
> past two years as a junior **2** .... in an electronics company
> in the Marketing **3** .... I feel now is the right time to apply
> for a higher position as I believe I have gained the necessary
> **4** ....
>
> I am a **5** .... engineer (see the enclosed **6** ....)
> and believe I have excellent management **7** ....
> My **8** .... at present is £25,000 a year.
>
> I realise that the **9** .... date for applications was last Friday,
> but I hope that you will still be willing to consider my application. I am
> available for **10** .... at any time. I look forward to hearing
> from you in the near future.
>
> Yours faithfully,
>
> *Jason Stephenson*

Speaking *Part 2*

Test spot

In Part 2 of the Speaking Module you will have to give a short
talk lasting 1–2 minutes. The examiner will give you a card to
read and then you will have 1 minute to prepare. It is a good
idea to make notes. You must talk about all the points on the
card. ···▸ TF 9

5   Look at this task.

> **Describe someone who has motivated you.**
>   **You should say:**
>   **who they are**
>   **what was special about this person**
>   **what other people say about this person**
>   **and explain why this person has motivated you.**

Use a mind map like the example opposite to make
notes of important points and then give your talk to
your partner. Time yourself – make sure you speak for
a maximum of two minutes, preferably a little less.

Had worked in advertising. Knew about the business world.

A TEACHER AT MY SECONDARY SCHOOL

Friendly, gave me confidence, extra help with exams.

Helped with university application. Made me interested in business studies.

Liked by most students. Not traditional enough, said parents.

Writing folder 3

Task 2: Understanding the question and planning your writing

In both the Academic and General Training Modules of IELTS you will be asked to write 250 words, giving your opinion on something or suggesting a solution to a problem. You should allow 40 minutes for this task.

Understanding the question

1 Look at the example Task 2 question below.

> Write about the following topic:
>
> **Working hours today are too long and people are not spending as much time as they should with their families or on leisure activities.**
>
> **What is your opinion on this?**
>
> Give reasons for your answer and include any relevant examples from your own knowledge or experience.

Advice

- Make sure you read the question carefully – there are often two parts to the question and you will need to answer both parts. If you don't, you will lose marks.
- There is no correct answer, so you can agree or disagree or a mixture of both, though it is usually a good idea to put forward both sides of the argument.
- Don't repeat the question in your introduction.
- Make a plan before you start writing. Make a list of ideas that you want to include and sort them into the different sides of the argument – for and against, or advantages and disadvantages.

Work with a partner. Which of the following ideas might be appropriate to include in your answer? Which would not be appropriate? Why?

Your answer could ...
1 say why you think people are spending more time at work
2 talk about just one type of job
3 explain what kind of job you want to have in the future
4 give examples of possible problems of someone who is always at work
5 talk about the effect of absent parents on the children
6 discuss the salaries of different jobs
7 say how much money you would like to make
8 mention a friend or a member of your family
9 say why a particular job would suit you
10 include a conclusion disagreeing very strongly with the statement.

Structuring the essay

You will gain marks if your essay is structured appropriately. This model may help you:

- an introductory paragraph followed by
- two to three paragraphs giving your reasons and examples from your own knowledge or experience followed by
- a concluding paragraph

The introduction

2   The introduction to your essay is very important and often the hardest part to write. Look at the three paragraphs below. Which ones do you prefer? Why?

A

I disagree with the statement that working hours today are too long and that people are not spending as much time as they should with their families or on leisure activities. Everyone knows that people today don't work as much as they used to. It is a fact that if people don't work hard, the economy will fail and there will be no jobs for anyone. I think my family is a good example of a family who work very hard.

B

In the twentieth century people believed that life in the future would be easier and that they would have more leisure time and spend less time at work. However, now we are in the twenty-first century we can see that this is not the case. In fact, people in most countries need to work even harder today than they did in the past.

C

The first thing we need to consider is where we are talking about when we say that people are working long hours. It is important to make clear that in many countries people have always worked long hours and to work shorter hours is not an option available to them.

Useful language

First of all, I would like to say that …
The first thing to consider when discussing X is that …
There is no doubt that …
One of the main arguments put forward for X is that …
I strongly agree/disagree with the statement that …
Although some people say that …, I believe that …

Giving reasons and examples from knowledge or experience

3   It is very important to give reasons and relevant examples from your own knowledge or experience. Read through the example below and then work with a partner and think of examples of your own which would be relevant to the essay task in exercise 1.

EXAMPLE: I think a person should not have to work more than 38 hours a week so that he or she can spend time with the family. Firstly, let's say the father, needs time to relax with his children, get to know them and see them grow. One example of a person working too much comes from my own family. My father used to work very long hours and never had the time to attend parents' evenings at school or see me play in concerts. This had a negative effect on the family unit.

Useful language

Firstly, …
The most important point is …
The next most important point is …
Secondly, …
Next, …
One/An example/illustration of this is …
I can illustrate this with an example from my own experience.
… such as …

The conclusion

It's important to have a conclusion – a short paragraph which summarises your arguments. You shouldn't introduce new arguments in your conclusion. It should summarise what you have already said earlier in your essay.

Useful language

Finally, …
To sum up, …
In conclusion, …

4   Write your answer to the task in exercise 1. Before you begin, read the question again and underline the important words. The question has two parts: what are they?

You can use one of the introductory paragraphs from exercise 2 or one of your own. Make sure you write 250 words or just over. If you write fewer than 250 words, you will lose marks.

Selling dreams?

Speaking *Parts 1 and 3*

1 With a partner, read this question and answer.

Question: Do you ever advertise products or companies, for example by recommending them to friends?

Answer: Yes, I sometimes do.

That answer doesn't show how good your English is. Here are some answers that have been expanded. By each of the beginnings (1–3), write the letters of the expansions (a–e) that can follow it.

1 Yes, I sometimes do.   ....
2 No, I don't.   ....
3 I've never thought about it. ....

a **For instance**, I told my friends about my mobile phone, because I thought it was very smart.
b **I suppose** I do, because carrying a plastic bag with a company's name on it is a form of advertising.
c **The reason is** that one of my friends does it all the time, and it gets very boring.
d **I'm not sure** if I would want to, but perhaps it's hard to avoid.
e **Maybe** I'll stop doing it, because I don't want to provide free advertising for companies.

Now answer these questions, using some of the phrases in bold above to develop your answer.

• Do you ever advise people not to buy certain products?
• Does advertising affect what you buy?
• Does advertising make you want things you can't afford to buy?

Reading

2 Whenever you read, try to work out the main point of each paragraph. The newspaper article on page 47 is about using members of the public to pass on advertisements on their computers. Read each of the first three paragraphs in turn, and answer questions 1 and 2. There is an example to help you.

Questions 1 and 2
*Choose the correct letter, **A**, **B** or **C**.*

Example:
What is the first paragraph about?
A the type of people who make films
B what happens in the writer's film
C how films are used in marketing

The answer is **B**. The paragraph describes a sequence of events (= *what happens*), and the last sentence, *"Cut!" shouts the director*, suggests that it's about a particular film, not films in general.

1 What is the second paragraph about?
   A deciding what a film should be about
   B choosing where to shoot a film
   C the reason for making a film

2 What is the third paragraph about?
   A how viral marketing started
   B the writer's concerns about viral marketing
   C a company that advises on viral marketing

Test spot

Choosing the best headings from a list, as in questions 3–6, is one of the task types in the Reading Modules.
Read each paragraph, consider all the headings in the box, and choose the one that fits the meaning of the paragraph best. Each paragraph should have a different heading. You won't use all the headings in the list. ⋯⟫ TF 4

Questions 3–6

For each of the last four paragraphs, choose the best heading from this list, and write its letter beside the paragraph.

A Some products benefit more than others from viral marketing
B It matters who sent it
C Getting the balance right
D The writer changes his mind about viral marketing
E How viral marketing has changed
F The response to the writer's viral

⏱ about 450 words

>> *How I made my first viral*

I'm sitting at a desk signing copies of my book. Suddenly, a man hits me on the head with a frying pan as hard as he can. I try to hide under the desk, but he's too quick and keeps hitting me. "Cut!" shouts the director.

5 The scene took place in a London bookshop. A company called the Viral Factory was making a 20-second film to promote my recently published book. The film was to be sent by email to people who know plenty of other people. The hope was that they'd send
10 it on to all their friends, and I'd become famous.

Viral marketing – promoting a product on the web – probably dates back to 1996, when it was used to advertise a free email service. Every time a customer used the service, the company's website address was
15 automatically included at the end. The company, Hotmail, signed up an amazing 12 million subscribers in only 18 months.

3 .... Today, viral marketing is a lot more sophisticated. It's not enough to simply put a website
20 address at the foot of an email. These days, only an instantly memorable short film will "go viral" – something attention-grabbing enough to make people want to pass it on immediately, something that gives the impression of having been caught on camera quite
25 by chance.

4 .... Viral marketing has two great advantages over most other advertising. It's extremely cheap, and it has enormous impact. With a television ad, there's no guarantee that viewers will actually watch it. But if a viral arrives in your email inbox from a friend, you'll be 30 curious and click on it. The message is then delivered straight into your brain.

5 .... Of course, if the clip is too obviously designed to advertise a particular product, people won't pass it on. No one wants to feel they are being used by a 35 business. On the other hand, nobody will buy the product if they don't know what it is. So the product name and a website address are normally put at the end of the clip. That's what I did in my viral. I didn't want it to be too obvious that the whole incident was a 40 marketing exercise.

6 .... So did it work? It's difficult to measure the success of a viral marketing campaign. In the few days after I launched my viral, traffic to my website increased dramatically, from a handful of visitors a day 45 to several hundred. Certainly, to judge by the number of people who asked if I was all right, it was a great success. The answer, incidentally, was no. Even though the frying pan was made of rubber, it still really hurt.

from an article by Toby Young

Vocabulary Word formation

3 Complete the spaces in this table with words that are related to the ones given, which come from the article above. Use an English–English dictionary to help you, and mark the stressed syllable in each word. In most cases, more than one noun is possible.

verbs	nouns	adjectives
		'viral
pro'mote		
'advertise		
		'memorable
	a'ttention	
		'curious
	suc'cess	

4 Complete each sentence with the most suitable adjective from the table in exercise 3.

1 People are usually .... to see film clips they have received from a friend.
2 The key to .... viral marketing is personal contact.
3 .... videos are ones designed to show a company's products to potential customers.
4 .... TV commercials are still talked about years later, even if they have had little effect on sales.
5 Although great care is taken when making commercials, ... viewers may still find mistakes in them.

5 Would you read virals sent to your computer? Would you send them to your friends? Do you think companies should be allowed to send virals?

1

In small groups, discuss what these quotes mean and say what you think about them. Remember to expand what you say.

> Telling lies does not work in advertising.

> If the advertising budget is big enough, you can make people believe anything.

> In our factory, we make lipstick. In our advertising, we sell hope.

Listening

2 🎧 You are going to hear a radio interview with Gary Phillips, the head of an advertising agency. Listen to the first part of the interview.

Questions 1–6
Complete the sentences below.
*Write **NO MORE THAN ONE WORD** for each answer.*

1 Early advertising provided only ....
2 In the late nineteenth century, manufacturers advertised because they needed to increase the .... for their goods.
3 Companies were able to make a large .... by selling luxury goods.
4 Increased .... meant that companies risked going out of business if they didn't advertise.
5 Persuasive advertising tries to involve people's ....
6 Persuasive advertising stresses the .... of buying particular products.

🎧 In the second part of the interview, Gary uses each of the products below (7–11) as an example of a different advertising technique. First make sure you understand the words in the box, using an English–English dictionary if necessary.

Questions 7–11
Which technique does each product exemplify?
Choose your answers from the box.

Example: *Answer:*
children's clothing   ....*H*....

7 running shoes   ....
8 furniture   ....
9 washing powder   ....
10 snacks   ....
11 engine oil   ....

Pronunciation *Sentence stress*

3 Read this sentence from the recording aloud, stressing *only* the words that are underlined.

<u>My</u> guest <u>this</u> evening <u>is</u> advertising expert Gary Phillips, <u>who's</u> going <u>to</u> tell <u>us</u> <u>how</u> advertising works.

It's difficult to read the sentence in that way, and hard to understand, because the wrong words are stressed.

🎧 Now listen to the sentence with the stress on the right words and repeat it.

4 In this extract from the recording, underline the words that should be stressed.

Interviewer: Welcome to the programme.
Gary: Thank you.
Interviewer: How did it all start?
Gary: When everyone lived in small communities, and knew the local farmer who grew and sold vegetables, advertising was unnecessary. But in a larger community it's a different situation.

🎧 Now listen and check.

5 Put each of these word classes in the right column in the table below.

adjectives   adverbs   auxiliary verbs
conjunctions   nouns   main verbs
prepositions

content words (usually stressed)	grammatical words (rarely stressed)

A	wide product range
B	humour
C	a claim that is suggested and not expressed
D	a name that young children can remember
E	celebrity endorsement
F	repetition
G	greater value for money
H	creating a brand

6 Words aren't given equal stress in sentences. Why do you think the words in boxes are given extra stress?

1 When everyone lived in small communities, advertising wasn't necessary. But in a larger community, it's a different situation.
2 For centuries adverts simply gave information. The big change occurred in the late nineteenth century. This was really the beginning of advertising designed to persuade people to buy.

Why do you think the words in *italics* below would *not* be given much stress?

3 My guest today is advertising expert Gary Phillips. Gary, have we always had *advertising*?
4 At the same time, in some countries there were plenty of people with money to spend on luxuries and other *inessential goods*.

Now read sentences 1–4 aloud, making sure you stress the right words.

🎧 Listen and check.

Grammar Relative clauses

7 Look at these two sentences which you heard in the recording. The relative clauses are underlined. Which relative clause is defining (gives essential information), and which is non-defining (gives extra information)?

1 My guest this evening is advertising expert Gary Phillips, <u>who's going to tell us how advertising works</u>.
2 Imagine a company <u>which makes children's clothing</u>.

8 In each of the sentences below, underline the relative clause, write *defining* or *non-defining*, and draw a box round the relative pronoun.

EXAMPLES: We learn by imitating people who are important to us. *defining*

My guest this evening is advertising expert Gary Phillips, who's going to tell us how advertising works. *non-defining*

1 A great deal of advertising is about the benefits that we hope to gain.
2 Ordinary people who appear in advertisements are usually intended to make the viewer or reader identify with them.
3 Jewellery and perfume, which are luxury goods, are usually very profitable for the manufacturer.
4 Consumers that see the same advertisements many times are likely to remember the name of the product.

Now complete this table with the correct relative pronouns.

	defining	non-defining
people	.... or	....
things	.... or	....

Which type of relative clause needs commas round it (or a comma and a full stop)?

G ⋯⊱ page 139

9 In groups of three, match pictures 1–6 with a type of advertising (a–f).

a small ads
b a commercial
c a flyer
d a banner
e a pop-up
f a poster on a hoarding

Now take turns to define one of the types of advertising, using relative clauses. The other people in your group should guess which type is being defined.

EXAMPLE: *This is an advertisement which is normally a single piece of paper, and which is given to people or put in places where people will see it.* (Answer: *a flyer*)

Test folder 4

Headings

(Academic Reading and General Training Reading Modules only)

You may be asked to choose suitable headings for some paragraphs or sections of the passage, which will be labelled alphabetically.

The headings are given Roman numerals, where i = 1, v = 5 and x = 10. The numbers one to twelve are: **i, ii, iii, iv, v, vi, vii, viii, ix, x, xi, xii**. Although you don't need to know this number system, you must copy the numbers correctly.

When this task is used, it is always the first one on a particular passage, and the headings are given before the passage.

Advice

- Skim the passage quickly to get a general idea of its meaning.
- Re-read the first labelled paragraph or section, and decide what it's about. Read all the headings, and write beside the paragraph all those that might be suitable. Make sure they fit the meaning of the whole paragraph, and don't simply use some of the same words.
- Do the same with the other paragraphs, in each case reading *all* the headings.
- Where you have chosen more than one heading, decide which one fits best. Remember that every paragraph or section will have a different heading and there will always be more headings than paragraphs. If you are given an example, make sure you don't use that heading for other questions.

1   This passage is similar to those in Section 3 of the General Training Reading Module, though shorter, about 600 words.

The article below has nine paragraphs, A–I.
Choose the correct heading for each paragraph from the list of headings on the opposite page.
Write the correct number i–xii next to each question 1–8.
Example: Paragraph **A** ....*x*.....

1	Paragraph **B**	....
2	Paragraph **C**	....
3	Paragraph **D**	....
4	Paragraph **E**	....
5	Paragraph **F**	....
6	Paragraph **G**	....
7	Paragraph **H**	....
8	Paragraph **I**	....

A Do we really want non-stop TV advertising without the boring programmes in between? Well, that's what more and more retailers are giving us, in the shape of in-store TV. Go into a supermarket or department store, and the chances are there will be plasma screens beaming the company's own TV channel at you.

B In between news clips, recipe tips and beauty advice, the screens show advertisements for products in the aisles. The news and other editorial sections of the broadcast play an important role in preventing shoppers from feeling they are the constant target of ads. 'Advertorial' pieces can be very effective: these are ads presented in the style of an editorial or journalistic report, and have been known to cause sales to treble or even quadruple.

C In the early years of in-store TV, too often screens were dotted randomly around stores, playing continuous adverts that were not tailored to the shopping environment. In terms of customer experience, it sometimes left a lot to be desired. This has been changing, though, as advertisers get more sophisticated at using in-store TV.

D In-store ads have to be particularly attention-grabbing because people are there to shop, not watch TV. Unless an ad is outstanding, no-one watches it for more than a few seconds. Advertisers have realised that this requires a different approach from standard television, and often customise ads just for in-store TV. One ad for

List of Headings

i   Satisfied shoppers
ii   How the technology has improved
iii Building on past experience
iv Why not everyone is happy
v   The advantages for advertisers compared with TV
vi The products that it suits best
vii Not just advertising
viii Information required
ix Giving shoppers input
x   A growing trend
xi Making customers notice the ads
xii Ads designed for different departments

2 This paragraph is from a more difficult passage that might be used in the Academic Reading Module. Consider each heading carefully, because they all have some connection with the paragraph, but only one fits it accurately.

Choose the correct heading from the list below.

List of Headings

i   Customers' rising expectations of what sellers should provide
ii Selling cars is different from selling certain other goods
iii What customers should do to find the best products
iv Manufacturers are improving their products to meet customers' demands
v   Customers and manufacturers need each other
vi How sellers can manage their relationship with customers to benefit themselves
vii Being dependent on customers puts a seller in a weak position

deodorant body spray certainly attracted attention. It was actually set in a store: a male shopper sprays on some of the product, making himself so attractive that women in the store run after him.

E Ads that communicate facts about a product or an offer appear to work better than the more emotional, slice-of-life advertising that dominates regular television. Shoppers are in the store to make purchases, and they want the ad to tell them specifically about a brand and what it is going to do for them.

F It is important to make sure customers are not bombarded with messages when they don't want to be, by ensuring that content is tightly tailored to particular store areas. Several TV channels need to be broadcast simultaneously: in the central aisle – which typically has five or six large plasma screens – the café, and so on. That allows advertisers to buy ad time in particular sections of the store: health and beauty, electronics or food, for instance, and reach customers just when they're deciding which brand of toothpaste or which DVD player to buy.

G A minority of customers feel that, rather than wasting money on in-store TV, the retailer should lower prices, or at least invest in more useful services. The biggest turn-off, though, for both customers and staff on the shop floor, is noise. However, if sound is not broadcast from all the channels, the noise levels should not cause unnecessary irritation. And directional sound can be used, which again curbs noise levels.

H As cable and satellite channels multiply, it has become more difficult for manufacturers and others to reach a mass audience on regular television. Through in-store TV they can reach the large numbers of people who still shop at the supermarket and big chain stores. The big plus is that the medium has been very successful at increasing sales.

I The biggest lesson is that in-store TV needs to communicate in an unobtrusive way. Analysing changes in shopping patterns at different times of day can help the retailer to show ads that are relevant to particular customer groups. As a result, the majority of customers feel that in-store TV improves their overall shopping experience. So the objectors are probably going to have to restrict their purchasing to the small shops that in-store TV hasn't yet penetrated.

Maintaining a positive relationship with buyers is an important goal for a seller, regardless of whether the seller is marketing cereal, financial services, or an electric generating plant. Through buyer–seller interaction, the buyer develops expectations about the seller's future behaviour. To fulfil these expectations, the seller must deliver on promises made. Over time, a healthy buyer–seller relationship results in interdependencies between the two parties. The buyer depends on the seller to furnish information, parts, and service; to be available; and to provide satisfying products in the future. For example, car buyers depend on car makers to provide quality vehicles, as well as service, guarantees, information about various car models, fair prices, and convenient dealer locations. The seller depends on the buyer to continue purchasing from the seller. A car maker depends on buyers to purchase its cars to supply it with the funds needed to meet its organisational objectives.

8·1 Time to waste?

1 Do you think people should spend their free time actively (for example, dancing or painting) or passively (for example, watching a film or listening to music)? Why? How do you spend your free time?

Reading

2 Read the extract from the programme of events at an arts centre.
Complete the table below.

⏱ about 350 words

*Write **NO MORE THAN TWO WORDS** from the reading passage for each answer.*

> ### Test spot
> First read the headings of the columns. Think about what word class would fit the heading and notes (if there are any). All the answers are words from the passage, but they may not be in the same order as in the questions. Make sure you write no more than the maximum number of words and copy them exactly as they are written in the passage. This type of task is similar to note completion. ⋯⋮ **TF 3**

name	type of event	main theme	notes
Jake Duff	EXAMPLE: **0** *comedy*	**1**	has been called **2** ....
Nick Robertson	**3**	supernovas	a **4** .... will be on sale
'Kate and Joe'	**5**	**6**	opportunity to talk to the **7** ....
Sharon Williams	**8**	seeing **9** .... in new ways	subjects are often reflected in **10** ....

This week at the Prospect Arts Centre

Monday and Tuesday at 7.30: Jake Duff

If you want to see a Shakespearean tragedy,
5 you're bound to be disappointed, but if it's comedy you want, look no further. Jake's hilarious look at rural life will make you laugh till you cry. Recently picked by
10 Ten-Street Magazine as best newcomer, Jake says he'd love to be named their 'Top Satirist'. To judge by his present form, he's sure to achieve this ambition very soon.

Wednesday at 7.30: Nick Robertson

15 Nick is a very popular regular at the Prospect, and if you attended last year's talk you'll remember his astonishing slides and clear explanation of how the solar system functions. This year Nick is turning his attention to supernovas, and it
20 promises to be an equally fascinating evening. His latest booklet, 'What is a galaxy?', will be available after the talk, and if you'd like to buy a copy, Nick will be happy to sign it for you.

Grammar Talking about the future

3 Match each sentence (1–8) with the right meaning (a–e).

1 The Arts Centre is holding a scupture exhibition soon.
2 The play begins at 7.30 p.m.
3 The actors are going to meet the audience after the performance.
4 The Arts Centre's falling income means it is going to make a loss this year.
5 Children will love the comedy show taking place next Saturday morning.
6 Because there's a special offer, I think I'll go to both this week's shows.
7 I expect Nick will give another talk next year.
8 Jake Duff's show is going to be a sell-out, judging by ticket sales so far.

a a prediction
b a decision made at this moment
c something already arranged or decided
d a future result of a present situation
e a timetable

Beside each meaning a–e above, write the tenses that can be used for it. You will need to use two of them twice, and one of the meanings has two answers.

Tenses: *will*   *be going to*   present simple
present continuous

Thursday to Saturday at 8.00: 'Kate and Joe'

The latest by Canadian playwright Geraldine Scott, 'Kate and Joe' is a moving exploration of growing up. Set in the industrial town where Scott lives, the play will have three performances here at the Prospect, before its extended run in Toronto. On Thursday the actors will be happy to stay and answer questions after the performance. This event is likely to prove very popular, so please book as soon as possible.

25

30

35

All this week: Sharon Williams

Sharon is well known for her fresh insight. In this new photographic exhibition, she moves away from her usual theme of people's emotional states. Through her use of polished metal, we see multiple reflections of everyday objects, apparently floating in air and transformed into abstract shapes. When this exhibition ends, Sharon is starting work on a major commission for the city council.

40

45

4 Look at sentences 1–10, in which the writer says how likely a future event is. Decide whether each sentence is closest in meaning to a, b or c.

a I think it's likely to happen.
b I'm not sure if it will happen.
c I think it's unlikely to happen.

1 If you want to see a Shakespearean tragedy, you're bound to be disappointed.
2 There are so many comedians these days that there's little chance of winning any of the top awards.
3 This year Nick is turning his attention to supernovas, and it promises to be a fascinating evening.
4 I'm convinced I'll enjoy watching live comedy.
5 Having a wide range of events at the Arts Centre may attract more people.
6 I doubt whether many people would want to go on stage with Jake.
7 There's a chance that the Arts Centre will have to close if it can't increase its ticket sales.
8 There'll probably be a queue to get in to Jake's performance.
9 I have no doubt that Sharon Williams's photographs will leave a lasting impression.
10 Maybe holding an exhibition by local artists will attract people.

G ⋯⋗ page 140

Speaking *Part 1*

5 With a partner, predict what each of these events will be like.

EXAMPLE: You've been invited to listen to an orchestra of very young children.
I doubt whether I'll enjoy it. On the other hand, there's a chance that they'll be better than I expect.

1 You've been invited to a performance by your favourite singer or actor.
2 You've been asked to sing in front of a large audience.
3 You've been invited to a film that you have already seen and don't like.
4 You've been asked to take part in a sport that you've never played before.

Use these phrases to start your sentences.

I doubt whether …   I'm sure …
I may …   There's a chance …
Maybe …   I'm convinced …

8·2

1 Here are five types of experience that people gain from hobbies and other leisure activities. Can you think of another activity which might provide each experience?

relaxation – *walking*
excitement – *paragliding*
communion with nature – *scuba diving*
companionship – *playing football*
creative expression – *writing short stories*

Listening

2 🎧 You are going to listen to a talk which is similar to Part 4 of the Listening Module. This one is about the study of leisure.

> ### Test spot
> Before listening, read the instructions carefully. Check how many answers you should write and the maximum number of words for each answer. Try and write your answers in the same order that you hear them, but it doesn't matter if you change the order. You should write the words exactly as you hear them. This is similar to note completion. ⋯� 3

Questions 1–9

Example:

List **TWO** leisure activities that are described as likely to provide relaxation.
Write **NO MORE THAN TWO WORDS** for each answer.

Listen to the first part of the talk. When the speaker mentions *the opportunity for relaxation* you know this is the relevant part of the recording. The answers are:

.... *yoga*
.... *stamp collecting*

Then keep listening and answer the following questions.

List **THREE** leisure activities that are described as providing 'flow'.
1 ....
2 ....
3 ....

List **TWO** leisure activities that are described as providing companionship.
4 ....
5 ....

List **TWO** leisure activities that are described as providing communion with nature.
6 ....
7 ....

List **TWO** leisure activities that are described as providing creative expression.
8 ....
9 ....

🎧 Listen to the rest of the talk, and answer short-answer questions 10–14. This task type is used in the Listening and in both Reading Modules.

Questions 10–14

> ### Test spot
> Read the questions and think about possible answers. Listen for a paraphrase of the question. Write down the words exactly as you hear them. Check that your answers are spelt correctly and make sense in relation to the question.

Answer the questions below.
Write **NO MORE THAN THREE WORDS** for each answer.

Example:

0 What is central to people's experience of leisure activities?

Answer: control

The question paraphrases *an essential aspect of leisure* in the talk.

10 What should organisers of activities aim to provide?

....

11 What do many participants want to do after an activity? ....

12 What name is given to shopping as a leisure activity?

....

13 What new attraction is now offered by shopping centres? ....

14 What do leisure activities help us to enjoy?

....

Pronunciation *Vowel length*

3 If you look at how dictionaries show the pronunciation of words, you'll see that both short vowels (e.g. the /ʊ/ in *full*) and long vowels (e.g. the /ɑː/ in *far*) are represented by one symbol. The symbols for short vowels are /æ/, /e/, /ɪ/, /ɒ/, /ʌ/, /ʊ/, /ə/. Most dictionaries add : to show long vowels: /ɑː/, /ɜː/, /iː/, /ɔː/, /uː/. Both short and long vowels may be spelt with one or two letters.

Diphthongs (e.g. the /aʊ/ in *about*) begin as one sound and end as another (*di-* means 'two'), and are represented with two symbols. The spelling often (but not always) has two letters.

You heard these words on the recording. Write them in the correct column.

f<u>u</u>ll   f<u>ar</u>   ab<u>ou</u>t   inst<u>ea</u>d   g<u>oa</u>l
t<u>i</u>me   m<u>ore</u>   th<u>ere</u>   m<u>u</u>sic   b<u>ir</u>d
sk<u>i</u>lls   y<u>ear</u>   st<u>u</u>dy   p<u>eo</u>ple   h<u>o</u>bby

short vowels /æ/, /e/, /ɪ/, /ɒ/, /ʌ/, /ʊ/, /ə/	long vowels /ɑː/, /ɜː/, /iː/, /ɔː/, /uː/	diphthongs /aʊ/, /eə/, /ɪə/, /əʊ/, /aɪ/, /eɪ/, /ɔɪ/
full	*far*	*about*

Look up the words in an English–English dictionary, such as the *Cambridge Advanced Learner's Dictionary*. Beside the words in the chart, write the pronunciation symbol for each underlined vowel.

🎧 Listen and repeat. Then, with a partner, read the words aloud, taking care with the pronunciation.

Speaking *Part 3*

4 In groups of three, choose a leisure activity, and write at least four questions about it. Here are a couple of examples to get you started.

Watching television
1 What are the most popular sorts of programmes?
2 Do you think the time that children spend watching television should be limited? Why, or why not?
3 ....
4 ....

Playing computer games
1 What are the benefits of playing computer games?
2 What do you think about the amount of time some people spend on computer games?
3 ....
4 ....

Collecting autographs of famous people
1 Why do some people collect autographs?
2 How easy is it to collect autographs?
3 ....
4 ....

Reading
1 ....
2 ....
3 ....
4 ....

Each of you should choose a leisure activity, and ask someone else in the class the questions.

Writing folder 4

General Training Writing Task 1: Writing a letter

In Task 1 of the General Training Writing Module you will have to write a letter. You will have 20 minutes to complete this task and you will need to write 150 words.

The letter will be about a particular situation/problem and you will have three points to write about.

Advice

- Remember you do not get extra marks for writing more than 150 words, but you will lose marks if you write less or many more.
- The instructions will ask you to write about three points. You must not leave out any of the points or add irrelevant material or you will lose marks.
- Your letter must be paragraphed – for example, a paragraph on each point and a concluding paragraph with a suitable ending.
- You do not need to include any postal addresses.

1   First of all, read the question below carefully. Who is the letter to?

You are studying in a large town where there are no leisure facilities for young people. Write a letter to the local council. In your letter
- *describe the problem*
- *make some suggestions for leisure facilities*
- *say why you think that these facilities will make the town a better place.*

2   Which of the following opening and closing phrases should you use in this letter? Why? When do you use the other two?

A Dear Peter
Best wishes

B Dear Mr Johnson
Yours sincerely

C Dear Sir/Madam
Yours faithfully

3   Compare these two opening paragraphs and say which one is more appropriate for the letter above. Give your reasons.

A

I am a nineteen-year-old student and I live in Hollworth. I am writing to explain the problems that young people who live in this town have. At present, there are very few things for young people to do and I believe you could help to improve the situation.

B

I want you to do something about the terrible problem we have here in Hollworth. There is nothing for young people to do in the evenings or at weekends. This is because you don't care about young people.

4   Read this answer to point 2 of the task above and say why it wouldn't get high marks.

I think it would be a good idea to have a swimming pool. Swimming is very good exercise and would benefit many people in the town, not just young people. I am sure you could easily raise the money when people find out what a good cause it is. There is a piece of land behind the cinema which would make a great place to have a swimming pool. It is very central and there is room for a car park as well. I am a very good swimmer and I won quite a few prizes when I was at school.

5   Read this conclusion to the letter above. Why is it unacceptable?

So, now you have my reasons and ideas. I hope you get back to me quickly and agree with my ideas. Drop me a line as soon as you can.

6   It is important that you use appropriate language. Look at these sentences from job applications, some of them written by IELTS candidates. Why would they be inappropriate in a formal letter? What would be a better way of expressing them?

EXAMPLE: I hope to hear a humble response from you soon.
Inappropriate – *humble* is not used in this way. It would be better to say:

I hope to hear from you soon or *I look forward to hearing from you in the near future.*

1   I want a job in your cinema as soon as possible.
2   Please, please, spare a thought to consider my application.
3   I found your Excellency's job advertisement in the paper last week.
4   I want you to answer this letter immediately.
5   I can't attend the interview next week as I am busy.
6   You forgot to send me an application form.
7   It is with regret that I must inform you that there are a number of deficiencies with your answer to my question.
8   Hope you like my CV.
9   Email me about my application any time.
10 May I take this opportunity to enlighten you about my many qualifications?

7   Read the question below and the letter in response to it, which is based on an answer produced by an IELTS candidate. Rewrite the answer, making sure that:

1   you have used the appropriate opening and closing phrases
2   you have answered all the points
3   everything you say is relevant – you may need to add or delete the information given
4   you have written in paragraphs
5   you have written the correct number of words
6   you have used appropriate language
7   your grammar is correct
8   your spelling is correct.

You are looking for a part-time job in a sports centre. Write a letter to the manager of the sports centre.

In your letter
- *introduce yourself*
- *explain what experience and special skills you have*
- *tell him/her when you think you could start.*

Dear Manager,

I am a twenty-year-old student and I am studing physical education at Pulteney College. I study there since two years. I need job, especially part-time job. This is because I need money for my accomodation which expensiv in this area. I share a house with three other students who are also studing physical education. I think I am suited to working in your sports centre becose I like sport, especially the running, the judo, the tennis and the basketball. I win the college award for Best Student in my first year. I have two more years before I am a qualified sports teacher. I can give you references from my teachers if you want. I can start whenever you want. I would prefer work at evenings and on weekends as I have classes on the daytime.

Write back soon.

Units 5–8 Revision

Topic review

1 Read these sentences and say which are true for you, giving more details. Try to expand your answers.

1 I have never taken any notice of adverts.
2 I think history and archaeology are fascinating.
3 In the future, people will spend more time on leisure activities.
4 You need to work hard to make money.
5 Qualifications are more important than experience when it comes to work.
6 I am more likely to watch TV than go to the theatre.
7 History as a subject is bound to disappear from the school timetable in the future.
8 A good salary is more important to me than long holidays.
9 I am going to spend next summer working.
10 I am the person who works the hardest in my family.

Grammar

Past simple / present perfect

2 Read the text below and circle the correct form of the verb.

Social trends in Australia

Between 1982 and 1994, the average hours worked by full-time workers **0** (increased) / have increased from 42 to 45 hours a week. This trend **1** levelled off / has levelled off during the late 1990s, and since 2000 the average number of hours worked by full-time workers **2** dropped back / has dropped back to around 44 hours a week.

Since 1982, the distribution of full-time hours **3** changed / has changed considerably. Between 1982 and 2002, the proportion of full-time workers working a 40-hour week **4** declined / has declined from 39% to 24%. The greatest increase in that period **5** was / has been in the proportion of full-time workers working 50 to 59 hours per week (from 10% to 16%). This trend towards longer working hours **6** was / has been relatively uncommon among other OECD countries at that time, most of which either **7** experienced / have experienced little change, or **8** continued / have continued the longer-term trend in reducing full-time working hours.

Relative clauses

3 Complete the sentences. Choose the most suitable ending from the box and make it into a relative clause using *who*, *which* or *that*.

> EXAMPLE: *I work on Madison Avenue, **which** is the centre of the advertising industry in New York.*

0 I work on Madison Avenue
1 My colleague is always late for work
2 The archaeologists have found the tomb of the king
3 We went to see the film
4 I am writing a book review
5 Archaeologists are people
6 I don't like advertisements
7 What was the name of the company

> it won an Oscar this year.
> it makes my boss really angry.
> ~~it is the centre of the advertising industry in New York.~~
> it might upset the author.
> it gave all its workers a bonus last year.
> he ruled the country in 4500 BC.
> they often have to work in difficult conditions.
> they don't tell the truth.

4 Add commas to sentences containing a non-defining relative clause. Sentences with defining relative clauses do not need commas.

> EXAMPLE: Richard Branson who is a very successful businessman was invited to speak at the conference.
> *Richard Branson, who is a very successful businessman, was invited to speak at the conference.*

1 My wife who lives in New York works in advertising.
2 The Dorchester Hotel which is near Hyde Park is very comfortable.
3 I know a lot of people who are archaeologists.
4 The boy who played the part of Peter in the play goes to my college.
5 The people who built the Pyramids must have worked long and hard.
6 My manager who is very strict about punctuality has been with the company for years.

Vocabulary

5 The twenty words below have all appeared in Units 5–8. Decide what they are with the help of the information given. Then use some of the words to complete sentences a–e.

- three words to do with history:
  1 s _ t _
  2 r e _ _ a _ _ h
  3 t _ _ b
- four words to do with work:
  4 s a _ _ r y
  5 p _ _ m _ t _ _ n
  6 _ _ t i v _ _ _ _ n
  7 m _ _ _ g _ _
- five verbs to do with money
  8 e _ _ n
  9 _ _ e n _
  10 w _ s _ _
  11 s _ _ e
  12 _ _ y
- six nouns to do with leisure
  13 p _ a _
  14 _ x _ _ b _ t _ _ _
  15 d _ _ c _ _ g
  16 p _ _ f _ _ m _ _ c _
  17 r _ l _ x a _ _ _ _
  18 a _ t _ v _ _ _

a I hope I can work my way up from tea boy to .... of the whole department.
b You should never ask someone how much money they .... from their job.
c We saw an excellent .... of *Macbeth* last night.
d Paola has spent the last four years doing .... into students' leisure habits.
e I went to a photography .... last night.

6 Complete each sentence with a verb from the box in the correct form. Use each verb once only.

> analyse   carry out   do   lead   reach
> support

1 A historian is a person who .... research into the past.
2 The company .... the conclusion that their advertising campaign wasn't working.
3 At the meeting, the Chairman .... the latest sales figures.
4 I'm afraid the statistics don't .... your theory about outsourcing.
5 The staff in the lab are at present .... an experiment which may .... to an exciting discovery.

Climate change

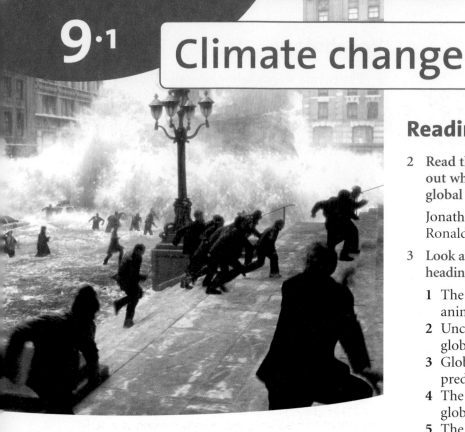

1 How much do you know about global warming? Do this quiz with a partner.

1 What has been the average global temperature change over the last 100 years?

A +0.6 °C   B +1 °C   C +3 °C

2 By how much has the sea level risen in the last 100 years?

A 0-5 cm   B 5-10 cm   C 10-20 cm

3 Which of the following is NOT an effect of global warming?

A a growth in population
B increased risk of flooding
C a change to animal habitats

4 When will we be experiencing the effects of global warming?

A not for another 50 to 100 years
B we may be experiencing them already
C never

Reading

2 Read through the article opposite quickly to find out which of the following people does NOT think global warming is a big problem.

Jonathan Overpeck   Jay Malcolm
Ronald Stouffer   Marianne Douglas

3 Look at headings 1–5 below. Which is the best heading for each paragraph A–E?

1 The effect of global warming on plant and animal life
2 Uncertainty among experts about the effects of global warming
3 Global warming: the position now and predictions for the future
4 The countries affected by a rise in sea level due to global warming
5 The debate about the causes of global warming

Test spot

There are two types of summary task in the Reading Modules. In one you need to find the answers in the text (and your answers must be actual words from the text). In the other you are given a box of answers to choose from. The summary may be on the whole text or just a section of it, and the answers may or may not be in text order but usually are.
Read the summary through first before trying to complete it. Don't try to complete the summary without reading the relevant parts of the text again carefully. Think carefully about the type of word that is missing – noun, verb, adjective, etc. ⟶ TF 5

4 As you complete this summary, remember that your answers must be words taken from the article.

Complete the summary below.
*Choose **NO MORE THAN THREE WORDS AND/OR A NUMBER** from the passage for each answer.*

The **1** .... temperature of the Earth has risen over the last hundred years. One effect is a reduction in the **2** .... in tropical oceans. An increase in carbon dioxide reduces the amount of **3** .... escaping from the atmosphere. As a result, animals are moving to different **4** ....

In the USA, research has been undertaken into the effect on sea levels if an **5** .... melted. This would destroy many heavily **6** .... places, especially in the worst-case scenario of a rise of **7** .... metres. The conclusion reached is that there is a need for people to reduce their use of **8** .... and change to different **9** ....

A disaster in the making

A

Most scientists agree that global warming presents the greatest threat to the environment. There is little doubt that the Earth is getting warmer. In the last century the average temperature rose about 0.6 degrees C around the world. From the melting of the ice cap on Mt Kilimanjaro, Africa's tallest peak, to the loss of coral reefs as oceans become warmer, the effects of global warming are often clear. Many experts warn that global warming will cause sea levels to rise dramatically. In the past 100 years the oceans have risen 10 to 20 cms – but that's nothing compared to what would happen if, for example, Greenland's massive ice sheet were to melt. 'The consequences would be catastrophic,' says Jonathan Overpeck, Director of the Institute for the Study of Planet Earth at the University of Arizona. 'Even with a small sea level rise, we're going to destroy a number of nations and cultures that have existed for thousands of years.' Overpeck and his colleagues have used computer models to create a series of maps that show the places most at risk of flooding.

Orlando
Cape Canaveral
St Petersburg
Tampa
FLORIDA
Fort Myers
Fort Lauderdale
Miami
Key West

Areas that would be under water if sea level rose by 3 metres

Areas that would be under water if sea level rose by 6 metres

B

Just as the evidence is clear that temperatures have risen in the last century, it's also well established that carbon dioxide in the Earth's atmosphere has increased about 30 percent, allowing the atmosphere to trap too much heat. However, the exact link, if any, between the increase in carbon dioxide emissions and the higher temperatures is still being disputed. Most scientists believe that humans, by burning fossil fuels such as coal and petroleum, are largely to blame for the increase in carbon dioxide. But some scientists also point to natural causes, such as volcanic activity. 'Many uncertainties surround global warming,' says Ronald Stouffer at the US National Oceanic and Atmospheric Administration's Geophysical Fluid Dynamics Laboratory. 'How much of it would still occur if humans were not changing the climate in any way?'

C

The current rate of warming is faster than ever before, however, which suggests it probably is not a natural occurrence. And a large number of scientists believe the rise in temperatures will, in fact, speed up. The UN Group on Climate Change reported in 2001 that the average temperature is likely to increase by between 1.4 and 5.8 degrees C by the year 2100. The climate change is likely to impact on ecosystems, agriculture and the spread of disease. 'Global warming is a serious threat to animal and plant life,' says Jay Malcolm, a forestry professor at the University of Toronto. 'As climates warm, more southerly species will begin appearing further north … species will find themselves in habitats where they don't belong. For example glaciers and sea ice in both the northern and southern hemispheres are already melting at a rapid pace, placing animals like polar bears at risk.'

D

A recent study suggested that Greenland's ice sheet will begin to melt if the temperature there rises by three degrees C. That is something many scientists think is likely to happen in another hundred years. The complete melting of the Greenland ice cap would raise sea levels by seven metres. Even a partial melting would cause a one-metre rise. Such a rise would have a devastating impact on low-lying islands, such as the Maldives, which would be entirely submerged. Densely populated areas like the Nile Delta and parts of Bangladesh would become uninhabitable, affecting hundreds of millions of people. A one-metre sea-level rise would flood the eastern seaboard of the USA.

E

Other scientists emphasise that such doomsday scenarios may be hundreds of years in the future. 'You can't say with any certainly that sea-level rises are going to have a huge impact on society,' says Stouffer. 'Who knows what the planet will look like 5000 years from now?' Most climate scientists, however, agree that global warming is a threat that has gone unchecked for too long. 'Is society aware of the seriousness of climate warming? I don't think so,' says Marianne Douglas, professor of geology at the University of Toronto. 'Otherwise we'd all be leading our lives differently. We'd see a society that used alternative sources of energy, with less dependency on fossil fuels.'

Grammar

Countable and uncountable nouns

1 Read the following sentences and think about the first phrase in each one. Then fill the gaps or choose the right option to complete rules a and b below.

   1 How much research has been done on carbon dioxide?

   2 How many scientists are looking into the problems of global warming?

   3 A large amount of information is available on climate change.

   4 A large number of countries are being affected by rising sea levels.

a Nouns like .... and .... are uncountable and cannot be plural. They are used with *How* .... and *a large* .... of and take a (*singular / plural*) .... verb.

b Nouns like .... and .... are countable and can be singular or plural. They are used with *How* .... and *a large* .... *of*.

Other words you can use with countable and uncountable nouns:

countable nouns	uncountable nouns
a/an	–
the	the
some	some
few	little
a lot of	a lot of
plenty of	plenty of
many	a great deal of
a number of	a good deal of

Notes: Some nouns can be both countable and uncountable depending on their meaning.

The following nouns take a plural verb: *clothes, glasses, goods, people, police, premises, savings, scissors, trousers.*

The following nouns ending in *-s* take a singular verb: *economics, mathematics, news, politics.*

 page 140

2 Decide if these nouns are countable or uncountable. Write C (countable) or U (uncountable) next to each word. Use a dictionary if necessary.

> ○→**knowledge** /ˈnɒlɪdʒ/ *noun* **1** [U, no plural] information and understanding that you have in your mind *He will easily find a job with his knowledge and skills.* ○ *He has **a** detailed **knowledge of** naval history.* ○ *He took the car without my knowledge* (= I did not know). **2 to (the best of) sb's knowledge** used to say that someone thinks that something is true, but cannot be sure *To the best of my knowledge, she's never worked abroad.*

pollution	activity	knowledge
university	accommodation	research
country	advice	climate
information	job	meal
news	scientist	work
weather		

3 Form sentences from the prompts, making any necessary changes.

   EXAMPLE: deal / research / do / into climate change last year.
            A great deal of research was done into climate change last year.

   1 Global warming / happen faster than people think.

   2 Information about ecology courses at universities / hard to find.

   3 lot / people / study / mathematics at my college this year.

   4 the company / put new equipment in the computer lab next year?

   5 The news this morning / not good.

   6 My work on climate change / be published next week.

4 Correct the mistakes that IELTS candidates have made with countable and uncountable nouns and the verbs that follow them. Then try to improve the sentences by using *many, a number of, a good deal of* or *a great deal of* instead of *a lot of* or *plenty of*.

   1 A lot of people thinks that many of the information about climate change have been wrong. Many research have taken place into whether it have been more influenced by natural occurrences such as volcanoes.

   2 A lot of gases trap the sun's heat in the atmosphere and causes a gradual warming of the Earth.

   3 A lot research have found that all people needs to do are use fewer fossil fuel.

   4 There are evidence that a car emit as many carbon dioxide a year as an entire house. A lot of energy can be saved by driving more smoothly and keeping the tyres inflated.

Speaking *Part 3*

5 With a partner, ask and answer these questions.

- What kind of things can you do personally to reduce global warming? e.g. recycling, using less electricity, etc.
- Do you think that ordinary people can stop global warming or is it up to the government? Why?
- Can joining a pressure group help?

Listening

6 🎧 You are going to hear a woman talking on the radio about a new book. Before you listen, read through the notes below and try to decide what kind of information you need to listen for.

Complete the notes below.
*Write **NO MORE THAN TWO WORDS AND/OR A NUMBER** for each answer.*

Saving the Planet

Approx. amount of money that each household could save a year: **1** US$ ....

Main topic of book: **2** ....

Ways to prevent global warming:

3 use modern types of ....
4 put your .... in a cool place
5 turn off ....
6 only shower for ....
7 unplug your ....

type of energy saving	amount saved
• keeping tyres inflated	**8** US$ ....
• eating less **9**	US$109
• buying food in	US$293
10	

Vocabulary

Collocations related to the environment

7 Vocabulary and collocations related to the environment often appear in IELTS. Link each word on the left with a word on the right. Use a dictionary to help you.

EXAMPLE: **1 f** global warming

1	global	**a**	gases
2	recycling	**b**	pollution
3	greenhouse	**c**	species
4	environmentally	**d**	modified
5	light	**e**	friendly
6	endangered	**f**	warming
7	genetically	**g**	waste

Writing extra

8 Write at least 150 words on the greenhouse effect, using the diagram and notes below. ⋯⟩ **WF 1**

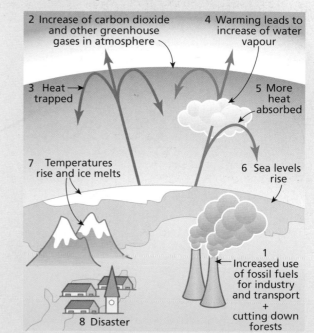

2 Increase of carbon dioxide and other greenhouse gases in atmosphere
3 Heat trapped
4 Warming leads to increase of water vapour
5 More heat absorbed
6 Sea levels rise
7 Temperatures rise and ice melts
1 Increased use of fossil fuels for industry and transport + cutting down forests
8 Disaster

Test folder 5

Summary completion

(Academic Reading, General Training Reading and Listening Modules)

A summary is usually of one part of the passage, but may be of the whole text.

In the Listening Module the questions follow the order of information in the passage. In the Reading Modules they may not.

The summary is worded differently from the passage, but the ideas are the same.

If you have to choose words from the passage, you will be told the maximum number for each answer.

If you have to choose words from a box, there will be more words than spaces, and they are usually different from ones in the passage.

Words must be spelt correctly to gain marks.

Advice

Reading Modules
- Skim the whole passage before you start working on any of the tasks.
- Read the instructions. If the answers come from the passage, check the maximum number of words for each space. Read the heading (if there is one) and the summary. Consider what information is likely to fit each space. Think about both the *meaning* and the *grammar*.
- Read the first gapped sentence. Find the relevant part of the passage – the heading will help you – and look for something that means the same. Find the words (in the passage or box) that fit the question. Copy them exactly. Continue with the next space.

Listening Module
- You will be given time to read the summary before you listen. Consider what information is likely to fit each space. Think about both the *meaning* and the *grammar*.
- Listen for each answer in turn. If you miss one, go on to the next question or you may miss that too.

All modules
- Check that your answers fit both the meaning and the grammar, that the spelling is correct, and that you haven't written more than the maximum number of words.

Reading

1 This passage is similar to those in the Academic Reading Module, but is only about 350 words. The task is typical of both Reading modules.

The Little Ice Age

Western Europe experienced a general cooling of the climate after the year 1150 and a very cold climate between 1560 and 1850 that brought dire consequences to its peoples. The period from 1150 to 1850 is sometimes called the Little Ice Age.

During this time, the cooler air of the Arctic began to spread southward. Together with other changes in the atmosphere over the North Atlantic, this directed a higher number of storms into northern Europe. The sea level seems to have been increased by ice melt during the preceding Medieval Warm Period (from about 900 to 1150), contributing to the flooding which caused the loss of hundreds of thousands of lives. Additionally, hail wiped out farmland and killed great numbers of livestock over much of Europe, due to very cold air during the warmer months. Glaciers in many parts of Europe began to advance, destroying farmland and causing massive flooding.

The climate change of the Little Ice Age had a serious impact on agriculture, as it reduced the growing season by up to two months. That is enough to affect almost any type of food production, especially crops highly adapted to use the full-season warm climatic periods. Varieties of seeds that can withstand extreme cold or warmth, wetness or dryness, were not available in the past. The impact on agricultural output was significant, with poor harvests leading to high food prices and famines. In one of the worst famines, millions of people died in France and neighbouring countries in 1693. Food prices reached a peak in the year 1816 – 'the year without a summer'.

The cooler climate during the Little Ice Age had a huge impact on the health of Europeans. Malnutrition led to a weakened immunity to a variety of illnesses, including bubonic plague – the Black Death – which killed a third of the population of Europe in the late 1340s. Cool, wet summers led to outbreaks of an illness called St Anthony's Fire, which caused terrible suffering, hallucinations and even death. This was due to a fungus which develops in grain stored in cool, damp conditions. Used to make bread, the grain passed the illness to whole villages.

Complete the summary below.
*Choose **NO MORE THAN TWO WORDS** from the passage for each answer.*

The Impact of the Little Ice Age

The increase in cold air affecting Europe led to more frequent **0** ..*storms*.. in the north of the continent. The sea level rose because of **1** ..ice melt.. caused earlier, and this led to **2** ..flooding.. in which many people died. Animals and crops were destroyed by **3** ..hail.. in the summer. As the climate cooled, **4** ..glaciers.. spread, causing great destruction.

In agriculture, the Little Ice Age led to a shorter **5** ..growing season.. , which had a particular impact on **6** ..crops.. that need long periods of warmth. A further problem was that **7** ..seeds.. were more vulnerable than those of today. In consequence, **8** ..harvests.. were poor. Large numbers of people died in the **9** ..famine.. that occurred in several countries. In addition, **10** ..malnutrition.. reduced many people's immunity to diseases. One illness, St Anthony's Fire, was caused by a **11** ..fungus.. that could grow in bread.

Listening

2 🎧 **This passage is similar to those in Part 4 of the Listening Module.**

Complete the summary below.
*Write **NO MORE THAN THREE WORDS AND/OR A NUMBER** for each answer.*

The Polar Front Jet Stream

The Polar Front Jet Stream is a wind at a height of up to **1** ..13.. kilometres above the earth's surface. It moves at approximately **2** ..400.. km per hour during the winter. The direction of movement is caused by the earth's **3** ..rotation.. . The jet stream is formed where cold polar air meets warm **4** ..subtropical.. air.

It was first identified by **5** ..pilots.. in the 1940s. Planes benefit in terms of both **6** ..speed... time... travel.. but **7** ..navigation.. is difficult.

Forecasters use jet streams to predict where depressions will form, and whether the British Isles will have potentially destructive **8** ..storms.. or only **9** ..showers.. .

Global warming may move the jet stream to the **10** ..north.. in the summer, creating **11** ..dry.. conditions in the British Isles.

3 🎧 **This passage is also similar to those in Part 4 of the Listening Module.**

Complete the summary below using words from the box.

disease	drought	dust	floods	hunger
ice	lava	migration	night	riots	snow
storms	sunlight	temperatures		

The eruption of Mount Tambora in 1815 filled the air with **1** .... The amount of **2** .... was reduced. The effects on the weather of 1816 included **3** .... in places where it was a rare occurrence, and **4** .... that severely damaged crops. Many Europeans suffered from **5** .... , and there were serious **6** .... in many towns. In the USA there was considerable **7** .... from affected areas to the more fertile Midwest.

Mount Tambora today

A place to work or live in

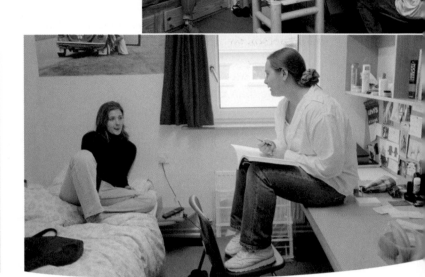

Speaking *Part 1*

1 With a partner, take it in turns to ask and answer the following questions. Remember to give a full answer – use *because* and *for example*.

- What type of accommodation are you living in at the moment?
- What's it like?
- What would your ideal room be like?
- What qualities would you look for in a flatmate?

Useful language

Accommodation
a hall of residence / a college room
a rented flat/apartment
a hostel
a family house / a home stay
a shared house

I like/love living with my/a family.
I don't mind staying in a hostel
What I would most like is ...
I'd like (to share with) someone who ...
I dislike/hate/can't stand sharing with anyone.
I can't afford to pay more.
I want to move soon.
On the other hand ...

Listening

2 🎧 You are going to hear a student asking about accommodation at a university. Read through the questions and try to decide what kind of information you need to listen for.

Complete the notes below.
*Write **NO MORE THAN THREE WORDS AND/OR A NUMBER** for each answer.*

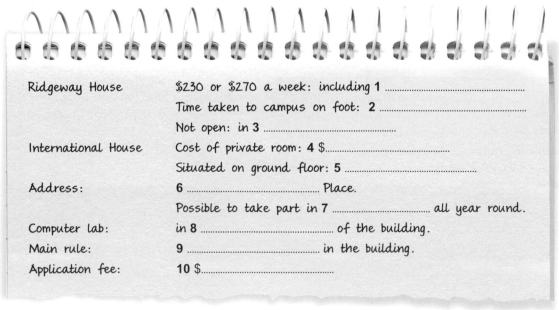

Ridgeway House	$230 or $270 a week: including 1 ....
	Time taken to campus on foot: 2 ....
	Not open: in 3 ....
International House	Cost of private room: 4 $...
	Situated on ground floor: 5 ....
Address:	6 .... Place.
	Possible to take part in 7 .... all year round.
Computer lab:	in 8 .... of the building.
Main rule:	9 .... in the building.
Application fee:	10 $...

Would you like to live in this college accommodation? Why, or why not?

Pronunciation *Polite intonation*

3 🎧 It is important to create a good impression by sounding polite during the Speaking Module. Listen to the beginning of the conversation from exercise 2 again and then repeat these words or phrases. Try to use the same intonation.

1 Can I help you?   4 Do sit down.
2 Yes, please.   5 Thank you.
3 I don't, I'm afraid.   6 Certainly.

Remember: phrases like *I'm afraid*, or *I'm sorry* soften a negative response.

4 🎧 Listen to eight short exchanges and decide if the *second* person sounds friendly or unfriendly. Write F (friendly) or U (unfriendly).

1   4   7
2   5   8
3   6

Vocabulary

Phrasal verbs and collocations with *house* and *home*

5 Rewrite the sentences using phrases from the box and making any other necessary changes. Use an English–English dictionary to help you.

to pull down a building / to pull a building down	a spacious house
to put someone up	a dilapidated house
to rent out a flat/house	a terraced house
to extend a house	a bungalow
to leave home	a detached house
to move house	a semi-detached house

1 My house is connected to another house.
2 Josh lived in eight different houses when he was a child.
3 Don't worry about finding a hotel – I can give you a bed for the night.
4 After they had children, they decided to add more rooms onto their house.
5 Tania's mother was very upset when Tania moved out of the family home.
6 The council are demolishing the old cinema.
7 Dr Thomas is very happy to allow students to have the flat for a reasonable amount.
8 I live in a house which only has one floor.
9 My aunt's house has a lot of space but it isn't in a very good state.
10 I have lived in houses which were part of a row and in houses standing alone.

Writing extra
General Training Task 1

6 Complete the letter using words from the box below. There are some extra words which you won't need.

agree	also	attention	because	conclusion
hear	hearing	however	is	know	limit
make	meet	next	past	receive	run
since	stop	when	where	would

Dear Professor Simpson,

I have been living in International House now for the **1** .... six months and feel very much at home as it is very comfortable and reasonably priced. **2** .... , I would like to draw your **3** .... to the following problems.

First of all, the computer room in the basement has been closed for the last two weeks **4** .... of a shortage of technical staff. **5** .... it not be possible to pay computer-science students to **6** .... the hall's computer room on a rota basis?

Secondly, noise levels from student parties have increased recently. I think it would be a good idea to **7** .... parties to Friday or Saturday nights and from 8.00 to 12.30 in term time. I am sure you will **8** .... that it is very hard to study **9** .... someone is having an all-night party in the middle of the week!

I look forward to **10** .... from you in the near future.

Yours sincerely,

7 Answer the following Task 1 question.

Write the following letter.

You are due to move into a rented apartment next month but you will not be able to because you have some problems.
Write a letter to the landlord. In your letter
- **explain your situation**
- **describe your problems**
- **tell him/her when you think you can move in.**
You should write at least 150 words.

Norman Foster – architect

Norman Foster was born in Manchester, England in 1935. His father was a shop manager in a poor area of Manchester but his parents managed to send him to a private school. However, there wasn't enough money to send him to university so his parents persuaded
5 him to get a job and earn some money after leaving school. Foster worked for two years in an office, before doing compulsory military service in the air force. He was beginning to develop an interest in architecture, so when he left the air force he went to Manchester University to study architecture. Designing buildings came naturally
10 to him. He decided to continue his studies at Yale University in the USA and became friends with another architect called Richard Rodgers. After they had finished studying, they decided to start Foster Associates. Since then, the firm has received more than 190 awards and won over 50 national and international competitions.
15 The latest is the Stirling Prize for 30 St Mary Axe in London.

30 St Mary Axe, or the Swiss Re headquarters, is London's first environmentally friendly skyscraper. It is situated in the city of London, and it is an easily recognisable building. The shape of the tower allows the maximum amount of natural light to come into the
20 building and this helps to reduce lighting bills. When it was first built, people weren't sure if they liked it or not and called it the Gherkin, but now it is very popular. It can be compared to the Chrysler building in New York, the wonderful art-deco skyscraper built in Manhattan in the 1920s. But it is much better than the
25 Chrysler, which would be quite ordinary without its spire. The Gherkin curves and glitters and reflects all over. Everyone agrees that it is an architectural masterpiece and its presence in London makes the people of the city feel very proud.

Grammar

-ing forms and infinitives 1

1 What do you think of this building? Do you know where it is and what it is used for?

2 Read the article above about the architect and the building.

-ing forms

3 The -ing form of a verb can be used in several ways. In which of these sentences from the article is the -ing form being used as a noun?

 1 <u>Designing</u> buildings came naturally to him.
 2 He was <u>beginning</u> to develop an interest in architecture.
 3 This helps to reduce <u>lighting</u> bills.

Infinitives

4 An infinitive is a form like *(to) do* or *(to) go.*

Find example(s) from the text of the following:

 1 an *-ing* form used after a verb, e.g. *enjoy doing*
 ....
 2 an *-ing* form used after a preposition, e.g. *after doing, good at doing*
 ....
 3 a verb/expression followed by *to* + infinitive, e.g. *I would like to do*
 ....
 4 an infinitive of purpose, e.g. *I went to town to do some shopping.*
 ....
 5 an infinitive after *too* or *enough*, e.g. *too hot to do*
 ....
 6 a verb which follows the pattern: verb + *someone/something* + *to* + infinitive, e.g. *I encouraged my friend to apply for university.*
 ....
 7 an infinitive without *to*, e.g. *My flatmates made me do the shopping.*
 ....

G ···⟩ page 141

5 Complete the sentences using a verb from the box in the correct form.

> | ~~buy~~ | finish | have | live | look | make |
> | pay | reduce | share | visit | work | |

EXAMPLE: Michelle has decided ....*to buy*.... Lizzie a lamp for her new flat.

1 It's not worth me .... for a house to buy – they are all too expensive.
2 Paul insisted on the builders .... the job on time.
3 I'm quite good at .... accommodation with other students during term-time.
4 Tania can't afford .... too much for a room in the hostel.
5 Can you imagine .... in an apartment on the top floor of a skyscraper?
6 Foster has succeeded in .... modern architecture popular in Britain.
7 I adore .... old buildings.
8 I used .... in an office just near the Eiffel Tower in Paris.
9 The hostel warden made us all .... noise levels in the evenings.
10 My sister has always wanted .... a houseboat on the River Thames.

6 The *Cambridge Learner Corpus* shows that the most common mistake IELTS candidates make is with *to*. Correct these sentences.

1 The architect made the builder to use triangular-shaped glass.
2 You had better to do your essay before to go out.
3 I gave up to live with my parents years ago.
4 Have you finished to do the cleaning?
5 He suggested to rent the apartment next year.
6 I object to pay such a high rent.
7 I look forward hear from you in the near future.
8 The college wouldn't let me to move out of the hostel.
9 I'm interested to go to see the house tomorrow.
10 The estate agent advertised in the paper to getting more people seeing the house.

7 With a partner, talk about why you think people do the following things.

EXAMPLE: study IELTS – *I think many people study IELTS to go to university.*

1 get married
2 smoke cigarettes
3 go to clubs
4 buy fast cars like Ferraris
5 join Internet chat rooms
6 have cosmetic surgery
7 recycle plastic and glass

8 With a partner, ask and answer these questions. Make sure you use an -*ing* form and ask *Why?* or *Why not?* when your partner answers.

1 Have you ever given up anything?
2 Do you dislike doing housework?
3 Are there some things you put off doing?
4 Do/Would you mind living away from home?
5 When will you finish studying?
6 Is there anything that you are particularly bad at doing?
7 What are you looking forward to doing this weekend?
8 Is there a hobby you'd like to take up?

Speaking *Part 2*

An exhibit in the Turbine Hall of Tate Modern art gallery

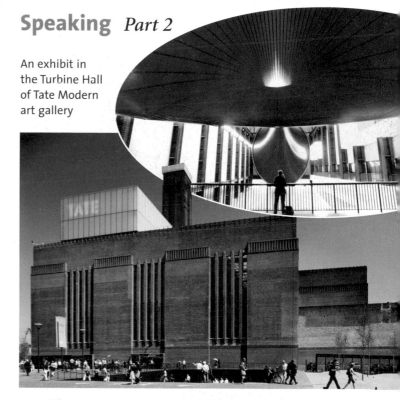

9 🎧 Listen to a student talking about the following topic.

> *Describe a building you like or dislike.*
> *You should say:*
> *where it is*
> *what type of building it is*
> *when you first saw it*
> *and explain why you particularly like/dislike it.*

Did the speaker cover all the points above?
Did she use a range of vocabulary?
Was what she said relevant?
What words did she use to avoid saying *big* repeatedly?

Now *you* answer the question above. You have one minute to make some notes and then you must talk for one to two minutes.

Writing folder 5

Academic Writing Task I: Handling data 2 – bar and pie charts and tables

In Task 1 of the Academic Writing Module you may be given one or more charts or tables and asked to explain what they show. You should spend 20 minutes on this task and you should write at least 150 words.

Advice

- Remember you do not get extra marks for writing more than 150 words, but you will lose marks if you write less.
- 'Other' is sometimes mentioned as a category on charts. Don't ignore it. Decide what it is referring to – in the chart below it refers to other private dwellings/housing – and then include the information if you think it is relevant.

1 Correct statements 1–7 about the charts, if necessary. Some statements are correct.

Bar chart

Private dwellings in Australia 1991–2001

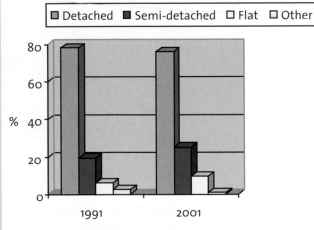

Pie chart

% of Canadian households 2002

1 In 1991, there were twice as many detached houses as semi-detached.
2 The percentage of flats increased slightly in the ten year period from 1991–2001.
3 The number of flats in 2001 was nearly double the number of semi-detached houses.
4 There was a fall in other types of housing from 1991 to 2001.

5 In 2002, the majority of Canadians lived in flats.
6 In 2002, a higher percentage of Canadians lived in semi-detached houses than in detached ones.
7 In 2002, more Canadians lived in detached houses than in flats.

2 With a partner, using the language given opposite, discuss what the table shows you and then write sentences summarising the information.

EXAMPLE: *It can be seen from the table that many more UK households with children had a PC than those without children.*

Home entertainment equipment – households in the UK (2000)

	with children	without children
DVD/Video	87%	78%
Video games	52%	14%
PC	41%	17%
Satellite TV	28%	18%
Video camera	23%	14%

3 Look at the chart and then complete the summary of the information in the chart using words or phrases from the box below.

Entertainment equipment in children's bedrooms, by age of children (UK 2002)

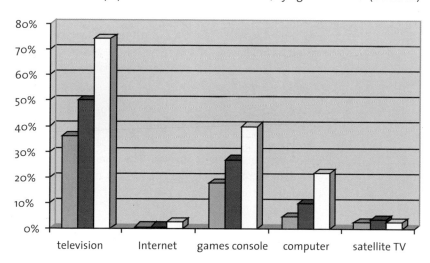

Overall, it would appear that the **1** .... children, that is children aged **2** ...., were more likely to have entertainment equipment in their rooms than **3** .... children. However, more 4–9 year olds did have **4** .... in their bedrooms than the other two age groups.

The **5** .... item of equipment for all age groups was the **6** ...., with over 70 per cent of all 10–15 year olds and **7** .... of 4–9 year olds being allowed to watch in their own rooms. A **8** .... was the second most popular item, with **9** .... of the older age group possessing this item of equipment.

Although just over 20 per cent of 10–15 year olds had **10** .... in their bedroom, a much smaller percentage of that age group were able to access the Internet. Very **11** .... younger children were allowed to use the Internet.

It is clear from the data above that, generally, the older **12** .... are, the more electronic equipment they are likely to have in their bedroom.

satellite TV	most popular	oldest
a computer	few	younger
40 per cent	children	games console
50 per cent	television	10–15

4 Make a chart giving information about the amount of home entertainment equipment the students in your class possess and then write 150 words describing your findings.

11·1 Animal life

robins   gulls   spider   worker bees

1   What similarities and differences are there between the lives of animals and of human beings?

Reading

2   Match each definition (1–7) with a noun or verb from the box (a–i). There may be more than one answer.

1   a group of people living together, or a person living alone
2   a couple and their children
3   parents, children, grandparents, uncles, aunts, etc., whether or not they live together
4   something done alone
5   something done in a group
6   to care for young animals or children until they are able to care for themselves
7   the way in which someone is treated and educated when they are young, especially by their parents

a   to bring up
b   a communal activity
c   an extended family
d   a household
e   a nuclear family
f   to raise
g   to rear
h   a solitary activity
i   upbringing

3   Most species of animals have a preferred way of living. This book extract introduces different patterns. Note that 'animal' is used to include birds, fish, insects and invertebrates. Skim the first section, and decide what the main topic of each paragraph (A–E) is. The passage is similar to those in the Academic Reading Module.

⏱ about 250 words

Social organisation among animals

Varieties of social organisation

A The palalo – a worm which lives on rocks in the sea – is one of very few animals which never have contact with other members of the same species. Others, such
5 as spiders, are normally solitary, meeting only to mate (that is, to reproduce).

B Some species form social links only for the period while they are rearing their young. Among birds, European robins raise their chicks in a pair, away from
10 other members of their species, while herring gulls form larger groups (colonies) consisting of many pairs living close together, each pair raising their chicks independently.

C Many species of fish and birds form large groups,
15 called schools and flocks, respectively, and swim or fly together. Hens attack each other, and eventually establish a hierarchy based on their individual strength. Those at the top of the 'pecking order' get to eat before the others.

20 D Finally, some animals spend most or all of their lives in social groups in which individuals co-operate. Lions, for instance, usually live in a relatively permanent group, called a pride, where some activities, such as hunting, are social, and others, like sleeping, are
25 solitary.

E Bees, wasps and ants live in stable, co-operative groups in which every activity is communal and organised. Worker bees (which are all female) have several jobs in succession, depending on their age.
30 They begin with cleaning duties, and later become soldiers to defend the hive against intruders. Finally they fly out of the hive to collect food. Theirs is a highly complex social organisation.

4 Now answer these multiple-choice questions about the extract you have just read.

Test spot

Remember to read each question carefully, find the relevant part of the text, consider *all* the options, and choose only one answer to each question. ⋯⋰ **TF 6**

*Choose the correct letter, **A**, **B** or **C**.*

1 Which of these animals spends most, but not all, of its life alone?
  A palalo
  B herring gull
  C spider

2 European robins and herring gulls are different with regard to
  A how many birds help to bring up each chick.
  B the social organisation in which pairs bring up their young.
  C how long they spend together.

3 What point is made about hens?
  A The best fighters eat different kinds of food from weaker hens.
  B They live in larger groups than most other species of birds.
  C Their social structure gives certain individuals advantages over others.

4 What is said about the life of lions?
  A They live in a group and do some activities together.
  B They live separately and come together for some activities.
  C They live in a group and do all activities together.

5 What point is made about worker bees?
  A They carry out different tasks as they get older.
  B They live in a social structure unlike that of any other animals.
  C They could not survive alone.

5 What do you think are the advantages and disadvantages for animals of living in groups? Consider

- bringing up the young
- finding food
- protection against other animals
- conflict

6 Now read the next section of the extract.
⏱ about 250 words

Advantages of social co-operation

frogs

Social co-operation can provide a number of benefits. Groups of male frogs sing to attract females, and large groups generally attract more females per male than smaller groups, making it easier for the males to find a mate.

5 The young can be reared more safely in social groups. Birds in a colony tend to lay their eggs at around the same time, so all the chicks emerge from the egg almost simultaneously. As an individual predator (an animal that kills and eats other animals) can only consume a
10 finite number of eggs or chicks, each individual is less likely to be eaten. Groups of adult elephants surround all their young, giving each one much greater protection than its parents alone could provide.

Groups are also more effective in bringing up the
15 young. In some species of apes and monkeys, female 'aunties' help to look after the young which are not their own, while learning how to raise their own young in the future. Lion cubs drink the milk not only of their mother but also of other lionesses in the group, and
20 the range of antibodies that different females provide increases their resistance to disease.

A group that spreads out in search of food is likely to be more successful than an animal searching alone. When one has found food, others may simply join it, but some
25 species have developed a highly complex form of communication. When a honeybee finds some food it returns to its hive and performs a complex dance to indicate the location of the food to others.

7 Which **FIVE** of these advantages of social co-operation are mentioned in the above passage?
  A Females can choose a mate more easily.
  B More eggs can be laid.
  C Eggs are more likely to survive.
  D There are more adults available to protect the young.
  E Individuals can develop skills for later use.
  F The young are likely to be healthier.
  G Individuals can eat food which others have found.
  H The group is more likely to live close to a source of food.

11·2

Grammar Articles

a/an and the

3 Look at these sentences.

When [1]a bee finds some food, it returns to its hive and performs [2]a complex series of movements. [3]The dance indicates where [4]the food is located.

Complete rules a and b by adding *a/an* or *the* to each space. Then give the number of the relevant examples (1–4) above.

> **a** Use .... when a singular, countable noun is used for the first time.
> (numbers .... from above)
>
> **b** Use .... when the noun refers, directly or indirectly, to something that has already been mentioned.
> (numbers .... from above)

4 Put *a/an* or *the* in each space.

> Binti Jua is **1** .... gorilla living in **2** .... zoo in Chicago, USA. One day she rescued **3** .... three-year-old boy who had climbed over some railings and had fallen close to her. Although zoo officials responded immediately, Binti reached **4** .... unconscious child first and carried him to **5** .... area where **6** .... officials could attend to him. **7** .... little boy recovered after spending four days in hospital.

No article

5 Look at rules **c** and **d**, which explain where no article is used.

> No article is used
>
> **c** with uncountable nouns:
> *Co-operation can be useful for many species of animals.*
>
> **d** with plural countable nouns used with a general meaning:
> *Lions, for instance, may live in a relatively permanent group called a pride.*

Listening

1 Do you know any stories which seem to be about animals but are really about people?

2 🎧 You are going to hear part of a lecture about animals in literature. This is similar to Section 4 of the Listening Module.

Complete the sentences below. Write **NO MORE THAN ONE WORD** *for each answer.*

1 Animals often appear in myths about the
.... of the world.

2 Writers of 'wild animal stories' wanted to show animals in a .... way.

3 Some stories are intended to increase
.... for animals.

4 Fables normally deal with ....
questions.

5 Animals in fables generally use human
....

6 Orwell's fable is about .... issues.

7 Most fables are meant for ....

8 In Kipling's story, the camel's laziness increases the .... of the other animals.

6 Decide which rule (**a–d**) explains each use of *a/an*, *the* or 'no article' in 1–10 below.

> Tess is ¹a dog, and every week she goes with her owner to ²a hospital in her home town, wearing ³a red ribbon in her collar. ⁴The patients enjoy playing with Tess, and even ⁵the nurses spend some time with her. They say she spreads ⁶happiness among ⁷the patients, and helps them to get better. ⁸Research has shown that ⁹animals can help ¹⁰people in this way.

G ···❖ page 141

Vocabulary Compound nouns

Many words, especially nouns, are formed by joining two independent words, for example, *honeybee*. Sometimes the meaning can be guessed from the meanings of the two parts. Usually the second part of the compound tells you more about the meaning of the word than the first, e.g. a *honeybee* is a type of bee and a *dogfish* is a type of fish – not a dog!

Sometimes compound nouns are separate words, e.g. *honey bear*, sometimes they are written as one word.

7 All the words in the box can form a compound beginning or ending with *work*, e.g. *workbook*. Decide what the other compounds are, and try to work out what they mean. Check in an English–English dictionary if you aren't sure.

~~book~~	force	home	load
place	sheet	shop	

8 Complete each sentence with the most suitable of the compound nouns from exercise 7.

EXAMPLE: A ....*workbook*........ is a publication containing a number of exercises to supplement a coursebook.

1 In Kipling's story the man's .... consisted of a horse, a dog and an ox.
2 The animals' .... was on the edge of the desert.
3 The horse, dog and ox had a heavier .... because of the camel's laziness.
4 A .... is a piece of paper with questions or exercises for students.
5 A training activity in which a number of people take part is sometimes called a ....
6 .... is useful because it gives students the chance to practise what they have learnt.

Pronunciation *Diphthongs*

9 Knowing about the sounds of English will help you to speak clearly. It is also useful to learn the different ways in which the same written letters can be pronounced.

Complete the tables below with words from the box to show the main ways of spelling the most common diphthongs. Write each one under the right heading, and give the spelling (in **bold** type) for the diphthong. There are some examples of diphthongs in Unit 8 (page 55).

~~although~~	approach	~~came~~	enjoy
~~find~~	flies	fly	goes
~~great~~	here	now	~~join~~
out	own	pair	right
say	share	so	spoke
there	they	wait	wearing
while	~~year~~		

1 /eɪ/ day

spelling	example
a_e	came
	great
ey	

2 /aɪ/ my

spelling	example
igh	
	find

3 /aʊ/ how

spelling	example
ou	

4 /ɪə/ ear

spelling	example
	year

5 /ɔɪ/ boy

spelling	example
	join

6 /əʊ/ no

spelling	example
	although
	spoke

7 /eə/ air

spelling	example
ere	
ea(r)	

🎧 Now you'll hear two words containing each diphthong, the one at the top of the column and the first example (e.g. *day* and *came*). Repeat each word.

Test folder 6

Multiple choice

(Academic Reading, General Training Reading and Listening Modules)

If you have to choose one answer, there will be three options (in the Listening Module, and occasionally in Reading) or four options (only in Reading).

If you have to choose *more than one* answer, there will be more options. In this case, the order of your answers isn't important: for example, if the answers are A, C, D, and you write D, A, C, they will still be counted as correct.

Each question normally focuses on one part of the passage. However, in the Reading Modules you may be asked one multiple-choice question about the whole passage.

The questions follow the order of information in the passage.

The options normally do *not* follow the order of information in the passage.

The questions and options are normally paraphrases of the passage.

Listening

1 🎧 This passage is similar to those in Section 4 of the Listening Module.

Which FIVE of these activities are said to be characteristic of sharks?

A travelling long distances
B diving deep
C feeding by day
D travelling alone
E attacking other members of their own species
F treating other species of sharks as equals
G threatening human beings
H defending their home

Reading

2 This passage is similar to those in the Academic Reading Module, but only about 600 words long. The task is typical of both Reading Modules.

How similar are animals and human beings?

Over the centuries, a number of animals have been charged with a crime, tried in a court of law, found guilty and punished – even executed. The last time was as recently as 1906. Animals were thought to be like human beings – able to decide their actions and morally responsible for the outcomes.

Then ideas about animals changed, and they were thought to lack awareness of their own internal states and relationships to others. They were therefore considered incapable of true suffering and of criminal behaviour.

But new research suggests that animals have far more complex cognitive and social skills than we thought. The focus in recent decades has been on wildlife, but it now seems that something similar is also true of farm animals: pigs, sheep, cows, chickens.

First for some findings. In 2004, researchers in Cambridge, UK, reported that when individual sheep were isolated from the flock of sheep that they belonged to, they experienced stress. This was shown by increases in heart rate, stress hormones and bleating – a sheep's call. But showing them pictures of familiar sheep faces reduced all three measurements. The same effect was not produced when they were shown pictures of goat faces or inverted triangles.

Donald Broom, professor of animal welfare at the University of Cambridge, says that cows often form long-lasting, co-operative partnerships. They also show a physiological response on learning something new. He and colleague Kristin Hagen put young cows in a situation where they had to press a panel to open a gate and gain access to food.

Those that learned the task were more likely to experience a sudden increase in heart rate and to run around than those that did not. This was called 'the eureka response', and resembles the human reaction to making a discovery.

Other research has shown that if offered a choice of two places to feed, pigs will avoid the one where they had previously been shut in for several hours after eating, and go for the one that they were released from quickly. None of these findings proves that animals feel pain or joy in the same way that humans do, but according to Broom, the evidence suggests that animals may be aware of what has happened in the past, and capable of acting on it in the future.

That awareness is the basis of collaboration among human beings – for instance, knowing not to attack a familiar face. In animal communities too, it now seems, animals with big teeth, or weighing several tonnes, will move carefully so as not to damage others. In the past, this was explained as their fear that if they accidentally hurt another animal, it will attack them. According to Broom, however, this is not true in every case. He claims that a great deal of this behaviour has a more general aim of ensuring that the society will function.

American animal rights lawyer Steven Wise has gone a step further. He argues that people have basic civil liberties because they possess a sense of self, plus the ability to want something and to have the intention of gaining what they want. The great apes, dolphins, African grey parrots and other animals also appear to have this ability. Now, he says, it seems to apply to some farm animals too. He claims that these animals therefore deserve basic rights such as freedom from being raised as food for human beings.

Wherever developments in our understanding of animals takes us, however, it seems unlikely that we will again try them for criminal behaviour.

Choose the correct letter, **A**, **B** or **C**.

Example:
The belief mentioned in the first paragraph is that animals
A can choose how to behave.
B behave worse than people.
C copy the behaviour of people.
Answer: A (*able to decide their actions*)

1 The belief mentioned in the second paragraph is that animals
   A behave better than people.
   B are not aware of other animals.
   C do not experience mental pain as people do.

2 What point is made in the third paragraph?
   A Further research is needed into comparing the skills of wild and farm animals.
   B Skills are being found among farm animals as well as wild animals.
   C Farm animals are proving to be more interesting than wild animals.

3 What is suggested by the research into sheep?
   A They suffer stress if they are placed with animals of different species.
   B They cannot distinguish between goats and abstract symbols.
   C They can recognise other sheep in photographs.

4 The experiment with cows was designed to find out
   A how they reacted to learning something new.
   B how fast they learned to solve a problem.
   C how they worked out a method of getting food.

5 Research into pigs has shown that they
   A forget previous experiences when they want food.
   B remember which types of food they like.
   C can base their behaviour on earlier experiences.

6 Professor Broom believes that animals try not to harm others
   A when the other animal is more powerful.
   B to avoid being attacked by another animal.
   C even if they will not benefit themselves.

7 Steven Wise argues that
   A the legal basis for human civil liberties also applies to animals.
   B animals should be given the same rights as people.
   C owning animals should be made illegal.

8 What do you think is the writer's main purpose in this passage?
   A to argue that animals should have the same rights as human beings
   B to present current research into animals to a non-specialist audience
   C to show differences between animals and human beings

1   In small groups, talk about why people do sports.

Reading

2   Now read this article, which is similar to the
    Academic Reading and Part 3 of General Training
    Reading, but shorter than an exam passage. As you
    read it, list the reasons that are mentioned for
    playing sports.

⏱ about 400 words

History of sport

The development of sport throughout history can teach
us a great deal about social changes, and about the
nature of sport itself. Sport seems to involve basic
human skills being developed and exercised for their
5 own sake, as well as for their usefulness. This suggests
that sport is probably as old as the existence of people,
and that it was a useful way of people increasing their
mastery of the environment.

Of course, as we go further back in history, the lack of
10 evidence makes this claim more difficult to support.
However, there are many examples in France, Africa
and Australia of pre-historic cave art – some of it over
30,000 years old. The existence of art is evidence of
there being leisure time available. It is therefore
15 possible that there was some activity at these times
resembling sport.

When the British explorer Captain Cook first visited the
Hawaiian Islands, in 1778, he reported that he saw the
native people surfing. Likewise Native Americans
20 played games and sports before the coming of
Europeans, such as ball games, running, and other
athletic activities. The ancient Mayan and Aztec
civilisations played ball games on courts of a type that
is still used today. It is reasonable to assume from
25 these and other historical sources that sport dates back
to the beginnings of mankind itself.

There is evidence that Chinese people engaged in activities
which meet our definition of sport as early as 6,000 years
ago. These activities seem to have developed as a form of
entertainment, as well as serving a practical function in
30 making people fit for work. In Ancient Egypt, too, sports such
as swimming and fishing were well developed and regulated
several thousand years ago. A wide range of sports were
played in Ancient Greece, among them wrestling, running,
discus throwing, and chariot racing. This suggests that the
35 military culture of Greece was an influence on the
development of its sports. It was the importance of sports
that led to the creation of the Olympic Games.

In the last two or three centuries, running and jumping,
which were originally done for food and survival, have
40 become activities done for pleasure or competition. The
Industrial Revolution and mass production brought
increased leisure in the 19th and particularly the 20th
centuries. This led to a major growth in spectator sports,
and made it possible for far more people to play and watch.
45 Recently, there has been a move towards adventure and
extreme sports as a form of escapism from the routines of
life, examples being white-water rafting, canyoning and
bungee jumping.

3 Look at the following periods and places and the statements below.

Match each period or place (**1–5**) with the correct statement (**A–E**) according to the passage.

1 Ancient Greece
2 19th and 20th century
3 pre-historic times
4 Ancient China
5 the Americas

A People invented sports that would create a sense of community.
B People played sports that developed their fighting skills.
C People did activities that suggest they may also have had opportunities for sport.
D People were already playing sports when Europeans arrived.
E People became more involved in sport because of economic changes.
F People played sports which spread into other parts of the world.
G People played sports for pleasure and to become strong and healthy.

Grammar

Should, had better, ought to

4 Look at these sentences, based on the listening passage.

Dad, you'd better not go zorbing if you feel ill.
You should book a few weeks in advance.
You ought to book at least six weeks ahead.
I'd better give my father details of both the bungee jumping and zorbing.

1 Which function could all four sentences have: informing, ordering, advising or suggesting?
2 Which of the following is mostly used in informal contexts: *ought to*, *should* or *had better*?

5 Look at this statement, and the five answers giving advice.

I've been playing tennis for the last three hours, and I'm exhausted.

a You'd better not play any longer.
b You shouldn't play any longer.
c You oughtn't to play any longer.
d You shouldn't play for so long.
e You oughtn't to play for so long.

1 Which sentences give specific advice about the present situation?
2 Which sentences give general advice for the future?
3 Which is normally used only to give specific advice about the present situation: *ought to*, *should* or *had better*?

Notes: *Should* is used much more than *ought to*. *Had better* is usually shortened to *'d better*, especially in speech, and very often follows a pronoun.

6 Write a sentence or two giving advice in each case below, using *ought to*, *should* or *'d better*, or their negatives, *oughtn't to*, *shouldn't*, *'d better not*.

EXAMPLE: I spend all my spare time playing football, and I never see my friends. *You shouldn't spend so much time on sport. You ought to call your friends.*

1 I want to do an activity that's really exciting.
2 I'm going surfing, but I don't know what to take with me.
3 I play a lot of football, but I'm finding it more difficult to run around.
4 I enjoy swimming, and now I want to do something different, but still in the water.
5 My friends want me to do a parachute jump with them, but I'm a bit afraid.

Should (and, less often, *ought to*) are used when the speaker thinks that something will probably happen. This is often something good or neutral, rather than bad. *Shouldn't* means that something (often something bad) *probably won't* happen; for example:
The team has been training very hard, so they should win their next game.
Admission to the match is by ticket only, so it shouldn't be too crowded.

7 Rewrite these sentences using *should* or *shouldn't*. One of them can't be changed.

1 It would be good to go skiing this week, because the weather will probably stay fine.
2 The two runners are both so good that the result is likely to be a tie.
3 I've got a slight injury to my arm, but it's unlikely to stop me playing football next week.
4 I've often gone riding before, so I'll probably manage to stay on the horse.
5 I've never ridden a horse before, so I'll probably fall off.
6 The team has just missed a goal, but it probably won't make much difference to the final score.

G ···⟩ page 141

8 In small groups, discuss how to improve at sports or other activities. Consider practice, training, mental preparation, encouragement from other people, watching champions, prizes …

Writing folder 6

Task 2: Connecting ideas 1

1 You can improve your written work by using a variety of connecting words. Decide whether the following words are closest in meaning to *and*, *but* or *so*, and write them in the correct column.

though	however
unfortunately	although
consequently	also
in addition (to)	what is more
therefore	as a result (of)
in fact	this means/meant (that)
despite (the fact that)	

and	but	so

Although the words in each column have a similar meaning to others in the same column, they can't be used in exactly the same way grammatically. Some are used to link ideas within a sentence and some to link ideas between sentences.

For example:
*I love football **and** I go to all my team's matches.*
*I love football. **What's more**, I go to all my team's matches.*
*I enjoy watching ice hockey **but** I wouldn't want to play it, as it is dangerous.*
*I enjoy watching ice hockey. **However**, I wouldn't want to play it, as it is dangerous.*

2 Decide which of the words in the table would fit in the following sentences. More than one answer is sometimes possible.

AND
1 a She has been a wonderful coach for the Scottish team. .... , she has done a tremendous amount to help young players.
 b Ice hockey has always been a popular spectator sport. .... , recently there has been an increase in the number of people playing the game.

BUT
2 a .... they had scored three goals by half time, they didn't win the match.
 b The team had scored three goals by half time, ... they didn't win the match.
 c The team had scored three goals by half time. .... , they didn't win the match.
 d .... the fact that the team had scored three goals by half time, they didn't win the match.
 e .... the team scoring three goals by half time, they didn't win the match.

SO
3 a Manchester United beat Liverpool and .... won the cup.
 b .... beating Liverpool, Manchester United won the cup.
 c Manchester United beat Liverpool. .... they won the cup.

3 Look at the example Task 2 question below (General Training or Academic) and then read the answer opposite. Don't worry about the missing words for now.

Write about the following topic.
People today spend far more time watching sport than actually doing any themselves. What are the factors influencing this change?
Give reasons for your answer and include any relevant examples from your own knowledge or experience.

I would argue that sport has never been as popular as it is today. In fact, it does not matter where people live, sport still has a great influence on their lives - whether they play or just watch.

1 .... , there is growing concern that people are beginning to prefer to be spectators rather than players. 2 .... , they are becoming overweight and unfit. This is undoubtedly the result of the way people live today in some parts of the world. By this I mean that they are always in a rush, suffer from too much stress 3 .... have to work long hours. 4 .... , they get home too late to do anything except make a meal, watch TV and go to bed.

5 .... , many small towns do not have suitable sports facilities, or if they do have a sports centre, it is often too expensive to go there often. Where I live, taking part in sport is still extremely popular, especially among young people. 6 .... there is no large sports centre in my town, the young people still play football and basketball. There are, 7 .... , some sports that it is only possible for us to watch on TV, like tennis and skiing. 8 .... , it seems to me that it is not what you play that is important - it is that you actually do play something.

I would like to conclude by saying that there may be some justification for claiming that fewer people are playing sport. It all depends where you live in the world. Playing sport as well as watching it is very much alive in my part of the world, and, 9 .... , I believe it will continue to grow in popularity.

4   In the essay some of the linking words and phrases are missing.
    Decide which of A, B or C would fit best in each space 1–9.

1 **A** However	**B** Despite	**C** Therefore
2 **A** In addition	**B** However	**C** Consequently
3 **A** therefore	**B** and	**C** but
4 **A** As a result	**B** Despite	**C** Although
5 **A** So	**B** Unfortunately	**C** In fact
6 **A** Although	**B** Consequently	**C** In fact
7 **A** also	**B** though	**C** so
8 **A** As a result	**B** However	**C** This means that
9 **A** so	**B** despite	**C** what's more

5   Complete the following sentences with a suitable phrase.

    1 Although footballers can earn a lot of money, …
    2 Despite the fact that extreme sports are very popular, they …
    3 The Olympic Games bring nations together every four years. What's more, they …
    4 Skiing is increasing in popularity, despite the fact that …
    5 The college is holding trials for their athletics team this week. In addition, they …
    6 The team won the local cup. Unfortunately, they …
    7 The team managed to overcome the opposition and win the town cup. What is more, they …
    8 The team won the local cup. As a result, they …
    9 Although …, the college is better known for its rugby team.
    10 A good diet is vital to sportspeople, so they …

Units 9–12 Revision

Topic review

1 How far do you agree with these statements? Give reasons for your answers.

   1 My favourite place to live is somewhere with a hot climate.
   2 When playing a game, the most important thing is to try to win.
   3 People shouldn't have animals or birds living in their homes.
   4 I try to reduce my contribution to global warming.
   5 There are no advantages to living alone.
   6 We can understand human behaviour better by studying the behaviour of animals.
   7 Sport is more exciting to watch than to play.
   8 People who can't afford to buy or rent a home should be given one free.
   9 I try to use environmentally friendly products when I have a choice.
  10 People should leave home when they are about 20 years old.

Grammar

Articles

2 Put *a/an*, *the* or nothing in each space.

Our earliest homes

If you were to ask a number of 1 .... people about the homes of our prehistoric ancestors, most would probably say that they lived in 2 .... caves. However, there is plenty of 3 .... evidence that early human beings also lived in areas where no caves existed. In fact, some of the earliest homes seem to be 4 .... round huts. In the Olduvai Gorge in Tanzania, there is 5 .... circle of 6 .... stones. This could be the foundation of 7 .... shelter that may date back nearly two million years.

8 .... earliest shelters may have consisted of a circle of 9 .... branches broken or cut from trees. 10 .... branches would have been leant against each other for support in the centre of 11 .... circle, creating a structure similar to a tent. They were probably covered with 12 .... animal skins or leaves. The first structures were probably very unstable, but in time, larger, stronger and more permanent structures are likely to have been created, which did not simply provide shelter, but became the centre of 13 .... family life, and a place where 14 .... possessions could be kept.

-ing forms and infinitives

3 Complete each sentence with the correct form of the verb in brackets.

1 We'd better .... another look at both houses before we decide which one to buy. (have)
2 I hope .... into a more conveniently located flat when I start my new job. (move)
3 Most sportsmen and women practise daily .... in peak condition. (keep)
4 If you've finished .... your assignment, we can have a game of tennis. (write)
5 I'm looking forward to .... the differences between domestic and wild animals. (study)
6 The climate is too complex for us .... sure of how our actions affect it. (be)
7 The tennis coach planned a practice schedule to help the players .... their skills. (improve)
8 Most people understand the importance of .... friends close by. (have)
9 It is hard .... that some animals have complex social organisations. (believe)
10 Any change to our climate will mean .... our way of life quite significantly. (adapt)

Countable and uncountable nouns

4 Complete each sentence with *much* or *many* and a noun from the box, making it plural if necessary. Use each noun only once.

accommodation	animal	country
news	person	pollution	research
time	evidence	university	work

EXAMPLE: How ....*much evidence*........ did they find of global warming?

1 How .... have we got before the game starts?
2 In .... there are laws to protect endangered species of animals.
3 You can take courses in different aspects of sport at .... nowadays.
4 I haven't found .... in this town that students can afford.
5 How .... have you carried out into the behaviour of lions?
6 As well as human beings, ... will be affected by climate change.
7 Do electric cars produce ....?
8 I've got so .... to do that I won't be able to go home for another few hours.
9 .... enjoy sports which are not competitive.
10 I haven't heard .... about recent developments in extreme sports.

Vocabulary

5 Complete each sentence with a suitable word from Units 9–12. Some letters are given, and each dash represents one letter.

1 Unless we increase the amount of waste re _ _ _ _ _ _ _ we do, we will soon be overwhelmed with our rubbish.
2 Sometimes efforts to protect en _ _ _ _ _ _ _ _ species succeed in saving them from becoming extinct.
3 When people have children, they may choose to ex _ _ _ _ their house rather than buy a larger one.
4 In many countries, the most common type of household consists of an ex _ _ _ _ _ _ family.
5 I recently took part in a w _ _ _ s _ _ _ where we discussed ways of reducing our impact on the climate.
6 Samuelson thought he had scored a goal, but the r _ _ _ _ _ _ ruled it off-side.
7 There were so many sp _ _ _ _ _ _ _ _ trying to get into the stadium without tickets that the police had to be called.
8 There is growing interest in ex _ _ _ _ _ sports, so new ones are being invented all the time.
9 Many elderly people choose to live in a bun _ _ _ _ _ because all the rooms are on the ground floor.

6 Complete this paragraph using phrases from the box. Use each phrase once only.

causes of	dependency on	effects of
effect on	increase in	loss of
melting of	threat to	

Scientists expect the 1 .... global warming to be dramatic. Higher temperatures are likely to cause the 2 .... the Greenland ice cap, and the resulting rise in sea levels will have a devastating 3 .... low-lying communities. An 4 .... extreme weather events, such as hurricanes, is also probable. Global warming is a serious 5 .... plant and animal life, as well as ourselves, and could lead to the 6 .... some species. The 7 .... global warming are not fully understood, but our 8 .... fossil fuels has certainly contributed to it.

Choices

1 Are these statements true for you? With a partner, answer *Yes* or *No* to each of them.

1 When I have to make a choice, I try to imagine what all the other possibilities are.

2 I spend hours shopping for clothes, trying to get something that looks perfect.

3 When watching TV or listening to the radio, I constantly click on to other channels so I don't miss anything.

4 I find writing very difficult in my own language because it's hard to get the wording just right.

5 I never settle for second best.

More than three *Yes* answers = You are probably a *maximiser*. *Maximisers* tend to be perfectionists.

More than three *No* answers = You are probably a *satisficer*. *Satisficers* are happy to make a quick decision and not worry about it afterwards.

Read the passage opposite to find out more.

Reading

2 Take about two minutes to skim the article to get a general idea of what it is about.

⏱ about 600 words

A

Barry Schwartz did not expect to feel inspired on a clothes-shopping trip. 'I avoid buying jeans; I wear one pair until it falls apart,' says Schwartz, an American
5 psychology professor. 'The last time I had bought a pair there had been just one style. <u>But recently I was asked if I wanted this fit or that fit, or this colour or that. I intended to be out shopping for five minutes but it took an hour, and I began to feel more and more dissatisfied</u>.'
10 This trip made him think: did more choice always mean greater satisfaction? 'I'd always believed that choice was good, and more choice was better. My experience got me thinking: how many others felt like me?'

B

15 The result was a widely discussed study that challenged the idea that more is always better. Drawing on the psychology of economics, which looks at how people choose what to buy, Schwartz designed a questionnaire to show the differences between what
20 he termed 'maximisers' and 'satisficers'. Broadly speaking, maximisers are keen to make the best possible choices, and often spend time researching to ensure that their purchases cannot be bettered. Satisficers are the easy-going people, delighted with
25 items that are simply acceptable.

C

Schwartz puts forward the view, which contrasts with what politicians and salesmen would have people believe, that the unstoppable growth in choice is in
30 danger of ruining lives. 'I'm not saying no choice is good. But the average person makes at least 200 decisions every day, and I don't think there's room for any more.' His study may help to explain the peculiar paradox of the wealthy West – psychologists and
35 economists are puzzled by the fact that people have not become happier as they have become richer. In fact, the ability to demand whatever is wanted whenever it is wanted has instead led to rising expectations.

D

40 The search for perfection can be found in every area of life from buying soap powder to selecting a career. Certain decisions may automatically close off other choices, and some people are then upset by the thought of what else might have been. Schwartz says,
45 'If you make a decision and it's disappointing, don't worry about it, it may actually have been a good decision, just not as good as you had hoped.'

E

One fact that governments need to think about is that people seem more inclined to buy something if there are fewer, not more, choices. If that's true for jeans, then it is probably true for cars, schools and pension funds. 'If there are few options, the world doesn't expect you to make the perfect decision. But when there are thousands it's hard not to think there's a perfect one out there, and that you'll find it if you look hard enough.'

50

55

F

If you think that Internet shopping will help, think again: 'You want to buy something and you look at three websites. How long will it take to look at one more? Two minutes? It's only a click. Before you know it you've spent three hours trying to decide which £10 item to buy. It's crazy. You've used another evening that you could have spent with your friends.'

60

65

G

Schwartz, who describes himself as a natural satisficer, says that trying to stop our tendency to be maximisers will make us happier. 'The most important recommendation I can give is to lower personal expectations,' he says. 'But no one wants to hear this because they all believe that perfection awaits the wise decision maker. Life isn't necessarily like that.'

70

3 **Questions 1–7**

The reading passage has seven paragraphs labelled ***A–G****. Which paragraph contains the following information (1–7)?*
NB *You may use any letter more than once.*

Example:
Look at question 1. The type of information and the topic of the information which you have to find has been underlined.

The answer is **A**. See the underlined words, where the writer talks about his shopping trip to buy a pair of jeans. Note that in this type of task the questions are not in the same order as the relevant information in the passage.

1 an <u>account</u> of a <u>personal experience</u>
2 why some advice may be rejected
3 a finding that confuses experts
4 the emotional effect of the result of making a choice
5 information about how Schwartz's research was undertaken
6 how a lack of choice affects decision making
7 a definition of two types of personality

Questions 8 and 9
Choose the correct letter, ***A****,* ***B****,* ***C*** *or* ***D****.*

8 Which phrase best describes Barry Schwartz's reaction to buying jeans?
   A annoyance at having spent more money than he intended to
   B delight at being able to find exactly what he was looking for
   C acceptance of the amount of time he needed to spend shopping
   D irritation at the end of his shopping trip

9 A suitable title for this article would be
   A When to make that decision
   B Too much choice
   C Decision making for the indecisive
   D A psychologist's choice

Vocabulary Collocations with adverbs

4 Adverbs are frequently used in academic writing; for example, *a widely discussed study*.

Complete each sentence with an adverb from the box.

anxiously	firmly	hardly	highly
hugely	justly	totally	widely

1 The psychologist was .... thought of by his students.
2 The government .... believes that choice has an important role to play in people's lives.
3 The shopping trip was .... successful – I bought three pairs of jeans.
4 Piet was .... waiting to hear if he had got a place at university.
5 They were .... wrong in their assumptions.
6 These trainers are .... available in the USA.
7 The class were .... proud of the questionnaires they had written.
8 I .... recognised Tim when he came into the room – he had changed so much.

Grammar Conditionals

1 🎧 You are going to hear four short extracts, where people talk about choices.

Which speaker (A–D) is talking about ...

1 something that always happens?
2 something that will probably happen?
3 something that is unlikely to happen?
4 something that could have happened in the past, but didn't?

2 🎧 Listen again. Which *if* sentence does each person use?

A If ....
B If ....
C If ....
D If ....

> **Note:** *If* can begin a sentence, or it can begin the second part of the sentence.
>
> There are other words that can be used instead of *if*.
>
> • *as long as* is used to make conditions
> *You can do the course **as long as** you have the required grades.* = You can do the course if you have the required grades.
>
> • *unless* = ***if ... not***
> *I'll go shopping with you tomorrow, **unless** it's raining.* = I'll go shopping with you tomorrow if it isn't raining.

G ⋯▸ page 141

3 Match sentences 1–10 with their endings a–j.

1 I would have bought a faster car,
2 If Marisa were unhappy,
3 If I sold my bike,
4 If there is a fire,
5 We can take the train,
6 Unless you take more exercise,
7 If you inherited some money,
8 If you had studied law,
9 I'll get a new coat,
10 I'll ring you straight away,

a if the flight costs too much.
b you should ring the emergency services.
c you won't feel better.
d I wouldn't get much for it.
e would you give any away?
f as long as I can find a bargain.
g you wouldn't have been any happier.
h if I have any problems.
i if I had had a choice.
j she'd say so.

4 With a partner, discuss how you could finish these sentences.

1 Unless you wear something smart, you ...
2 I would have bought a new CD ...
3 If I were you, ...
4 If I had had the chance, ...
5 As long as you let me choose the film, I ...
6 If I had to choose between studying at home and studying abroad, I ...
7 I won't go shopping unless ...
8 I'll buy ... if ...

5 The following sentences show common errors that IELTS candidates have made with conditionals. Correct the errors.

1 It be best if the children were in bed when we go out tonight.
2 You will not go wrong if you chose her for your secretary.
3 If I ever will have money, I will be spend it wisely.
4 What would happen if the cheque would go missing?
5 If you would choose to live in the town centre, you'd need to pay more.
6 Unless we will hurry, we will be late.
7 I would appreciate it if you would have written back to me.
8 I would be grateful if you reply as soon as possible.

Listening

6 Look at the photographs above. Where would you prefer to do your shopping, at A or B?

7 🎧 You are going to hear a tutorial with a number of people speaking, which is similar to Part 3 of the Listening Module. Listen once and say how many people are speaking. Does the number of people make a difference to your understanding?

8 Read through each set of questions very carefully before you listen to the relevant part of the recording.

🎧 **Questions 1–3**
*Choose the correct letter, **A**, **B** or **C**.*

1 At the start of the tutorial, the tutor wants to know how the students would feel about having
   A no choice.
   B too much choice.
   C a few choices only.

2 The tutor says that the economy works because
   A people copy what others buy.
   B some people have more than others.
   C not everyone is the same.

3 What point is the tutor making about American TV?
   A There are too many channels.
   B People rarely watch all the available channels.
   C Most Americans watch too much.

🎧 **Questions 4–10**
Complete the notes below.
*Write **NO MORE THAN THREE WORDS** for each answer.*

Tutorial Notes

If you are buying 4 .... , then choice is a good thing.

Mobile phone contracts are an example of what is called 5 '..' .

You might buy a loaf of bread on the basis of 6 .... and

....

When you buy a house, the 7 .... is the most important factor.

Three strategies:
- to buy the same as 8 ....
- to buy the latest thing – being known as a 9 ....
- to buy something unique – such as 10 ....

Speaking *Part 3*

9 Discuss these questions with a partner. Make sure you give reasons for your answers.

   1 Do you believe the theory that too much choice is bad for you?
   2 What choices did you have to make today?
   3 Have you ever had to make a really difficult choice?
   4 If you have to choose between two things, how do you personally make that decision? Do you toss a coin, decide on the evidence ...?

Useful language
Clarification
What I mean is that ...
Let me put this another way ...
What I'm trying to say is ...
My point is that ...

Test folder 7

Locating information

(Academic Reading and General Training Reading Modules only)

You might be asked which paragraph or section of a passage contains certain information.

The answers only come from those paragraphs or sections that are labelled alphabetically.

The information in the questions doesn't come in the same order as in the passage.

The questions generally say what *type* of information you must find, such as an explanation, an example, a recommendation, how, why, etc. They are not paraphrases of the information itself.

Advice

- Skim the whole passage before you start working on any of the tasks. Read the instructions carefully.
- Read the questions and think about what they mean. Underline the key words in the questions, both the *type* of information (explanation, how, etc.) and the *topic* itself.
- Read the first labelled paragraph carefully. Read all the questions, and write the paragraph letter by any questions that match information in the paragraph. Remember to check both the *type* of information and the *topic*.
- Continue with each of the labelled paragraphs in turn. Where you have more than one possible answer, re-read those paragraphs and choose the one that fits the question best.
- Your answers should be A, B, C, etc: don't write line numbers or anything else.
- Unless the instructions tell you that you can use any letter more than once, make sure all your answers are different.

1 This passage is similar to those in the Academic Reading Module, but only about 550 words. The task is typical of both Reading Modules. The idea of different 'thinking hats' comes from the idiom 'put your thinking cap on', which means 'think hard'.

Six Thinking Hats –
Looking at a decision from all points of view

A Faced with a number of choices, we may find it hard to make a decision, or may always approach problems in the same way. Emotional people, for example, may not consider decisions calmly and rationally. Many successful people think from a very rational, positive viewpoint, and this is one reason for their success. Often, though, they fail to look at a problem from an emotional, intuitive, creative or negative viewpoint. By always using a positive approach, they may underestimate possible difficulties – such as resistance to their plans – and be under-prepared for dealing with future problems.

B 'Six Thinking Hats' is a valuable technique for increasing the effectiveness of decision-making. Created by Edward de Bono, it makes you consider the decision from a number of perspectives, forcing you to add different ways of thinking to your usual approach. This gives you a fuller view of a situation. As a result, your decisions and plans will be ambitious, creative and sensitive to the needs of others. They will be carried out effectively, and you will be prepared for the unexpected. You can use Six Thinking Hats with other people or on your own. With others, it has the benefit of blocking the confrontations that happen when people with different thinking styles discuss the same problem.

C Each 'Thinking Hat' is a different style of thinking. With the White Thinking Hat you focus on the data available. Look at the information you have, and see what you can learn from it. Look for gaps in your knowledge, and either try to fill them or take account of them. This is where you analyse past trends, and try to work out from historical data what might happen in the future. 'Wearing' the Red Hat, you look at problems using intuition, instantaneous reactions, and emotion. Also try to think how other people will react emotionally. Try to understand the responses of people who do not fully know your reasoning.

D Using Black Hat thinking, look at all the bad points of the decision. Look at it cautiously and defensively. Try to see why it might not work. This is important because it highlights the weak points in a plan. It allows you to eliminate them, alter them, or prepare contingency plans to deal with problems that might arise. Black Hat thinking helps to make your plans 'tougher' and better able to survive difficulties. It can also help you to spot fatal flaws and risks before you start on a course of action.

E The Yellow Hat encourages you to think positively. It is the optimistic viewpoint that helps you to see all the benefits of the decision and the value in it. Yellow Hat thinking helps you to keep going when everything looks gloomy and difficult. The Green Hat stands for creativity. This is where you can develop creative solutions to a problem. It is an unstructured way of thinking, in which there is little criticism of ideas. A whole range of creativity tools can help you here.

F The Blue Hat stands for process control. This is the hat worn by people chairing meetings. When running into difficulties because ideas are running dry, they may direct activity into Green Hat thinking. When contingency plans are needed, they will ask for Black Hat thinking, and so on.

*The passage has six paragraphs labelled **A–F**.*
Which paragraph contains the following information?
***NB** You may use any letter more than once.*

Example:
Read paragraph **A**. The last sentence contains the information in question 2, so the answer to 2 is **A**.

1 a method of thinking which discourages objections to suggestions
2 a potential disadvantage of considering a problem from only one angle *A*
3 possible benefits of identifying negative aspects of a plan
4 how the Six Thinking Hats technique can help to prevent conflict in a meeting
5 a method of thinking where one person in a group changes the style of thinking that is required
6 a description of decisions made using the technique
7 how to use what you already know
8 a way of making you feel more cheerful

Do roles limit our choice of how we behave?

A We all have many roles and often switch between them, as we interact with different people in different situations. In the course of a single day, one person may need to act as manager, husband, father, son, friend, and so on.

B Associated with each role is a distinct pattern of behaviour which is considered typical of a person in that particular position, and this becomes part of the role. Fathers are expected to behave in certain ways, and managers in others, which perhaps include making decisions quickly, 'looking the part' by dressing differently from those below them in the company hierarchy, and speaking in a certain style. Clearly expectations are a product of a particular time and place: expectations connected with the role of manager or adult daughter may be different from what is expected in other cultures, or in the same culture a century ago. These expectations affect how people behave in roles, how they feel they ought to behave, and how they believe other people should respond to their actions.

C Roles are normally taken in relation to an appropriate other person, in an appropriate context.

Doctors are expected to take our pulse, maintain a degree of professional distance and wear white coats when we encounter them in hospitals, but they are not expected to do this all the time – when we meet them at parties or in the street, for instance.

D Expectations about the behaviour associated with particular roles influence our actions. Although we have some degree of choice in our conduct, the expectations and patterns of behaviour connected with our roles encourage us to conform with the norm. Managers, for instance, may feel under pressure to behave in an authoritarian manner, even if this conflicts with their personality and general approach to interaction with other people. Choosing to behave in a way that conflicts with other people's expectations can create a wide range of problems.

E On the other hand, expectations simplify social contact, as they make it unnecessary to analyse every individual situation we find ourselves in. Instead, once we know the relevant role of the other person, we assume that they will behave in certain ways, and that we, too, need to behave in certain ways.

2 **This is similar to passages in the Academic Reading Module but is only about 375 words. The task is typical of both Reading Modules.**

*The passage above has five paragraphs labelled **A–E**.*
Which paragraph contains the following information?
***NB** You may use any letter more than once.*

1 examples of situations in which particular role behaviour is considered unsuitable
2 how clothing might be chosen to differentiate between people at different levels within an organisation
3 a suggestion that people may be uncomfortable with the way they are expected to behave
4 an example of an individual taking a number of roles
5 how a person's role affects other people's response to them
6 a claim that the behaviour expected as part of a particular role is not always the same

The importance of colour

1 What do you think about the colours used for the iPod Mini, car and ketchup above?

Listening

It is important to listen for what is relevant to the questions. You don't need to understand everything.

2 You are going to hear a man talking about how the colour of a consumer item affects how popular it is with the public. Read each set of questions and try to guess what the answers might be before you listen.

🎧 Questions 1–4

Which colour is the most popular for items **1–4**?

A	black
B	blue
C	green
D	grey
E	red
F	silver
G	white

Write the letter **A–G** next to each item.

1 business suits
2 offices
3 national flags
4 the iPod Mini

🎧 Questions 5–8

Write the name of the colour in the right place on the key to the chart below.

Global colour trend data – Cars 2004

red 5 .... 6 .... 7 .... 8 .... green

🎧 Questions 9 and 10

Complete the lines on the graph.

You won't have to draw in the IELTS Listening Module, but this exercise will help you to listen for detailed information.

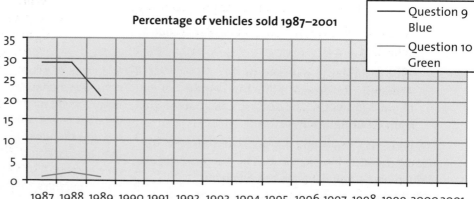

Percentage of vehicles sold 1987–2001

—— Question 9 Blue
—— Question 10 Green

3 The verbs in the box are used to describe changes. Put them in the right column of the table below.
···⟩ WF 2

to be consistent	to make progress
to be steady	to pick up
to decline	to plummet
to fall	to remain constant
to grow	to remain unchanged
to improve	to rise
to level off	to weaken

to go down	to remain stable	to go up

4 Look at the graph you completed for Questions 9 and 10 in exercise 2. Work with a partner and use the vocabulary above to describe the graph. Then, write a paragraph for the blue and green vehicle data.

Pronunciation *Linking words*

English links words together smoothly so a final consonant of a word can sound like the first consonant of the next word, particularly if the next word starts with a vowel. This means that it can be hard to tell the difference between, for example, *I scream* and *ice cream.*

5 🎧 First listen to the examples. Then listen to the rest of the recording and notice how the words are generally linked together. Then, read it through to your partner.

EXAMPLES: black‿orange, red‿apple, green‿egg

Although blue can be quite a popular colour generally, it is the least attractive colour when it comes to food because of the way we have learnt to look at blue-, black- or purple-coloured foods. Psychologically, these foods resemble food spoilt by bacteria or food which is poisonous. However, one food giant is aiming to boost ketchup sales by introducing blue ketchup. The flavour remains unchanged and the price is a little higher than for the red ketchup, but it is popular with children.

Speaking *Part 3*

6 What colour do you normally wear? Look at the chart below and see what personality type you are. Use an English–English dictionary to check you understand the adjectives describing personality.

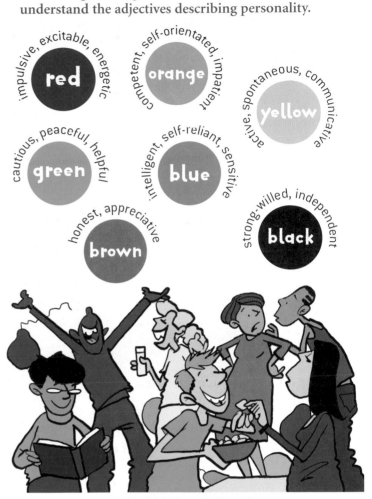

7 With a partner, discuss the following questions. Make sure you give reasons and expand your answers.

1 Do you think you can tell what someone's personality type is by the colour they normally wear?
2 In your country, do any colours have a particular significance? What colour do people wear at weddings or funerals, for instance?
3 What do you think is the role of colour in our lives?
4 How important is colour in advertising?

Useful language
I haven't thought about it before, but it seems to me …
… plays an important part/role in …
On the whole …
As a rule …
For the most part …
Generally …

Listening

1 🎧 Listen to a girl talking about what happened at college today. What colours are mentioned? What is said about the colours?

2 🎧 Listen again and answer these questions.
   1 What subject is the student studying?
   2 Is she usually late for seminars?
   3 Why was she late this morning?
   4 What did Dr Stanley do when she entered the room?
   5 What did Dr Stanley go on to talk about?
   6 Why did Dr Stanley stop?
   7 What did the girl do to try to keep awake?

Grammar -ing forms and infinitives 2

3 Look at the pairs of sentences below. They are taken from the recording. Why does one sentence use an -ing form and one an infinitive with *to*?
   1 a I didn't remember to switch my alarm clock on.
     b I remember getting into bed but that's about all.
   2 a Dr Stanley stopped talking and just looked at me.
     b He then stopped to show us a video.

4 Discuss with your partner the difference in meaning, if any, in the following pairs of sentences.
   1 a I tried to keep awake, but it was no good.
     b I tried opening the window to get some air in the room.
   2 a He went on talking while I found a seat.
     b He went on to say that many people suffer from colour blindness.
   3 a They began painting when I came into the room.
     b They began to paint when I came into the room.
   4 a I like studying zoology.
     b I like to get up early in the morning.

G ⋯⟶ page 142

5 Complete these sentences using the verb in brackets and your own ideas.
   EXAMPLE: When I was on my way to college, I stopped … (look)
   When I was on my way to college, I stopped to look in a shop window.
   1 When I couldn't wake up in time for school, I tried … (ask)
   2 When I realised I had forgotten my wallet, I tried … (borrow)
   3 When I was young, I remember … (go)
   4 I asked them to keep the noise level down, but they went on … (play)
   5 At the weekends, I like … (go shopping)
   6 Next time, you must remember … (take)

6 With a partner, discuss these questions. Use the right form after the verb.
   EXAMPLE: (answer to 1) *Seeing my brother come home covered in sticky brown mud.*
   1 What is your first colour memory?
   2 What sort of things do you forget to do?
   3 What would you do if had an argument with your best friend? (Use *try*.)
   4 What do you like to do first thing in the morning?

Vocabulary Confused words

7 The following sentences contain words that IELTS students often confuse. Circle the correct alternative, then write another sentence showing how the other word is used. Use an English–English dictionary to help you if necessary.
   EXAMPLE: If you're a banker, it's a good idea to wear ⟨sensible⟩/ sensitive dark suits to work.
   Steve is very sensitive about being colour-blind.
   1 I *borrowed / lent* Tony the book about personality and colour.
   2 *Remind / Remember* me of the colour you've decided to have.
   3 You can't take the paint back to the shop without a *recipe / receipt*.
   4 The seller *raised / rose* the price of the painting by twenty per cent.
   5 Many famous artists have painted the *countryside / nature* around my town.
   6 You need to *check / control* whether you can get shoes the same colour as your dress.
   7 What *affect / effect* will painting the common room bright red have?
   8 It is not *economic / economical* to use cheap paint.

9 *In the end / At the end* of the fashion show, she decided to wear only red.
10 *Standards / Levels* of living have risen in Europe since 1950.
11 The *journey / travel* to the Blue Mosque took four days.
12 The *discovery / invention* that some colours appeal more than others was significant.

Comment adverbs

Comment adverbs are very common in both academic writing and speaking. They allow the writer/speaker to indicate how likely they think something is and what their attitude or opinion is, or what viewpoint they are speaking from. Look at these two examples.

> ***Interestingly***, he went on to say …
> [I think this is interesting]

> ***Psychologically***, these foods resemble food spoilt by bacteria. [from the psychological point of view, i.e. in our minds]

8 **Replace the underlined part of each sentence with one of the comment adverbs from the box. More than one choice may be possible.**

disappointingly	generously	honestly
interestingly	logically	obviously
personally	statistically	surprisingly
wisely		

1 Although there would appear to be a lot of blue cars on the road, <u>from the point of view of percentages</u>, silver is more popular.
2 <u>In my opinion</u>, I can't see any reason for not eating blue food.

3 Matt gave <u>a lot of money</u> to help redecorate the children's playroom.
4 If A = B, then <u>it follows that</u> B = A.
5 <u>I was very interested to find out that</u> red is a lucky colour in China.
6 You are, <u>it goes without saying</u>, wrong in thinking all animals can see in colour.
7 <u>It's a pity but</u> very few people went to the exhibition on the history of colour.
8 <u>To be frank</u>, I think driving a red car would make you more likely to have accidents than driving a black one.
9 <u>You may not know this but</u> 8% of men are colour blind.
10 Tania, <u>in what was a very good decision</u>, decided to apply to study biology rather than art.

9 **In small groups, choose a colour and talk about it, using as many comment adverbs as you can. Use the adverbs opposite and the extra ones below.**

clearly	kindly	stupidly
undoubtedly	luckily	wrongly
probably	unbelievably	

EXAMPLE: My father generously painted my bedroom purple a couple of years ago, as a surprise for me. Clearly, it was kindly meant, but personally, I don't believe anyone can get a good night's sleep in a purple room. Unbelievably, my mother then went on to buy me black bed covers. Luckily, I went to college soon after and my sister got my room.

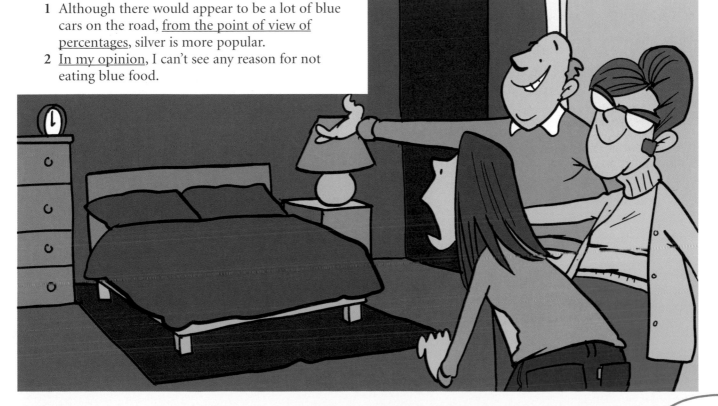

Writing folder 7

Task 2: Making a general statement, giving examples and using comment adverbs

Making a general statement

It is often necessary in academic writing to make general comments as you may not know exact figures or information. You should try to avoid definite statements using *all*, *always* or *never*.

1   Compare the sentences below. Which one is more general and formal?

   A Advertising agencies use colour to sell a product.
   B It is widely recognised that the majority of advertising agencies use colour to sell a product.

2   Using the language in the box below, make the following statements more general.

   1   Blue is a cold colour and shouldn't be used to paint living rooms.
   2   The colour of the packaging influences customers' choice of products.
   3   Green is the colour of environmental awareness.
   4   Driving a red car means that you like speeding.
   5   More women than men wear bright colours.
   6   Red is the best colour for a national flag.

Useful language

There is a tendency for ...
It appears/seems that ...
It would appear/seem that ...
It is (often) said that ...
It has been suggested/claimed that ...
It is generally agreed/believed/assumed/recognised that ...
It is widely accepted/believed/assumed that ...
... tends to be ...
... is recognised/believed/thought to be ...
In a majority / a large number of cases, ...
Broadly/Generally speaking, ...
On the whole, ...

Giving examples

The instructions for Task 2 in both the Academic and General Training Writing Modules state:

Give reasons for your answer and include any relevant examples from your own knowledge or experience.

3   Finish this paragraph using the words in italics and phrases from the Useful language box below.

Colour blindness does not seem to affect a person's day-to-day life. People who are colour blind tend to adapt, and some people go through life without even knowing they are colour blind. The only problems that people with defective colour vision face are in some career choices.

pilot, police officer, fire fighter, train driver, red and green lights

Useful language

A pilot, for instance / for example, needs to ...
For instance / For example, a pilot needs to ...
An illustration of X is ...
The following are examples of X: ... and ...
such as

Don't use abbreviations such as *e.g.*

4 Discuss the following statements with a partner and give examples from your own knowledge or experience.

1 When you consider animals, the male is usually more colourful than the female.
2 Colour helps companies to sell their goods.

Choose one of the statements above and write a paragraph, giving examples.

Comment adverbs

5 Complete the following paragraph using one of the adverbs, A, B or C in each space.

> **1** .... I believe that both men and women should pay more attention to the way they dress, especially when it comes to the colours they wear. I shall first of all discuss the choices men have when it comes to clothes. **2** .... men feel they need to wear something conventional to work like a dark suit, but **3** ...., there is still room for individuality in their choice of shirt and tie. **4** ...., men should have the same choices as women when it comes to dress and not feel that they are forced to wear something they do not like or feel comfortable in. **5** ...., many men do not feel they can challenge the system and introduce more colour into their clothes.

1	**A** Unfortunately	**B** Personally	**C** Apparently
2	**A** Understandably	**B** Frankly	**C** Totally
3	**A** statistically	**B** unbelievably	**C** clearly
4	**A** Honestly	**B** Ideally	**C** Interestingly
5	**A** Disappointingly	**B** Wisely	**C** Personally

6 Answer the following Task 2 question. Remember to generalise, exemplify and use comment adverbs.

You should spend about 40 minutes on this task.
Write about the following topic:

The world would be a poorer place without colour.

To what extent do you agree with this statement?

Give reasons for your answer and include any relevant examples from your own knowledge or experience.

Write at least 250 words.

Remember ...
- to make a plan
- to make sure you have an introduction, two or three paragraphs giving reasons and examples, and a conclusion
- to check for errors – spelling, grammar, punctuation
- to check you have written enough.

Social interaction

Speaking *Parts 1 and 3*

1 In small groups, discuss these questions.

- Do you like meeting new people?
- Do you like meeting people from other countries?
- How do you make guests feel welcome?
- What usually happens when people in your country invite guests to their home?

Reading

2 You are going to read a passage by a British woman who spent most of 2001 staying with a family in a foreign country in order to study everyday life there. In small groups, think about the problems that she may have had and also the things that she may have enjoyed. Then read the passage quickly to check if any of your ideas are mentioned.

⏱ about 700 words

Different forms of hospitality

As a British woman social anthropologist, I once spent a year in Moldova, in eastern Europe, studying everyday life in the country. I stayed with a Moldovan family, to see from the inside how people managed their lives. I had a
5 wonderful time, and made many new friends. What I observed is of course based on my own experience, at a particular place and time.

I often found it surprisingly difficult to see life there through the eyes of a Moldovan. This was because the
10 people I met were extremely hospitable and I was treated as an honoured guest at all times. As my hosts, they wanted me to enjoy myself, and not to get involved in shopping, cooking, or other domestic chores. Most mornings I was encouraged to go out to explore the city,
15 or carry out my research, and I returned later to find that my elderly landlady and her sister had travelled across the city on buses to the central market to bring back heavy loads of potatoes, a whole lamb, or other large quantities of produce.

20 I was often invited to people's homes, and was always offered food on entering. Most of the adults I met enjoyed inviting friends, family, neighbours, colleagues and even strangers into their homes, where they treated them to food, drink, and a lively, hospitable atmosphere. Hosts hurried to serve guests as well and as quickly as possible. 25 When a household was expecting guests, large amounts of food were prepared in advance, usually by the women. Wine had already been made, generally by the men, who were also responsible for pouring it. Unexpected visitors were still offered as much food and drink as the household could 30 provide in the circumstances.

At the time of my visit, it was not always easy to buy food. Grocery stores tended to be rather expensive and difficult to find, and so people usually shopped in markets instead. Because few of the people I knew 35 owned cars, most had to make frequent trips to the market on foot or crowded buses. People regularly travelled to several locations to purchase food and other necessities. City inhabitants were also involved in complex food exchanges with their home villages. 40

There were many similarities to my experience of Russia during visits in the 1990s. Here too, I found that people often put enormous effort into providing very generous meals for guests. In fact, my Russian hosts seemed to feel that they could only succeed in ⁴⁵ their role as host if their guests tried all the courses of the meal, and consumed far more than they would normally.

My impression was that there ⁵⁰ was a clear, generally accepted understanding of how hosts should behave. They were expected to provide large amounts of food, and to ensure that guests ate a great deal. ⁵⁵ All the chores – the shopping, preparation, washing up – were the responsibility of the hosts, and a guest's offer to help was usually politely refused. Guests were unlikely ⁶⁰ to be allowed into the kitchen.

In England the roles of host and guest tend to present a different picture, in ways that some might welcome and others regret. The two roles are less ⁶⁵ strictly defined as the English move towards more casual notions of hospitality than in the past. Perhaps to make guests feel at home, they may be invited into the kitchen to talk, ⁷⁰ and an offer to help with the cooking may well be accepted. Although traditionally cooking was women's work, nowadays far more men either help with or take charge of the food ⁷⁵ preparation.

In general, guests are expected to eat as much, or as little, as they like – so many people are on a diet that this is accepted as an adequate ⁸⁰ reason for not eating much. Hosts usually don't feel that their food, cooking skills or hospitality are being criticised if a guest refuses second helpings. And after the meal, a guest ⁸⁵ who offers to help with the washing up may be disappointed to find that their offer is accepted! Unexpected visitors will probably be offered a cup of tea or coffee, and perhaps a ⁹⁰ biscuit, but an offer of food is not regarded as essential.

3 Questions 1–8

Complete the summary below using words from the box.

A year in Moldova

The writer spent a year in Moldova as a member of a local 0 ....household...... , and studied the 1 .... of daily life. As a 2 .... , she was not expected to help with domestic 3 .... She found that making and serving 4 .... was seen as men's work, while women were responsible for other aspects of providing 5 .... Buying 6 .... generally required long journeys to 7 .... by 8 ....

bus	car	customs	duties	groceries	guest	homes
host	~~household~~	markets	meals	people		problems
resident	shops	villages	wine			

Question 9

What does the writer say about hospitality in Russia?

A People see it as their duty to invite guests, even if they do not enjoy being a host.

B Certain food is kept for special occasions when guests are present.

C Foreign visitors are likely to be treated differently from Russian guests.

D Hospitality is seen as an occasion for guests to eat more than usual.

Questions 10–13

*Which **FOUR** of the following activities by guests in England are mentioned by the writer?*

A bringing food or drink

B helping to prepare food

C eating a small amount

D praising the host's cooking

E refusing food

F helping to wash up

G inviting hosts to their home

Speaking *Part 2*

4 Look at this task.

> **Describe an occasion when you were a guest in someone else's home.**
> **You should say:**
> **why you went to that person's home**
> **what you did while you were there**
> **how that person behaved towards you**
> **and explain how you felt about being a guest.**

In small groups, think of as many ideas as possible, for example:

- *why you went to that person's home:*
  I visited my grandparents, as I do every week.
  I went home with a friend, whose parents invited me to join them for lunch.

- *what you did while you were there:*
  I helped my host to cook dinner.
  We chatted, then went out for a walk.

1 In small groups, discuss how people in your country feel about these aspects of social interaction.

- Eye contact
- Shaking hands
- Punctuality
- Personal space

Listening

2 🎧 You are going to hear part of a seminar for business students about customs in Japan, Arab countries and the USA. Read the questions before you listen. Even if you think you know the answer, listen to check what the speakers say.

According to the speakers, where is each type of behaviour (**1–8**) usual?

A Arab countries
B Japan
C USA

Write the correct letter, **A**, **B** *or* **C**, *by each question.*

Example:

0 saying 'no'   *C*
   Bill says, 'In the US … many people pride themselves on saying what they mean. If they want to say 'no', they come straight out with it.'

1 looking away
2 strong handshake
3 keeping visitors waiting
4 arriving late
5 social conversation in business meeting
6 personal space of around 30 cm
7 nodding the head to greet someone
8 keeping distance from strangers

3 🎧 Listen to part of the recording again.

Complete the sentences below.
Write **NO MORE THAN THREE WORDS** *for each answer.*

1 According to Helen, people feel more .... with the customs that they are familiar with.

2 According to Bill, Americans usually give negative information quite explicitly and ....

3 If you look at an American who is speaking to you, they will consider you ....

4 In Japan, people show .... by looking away from the speaker.

5 In the USA, shaking hands firmly is interpreted as showing ....

6 In Arab countries, time is regarded as a ....

7 If you keep an American waiting for half an hour or more, they may think they are not .... to you.

Grammar Talking about possibilities

May and *might*

Look at this question and the answer.

Question: *Could you speculate on how customs in your country will change in the next twenty years?*
Answer: *We might start having our main meal in the evening instead of at lunchtime.*

Candidates are often asked to speculate about the future in the Speaking Module. You can use *may* or *might* to refer to present or future possibilities. *May* is usually slightly more sure than *might*.

4 Rewrite the following answers to the question above, *using may/might* (*not*).

1 Customs will possibly become more similar to those in other countries.
2 Maybe shaking hands won't be so common in future.
3 It's possible that people will copy the customs they see in foreign TV programmes.

May have done and *might have done* refer to possibilities in the past. This question is one that could be asked in the Speaking Module. Rewrite the answers (4–6) using *may/might (not) have*.

How different do you think customs were fifty years ago?
4 Perhaps people didn't eat much foreign food.
5 Maybe people were more hospitable.
6 One possibility is that people didn't spend much time enjoying themselves.

IF IT'S TUESDAY THIS MUST BE BELGIUM

Must and *can't*

The American comedy film *If it's Tuesday, this must be Belgium*, is about a group of Americans who tour Europe, visiting nine countries in eighteen days. Here *must* expresses a deduction, or logical conclusion, not a fact: the speaker doesn't *know* that they are in Belgium, but they can work it out from their tour schedule.

5   Match each explanation (1–4) with the right example (**a–d**).

A deduction (logical conclusion), or strong belief that
1   something in the present is true
2   something in the present is impossible
3   something in the past is true
4   something in the past is impossible

a   That *can't be* Daniel – he's away on a business trip at the moment.
b   You get so many invitations to people's homes, you *must have* a lot of friends.
c   You *can't have seen* my aunt in Montreal – she didn't live there when you visited Canada.
d   This meal is delicious! It *must have taken* you a long time to cook it.

G ⋯⋮ page 142

6   In small groups, decide what you might say to the person in each of these situations. Start each sentence with *You must* or *You can't*.

EXAMPLE: Somebody has tried to connect up their new computer, but it doesn't work.
You can't have read the instructions.

1   Your friend tells you he hasn't slept for two nights.
2   Somebody tells you that Kazumi Ohno is a doctor, but Kazumi had already told you he is a dentist.
3   You've arranged to meet a friend's mother, Sally Green, for the first time. A woman is waiting in the right place at the right time.
4   You send an email to your friend Nur, but it is returned with the message that the address does not exist. You tell another friend about this. (Begin *Nur must …*)
5   You left a message for your friend Hasan asking him to call you urgently, but you haven't heard from him. Another friend asks you if you have heard from Hasan. (Begin *No – he can't …*)

Vocabulary

Collocations with *big, large* and *great*

Look at these phrases from the reading and listening passages:
   large amounts of food
   a great deal of information
   a big difference

Some nouns can collocate with more than one of the adjectives, often *big* and one of the other two.

7   Write *big, large* and *great* at the top of the appropriate column, A, B or C. Which one is not normally used with physical objects?

A:	B:	C: ....
a ... amount	a ... advantage	a ... advantage
to a ... extent	a ... surprise	a ... impact
a ... proportion	a ... impact	(a) ... difficulty
a ... measure (e.g. of agreement)	(a) ... difficulty	a ... problem
a ... number	a ... problem	a ... difference
a ... quantity	a ... difference	a ... city
a ... sum (e.g. of money)	a ... deal (of ...)	a ... family
a ... family	... importance	a ... house
a ... house	a ... honour	
	(a) ... success	
	to take ... care of	
	a ... distance	

8   Choose the most suitable nouns from the table in exercise 7 to complete this passage. Use a different noun for each space. As the style is fairly formal, *big* isn't used here.

It's a great **1** .... to be here to talk to you today about my research in China. In fact, I was very surprised to receive the invitation, as my work in social anthropology is to a large **2** .... unknown. I've had a large **3** .... of articles published, but mostly in academic journals.

Choosing to carry out my research in China was a difficult decision. It meant I would have to spend a large **4** .... of time, and a large **5** .... of money, learning the language. Luckily I have the great **6** .... that I'm half Chinese, and speak some Cantonese. It also meant spending a year at a great **7** .... from my family. However, I'm very glad I chose to go there, and my year in China was a great **8** .... in terms of my research.

Test folder 8

Classification

(Academic Reading, General Training Reading and Listening Modules)

You may be asked to classify several pieces of information from the passage, choosing among the same options (normally three) in each case. The options are all of the same type, for example, three time periods, three countries, three opinions, and so on. They could also be, for example, *before 1950 / after 1950 / both or satisfied / dissatisfied / neither*.

In the Listening Module the questions follow the order of information in the passage. In the Reading Modules they do not.

Advice

Reading Modules

- Skim the whole passage before you start working on any of the tasks.
- Read the instructions carefully and think about the meaning of the three options. Check what letters you should use for your answers: they may be A, B and C, or three other letters.
- Read the first question, and underline the key words. Find the relevant part of the passage. Read it carefully and consider all three options before choosing the correct one.
- Read the next question and find the relevant part of the passage. Remember that it might be *anywhere* in the passage.
- Always give an answer – you won't lose any marks if it's wrong.

Listening Module

- Use the time you are given to read the instructions carefully and think about the meaning of the three options. Check what letters you should use for your answers: they may be A, B and C, or three other letters.
- Listen for each answer in turn. Consider all three options before choosing your answer.
- Always give an answer – you won't lose any marks if it's wrong.

Listening

1 🎧 You will hear a short conversation similar to Section 1 of the Listening Module.

What is the relationship of the following people to the man?

Write   **C**   if the person is the man's colleague
          F   if the person is the man's friend
          R   if the person is the man's relative

Write the correct letter, **C**, **F** or **R**, after each person.

Example: Douglas   *Answer:* F (*We met a few years ago … We've stayed in touch*)

1 Rachel   ....
2 Suzanne   ....
3 Jack   ....
4 Melanie   ....

2 🎧 This task is similar to Section 3 of the Listening Module.

What does the student decide about including each topic in her current assignment?

*Write the correct letter, **A**, **B** or **C**, after each topic.*

A She will include it.
B She will not include it.
C She may or may not include it.

1 families   ....
2 social groups   ....
3 work teams   ....
4 acquaintances   ....
5 friends   ....

Reading

Read this passage, then answer the questions below.

How English family life has evolved since the eighteenth century

The majority of English families of the pre-industrial age – roughly until the mid-eighteenth century – lived in a rural location. Many of them owned, or had the use of, a small piece of land, and virtually all family members were engaged in agricultural work in one form or another, usually growing food for their own consumption and sometimes also producing food or other goods for sale.

The labour was controlled by the husband, the undisputed master of the household, even though his wife and children, too, had an economic value as their contributions to the family income were likely to make the difference between starvation and survival.

Children worked from an early age, girls helping their mothers, and boys their fathers. School was an occasional or irrelevant factor in their lives. Instead, children learned by doing what their parents showed them. Knowledge – of caring for animals, growing vegetables, sewing – was handed down from parent to child.

Most people also engaged in handicraft production in the home, the family being paid by a company to work with cloth, wood or leather. In general, this work could be put aside and taken up again when there was a break from household chores or agricultural work.

The process of industrialisation in the second half of the eighteenth century and during the nineteenth transformed life for the majority of the population. The use of steam to power machinery required large buildings, and this resulted in the construction of numerous factories in many towns and cities. <u>These in turn encouraged</u> <u>migration from the countryside in search of work</u>. If electricity had preceded steam, domestic industry might have survived more fully.

The new economic forces had a series of effects on the family. One of the vital economic ties holding it together was removed when it ceased to be a business partnership. Men, women and children were employed as individuals for a wage, often by different employers. When home and workplace were physically separated, husbands, wives and children were also physically separated for a good part of their time, especially as working hours were generally very long. Despite this, men were still regarded as the head of the household.

Few children now worked with their parents at home, and so could not learn by watching them at work. They had generally become greater economic assets than before, often taking jobs which were open to children rather than to adults, such as sweeping chimneys. Gradually the already bad economic situation of families worsened, as children's working hours were limited and their employment prohibited. Worst of all, from the family's economic perspective, education became compulsory before it became free.

---

3   You might find a task like this in either of the Reading Modules. Remember to choose your answers according to the passage.

Classify the following situations as being said to occur

A   in the pre-industrial period
B   in the industrial period
C   in both periods

Example: <u>Workers</u> were <u>attracted</u> to <u>urban</u> centres.   *B*

(The relevant part of the passage is underlined.)

1   People carried out work for a company in their own home.   ....
2   Most incomes were low.   ....
3   Children worked with their parents.   ....,
4   Husbands and wives worked apart.   ....
5   School attendance was irregular.   ....
6   Children contributed to the family income.   ....
7   Restrictions were placed on children's work.   ....
8   People were likely to live in the countryside.   ....
9   Families were dominated by men.   ....

16·1 Books, writing and signs

1   In small groups, describe and discuss these signs.

- Do you know what they mean? If not, try to work them out.
- Do you need to understand a particular language to understand them?
- How easily can they be understood by someone seeing them for the first time?
- Can you think of ways in which they could be interpreted wrongly?

Useful language

The sign consists of … / The sign shows …
It means …
The meaning is obvious, as …
The meaning isn't very clear, because …
It looks like …

Reading

2   Read this extract from a book. As you read it, decide which writing system the signs above would fit into best.

⏱ about 600 words

A variety of writing systems

Writing is something we do every day, and we rarely give it a second thought. Yet linguists disagree about how to define the activity, and how best to describe some of
5 *the world's writing systems.*

Writing appears to have developed independently at different times in several parts of the world, among them Mexico and Central America, China, and Mesopotamia (present-day Iraq). One of the earliest
10 writing systems evolved to record ancient Egyptian around 5,000 years ago. The signs are called hieroglyphs, and are of three types. Some represent ideas or objects from the real world, such as *beetle* (a type of insect) and *swallow* (a type of bird), others
15 indicate sounds, and the third group are used to distinguish between two words that are otherwise identical: *carve* and *retreat* are represented by the same hieroglyph, but a knife symbol is added to show when the former meaning is intended, and a
20 pair of legs to indicate the latter. Some hieroglyphs are pictures, such as a drawing of a beetle or swallow; some were originally pictures and became more abstract; and yet others are symbols. Because of its complexity, the Egyptian system was much
25 more suitable for communication than earlier systems, which could express only a limited range of meanings. Hieroglyphs remained in use in Egypt for about 3,000 years – for some of the time used alongside alternative writing systems – before being
30 replaced by an alphabetical system.

Chinese has been written for nearly 4,000 years. Like many Egyptian hieroglyphs, the signs were originally pictures, and gradually became more

Chinese has been written for nearly 4,000 years. Like many Egyptian hieroglyphs, the signs were originally pictures, and gradually became more

104   UNIT 16

abstract. The writing system consists of characters representing words, sections of words, or ideas. Chinese characters are used throughout the country, as well as in the unrelated languages of Japanese, Korean and, until the twentieth century, Vietnamese. They can be compared with mathematical symbols, such as = or +, which have the same *meaning* in all languages but represent different *words*. There are thousands of Chinese characters to learn, and they take a considerable time to draw and to type: a traditional Chinese typewriter can contain over a thousand keys, and even a skilled typist is only expected to type about eleven words per minute.

A totally new development in writing appeared in the Middle East about 3,700 years ago, when Egyptian hieroglyphs were well established. This was the North Semitic alphabet, which evolved in Palestine and Syria. The Phoenicians, a trading nation living on the coast of modern Lebanon, adapted it to form their own alphabet. This in turn spread into northern Africa to become the writing system of the Arabs, and northwest to Greece. The Greek letters were further modified to become the Cyrillic alphabets of Russia and part of the Balkans. The Romans adapted the letters into the alphabet still used for many languages, including all those of western Europe and the written languages of North and South America, which are, of course, European in origin.

Alphabets are the most adaptable of all writing systems. A small number of symbols representing significant sounds in a language, not pictures or ideas, can be combined in different ways to represent all the words of the language. While most alphabets contain between 20 and 30 letters, the smallest, used in the Solomon Islands, contains only 11. Khmer, the official language of Cambodia, has the largest alphabet, with 74 letters. Alphabetical systems are very flexible, and can easily be used in computers, and so the Latin alphabet is used in both China and Japan alongside the traditional writing systems.

Although alphabets are based on sound, there is rarely great consistency between spelling and pronunciation. Finnish and Macedonian are among the most regular. English, however, is far more irregular, in part because the writing system has not kept pace with changes in pronunciation over the centuries.

3 Remember to answer these questions according to the passage, even if the information given there is incomplete.

Questions 1–6
Classify the following statements as referring to

A Egyptian hieroglyphs
B Chinese characters
C both
D neither

Example: Producing the signs is a slow process.
Answer: B

> they take a considerable time to draw and to type (lines 43–44). Although this is also likely to be true of hieroglyphs, it is not mentioned in the passage.

1   Pictures developed into abstract symbols.
2   This system has been used by more than one language.
3   Some of the signs represent sounds.
4   Signs may refer to all or part of a word.
5   The system was introduced from another country.
6   In this system, some words require two signs to make the meaning clear.

Questions 7–13
Do the following statements agree with the information given in the reading passage?

Write

TRUE   *if the statement agrees with the information*
FALSE   *if the statement contradicts the information*
NOT GIVEN *if there is no information on this*

7   Alphabets developed later than Egyptian hieroglyphs.
8   The first alphabet was created by the Phoenicians.
9   The Arab and Greek alphabets developed from the same writing system.
10 The Greek and Russian languages have the same origin.
11 The more words there are in a language, the more letters there are in its alphabet.
12 In most languages, spelling closely represents pronunciation.
13 English pronunciation has changed more than spelling.

Writing folder 8

Task 2: Being relevant and avoiding repetition

Being relevant

1 Read this example Task 2 question (suitable for both Academic and General Training). Underline the key words in the question.

Write about the following topic:

> **With the increase in use of the Internet, books will soon become unnecessary.**
> **To what extent do you agree or disagree with this statement?**

Give reasons for your answer and include any relevant from your own knowledge or experience.

You should write at least 250 words.

Now look at this answer to the question above. How well does the candidate answer the question? Circle the key points that answer the question and cross out any information that is irrelevant.

It has been suggested that in the future the Internet will totally take over the role that has always been taken by books. Personally, I believe that this will, in fact, happen sooner than people think.

It is often said that books are useful, but if we are talking about communicating news to the public, then in this case books are not so useful. I don't often read books, even though I know they might help me. I find them boring, because most novels are really silly love stories.

Personally, I think the Internet is very useful and I use it all the time, both at college and at home. I have had a computer for ten years and the one I have at the moment is an Apple Mac. It is particularly useful for finding information quickly and for keeping in touch with friends via email. I also use it to talk to people in chat rooms. People in chat rooms are really interesting and I have met many friends there. They give me a chance to practise my English, which I find really interesting. All the information I need I can find on the Internet. Some people say that it is hard to read from a screen, but I don't have this problem.

So in conclusion, I think the Internet is a good thing.

226 words

2   Think about how you would answer the question in exercise 1. With a partner talk about the questions below, particularly those referring to the second and third paragraphs – try to use the expressions in the Useful language box.

First paragraph
First reaction to the statement – for, against, unsure?

Second paragraph
How much has use of the Internet increased?
Who uses the Internet? Where in the world is it used?
What are its strengths?
What are its weaknesses?
Examples from your knowledge and experience

Third paragraph
What are books used for?
Advantages of using books?
Disadvantages of using books?
Examples from your knowledge and experience

Conclusion
Restate opinion while accepting some aspects of opposite opinion.

Useful language

Giving reasons
Use of the Internet is spreading fast **because of** the decreasing cost of computers.
Thanks to computers becoming more affordable, use of the Internet is spreading fast.
One result of the decrease in the cost of computers is the rapid spread of the Internet.
Because computers are rapidly coming down in price, the use of the Internet is growing.

While I agree that, … nevertheless / on the other hand I feel / I (still) feel …
Although it is true that …, I don't think that …
Finally I must restate my opinion that …

Avoiding repetition

3   Look at the answer in exercise 1 again. Underline any adjectives that are repeated. Which of the adjectives below would be suitable replacements?

absorbing	beneficial	effective
efficient	fascinating	friendly
helpful	informative	predictable
sociable	tedious	uninspiring
valuable	worthwhile	

4   Circle any linking words that are repeated. What other linking words could you use?

5   In the answer in exercise 1 the candidate has avoided repetition by using pronouns. This is generally a good thing to do. List the pronouns used and say what they refer to.

6   Write your own answer to the Task 2 question in exercise 1, using your own ideas and making sure they are relevant and clear, and that you give examples to support your views. Try to vary the words you use and look back at Writing folders 3 and 6 for useful phrases. You should take 40 minutes to answer this question.

Units 13–16 Revision

Topic review

1 How far do you agree with these statements? Give reasons for your answers.

 1 Some people always seem to make the right choice, and others always make the wrong one.
 2 Choices in a family should be made by the parents and not by young children.
 3 People don't want to eat food that is an unusual colour.
 4 We sometimes buy a product because of its colour rather than because we need it.
 5 Our colour preferences are strongly influenced by fashion.
 6 It is harder to know what someone from another culture is thinking than someone from our own.
 7 It is important when visiting a foreign country to know how to be polite in that culture.
 8 We should learn in school about the customs of other countries.
 9 It is more useful to be able to write emails and text messages well than to write letters.
 10 Books and magazines are likely to disappear and be replaced by electronic texts.

Grammar

-ing forms and infinitives

2 Complete this passage with the -ing form or infinitive of the verbs in brackets.

Too much choice

As societies become wealthier, the number of choices people need to make seems 1 (grow) .... I once spent two years in a country where buying milk meant 2 (get) .... to the store at six in the morning and 3 (be) .... thankful if there was any milk – or indeed, anything else – on the shelves. When I returned to my own, more affluent, country, I soon stopped 4 (worry) .... about whether there would be anything to buy. There were now five or six types of milk 5 (choose) .... from, and it was more a question of not wasting time choosing, and just remembering 6 (buy) .... full-cream for my cat and semi-skimmed for myself.

I'd like 7 (say) .... that I appreciated the choice of food and clothing – not to mention telephone, gas and electricity companies – but 8 (be) .... honest, I generally spent too long trying 9 (make) .... up my mind. I soon regretted 10 (complain) .... about the lack of choice during my two years abroad.

Conditionals

3 Put the verb in brackets in the right tense.

 1 I haven't got much money, so I won't buy any clothes unless I see something that really (catch) .... my eye.
 2 If I'd learnt more about the local culture before I went to live abroad, I (be) .... more sensitive to differences from my own country while I was there.
 3 A lot of books don't appear unless the writers (pay) .... for publication themselves.
 4 I (not mind) .... Kevin wanting to buy a new car so long as he doesn't expect me to lend him any money for it.
 5 I'd work in a library if I (be) .... sure of earning enough to live on.
 6 You're welcome to come to the cinema with me as long as you (be) .... ready to leave in ten minutes.
 7 I enjoy shopping as long as I (not have) .... to queue.
 8 If everyone had a car, the roads (be) .... even more congested than they are now.
 9 Giovanna would have studied Ancient Egyptian if there (be) .... a course at a nearby university.
 10 If the person you are talking to (keep) .... moving away from you, it is best not to try to move closer to them.

Non-finite clauses

4 Complete this passage with the *-ing* or *-ed* form of the verbs in brackets.

A valuable red dye

Cochineal is a traditional red dye **1** (use) .... by the Mixtec Indians of southern Mexico before the arrival of the Spanish. **2** (Obtain) .... from an insect that spends its life **3** (suck) .... on certain plants, cochineal was used to dye clothing various shades of red, while indigo was used for blues. Coloured clothing was important in Mixtec society, **4** (indicate) .... the social status of the wearer.

The Mixtecs farmed cochineal with great skill, **5** (light) .... fires on cold nights to prevent the insects from freezing and even **6** (build) .... temporary shelters to protect them from heavy rain.

When the Spanish arrived in Mexico in the sixteenth century, they were impressed by the bright crimson dye, which was superior to anything found in Europe. **7** (Realise) .... that there would be a ready market across the Atlantic, they began to ship textiles **8** (dye) .... with cochineal to Europe. Cochineal dye became so fashionable that before long it was a major import from Central America, second only to gold in importance.

Vocabulary

5 Complete the description of the chart below. In each case, choose one of the three alternatives.

This chart shows the annual breakdown of book loans from British libraries into the categories adult fiction, adult non-fiction and children's books. The period covered is from 1992 to 2001.

Adult fiction accounted for over half of loans every year, starting from nearly 60% in 1992. However, this figure tended to **1** *improve / be consistent / slide* over the period as a whole. It **2** *picked up / fell slightly / remained constant* in 1997, then **3** *plummeted / levelled off / picked up* before **4** *declining / growing / rising* again. Adult fiction ended the period at fractionally over 50% of loans.

Around 20% of loans were in the adult non-fiction category. This percentage **5** *picked up / was fairly steady / declined* between 1992 and 1999. In the following year, the proportion **6** *rose / slid / declined* fairly sharply to about 24%. The category **7** *fell / was consistent / picked up* in 2001.

At the beginning of the period, children's books accounted for a marginally higher share of loans than adult non-fiction. Their share **8** *was unchanged / made steady progress / deteriorated* in the following few years, mostly at the expense of adult fiction. The trend continued until 1996, when about 28% of loans were of children's books. This category saw little change until 2000, when the percentage **9** *declined / rose / expanded* to 25%, but it again recovered, reaching about 27% in 2001.

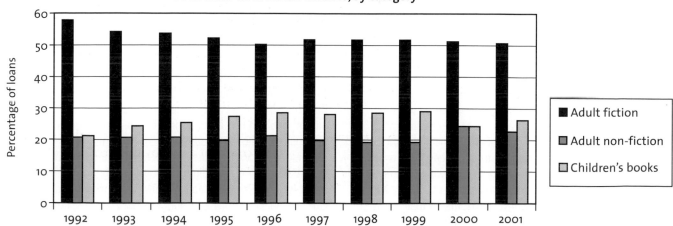

Book loans from British libraries, by category

- Adult fiction
- Adult non-fiction
- Children's books

17·1 The body clock

Speaking *Part 1*

1 Ask and answer these questions with a partner. Try to use some of the phrases from the Useful language box.

- What time in the morning would you get up if you could choose?
- What are you like in the morning – chatty, friendly, grumpy or totally silent?
- Tell me about your typical routine in the week and at weekends.
- Do you ever go shopping late at night? Why, or why not?
- Do you think your country is becoming more of a 24/7 society*?

* a society where shops and other facilities are open all day and night

Useful language

It depends on what I've been doing the night before.
It's difficult to say because I ...
As far as getting enough sleep is concerned, I ...
On the one hand I think that it's good that shops are open 24/7. **But, you could argue that** ...
I get up early **but, in spite of** this, I ...

Reading

2 Read through the passage quickly and answer these questions.

1 Why do we have a body clock?
2 What are a 'lark' and an 'owl'? Which are you?

⏱ about 650 words

WHO NEEDS SLEEP?

It's 2 a.m. The time when you should be in bed, sound asleep. But pull back the curtains and you might be surprised by the number of lights on in your street. Night-time is no longer just for sleep. It has become the new daytime, offering us the chance to catch up on everything we
5 didn't manage to cram in during what used to be our waking hours. Now, instead of sleeping, we can check our bank balances by phone, buy groceries, surf the net for cheap flights or go to the gym.

Such flexibility, however, has a price. Our bodies are run by circadian rhythms, a prehistoric internal clock that regulates when we feel
10 sleepy or awake and affects our body temperature and level of alertness. It makes our brains and bodies active during the day and allows them to recuperate through the night. So robust is this clock that even two weeks on a nightshift without a break will not destroy its intrinsic rhythm, and when scientists keep human
15 volunteers in isolation, without cues of what time it is in the day, they still show daily cycles of temperature changes, sleep and wakefulness, and hormone release. Continually working against our body's natural rhythm is likely to cause ourselves both physical and psychological damage and, research shows, may actually increase
20 our risk of health problems such as stomach ulcers.

Consultant Tom Mackey believes that our normal circadian rhythms are increasingly being completely distorted. 'More and more of us are being pressured into doing things at odd hours. This is going to have an impact on quality and length of sleep. If people don't go to bed at a reasonable time, say around 11 ⟨25⟩ p.m., and have between six and eight hours of sleep, they will be unable to concentrate and liable to swings in mood. You need sleep for rest and repair. If you bombard your mind with information for too long, then everything gets disorganised – you become unable to manage daytime activities.' ⟨30⟩

The circadian rhythms that run the sleep/wake cycle are as old as evolution itself. Our prehistoric ancestors would have needed their biological clock to get them out hunting during the day and probably in bed around nightfall to avoid predators. Our night vision is not as good as that of nocturnal animals – our ⟨35⟩ natural rhythm was to sleep as the sun went down. The invention of the electric light obviously changed that. Like most biological systems, circadian rhythms are not made to measure. Our internal clock runs a bit longer than 24 hours, hence its Latin name, circadian, which means 'about a day'. ⟨40⟩

3 Questions 1–5

Do the following statements agree with the information given in the reading passage?

Write

TRUE *if the statement agrees with the information*
FALSE *if the statement contradicts the information*
NOT GIVEN *if there is no information on this*

1 There is a greater demand at night for some services than for others.
2 People who are kept in isolation show some reaction to day and night.
3 Damage caused by working against the body's natural rhythms is limited to our bodies.
4 In prehistoric times, people's biological clocks probably controlled their lives.
5 Larks are more likely to be ill than owls.

Questions 6–8

Complete each sentence with the correct ending A–G from the box below.

6 Our internal body clock
7 A lark
8 Jet lag

> **A** can be altered over time.
> **B** is alert on waking.
> **C** causes the body temperature to rise at night.
> **D** programmes us to be awake in daylight hours.
> **E** can result in tiredness.
> **F** experiences high body temperatures.
> **G** is more problematic at night.

That humans tend to vary in their circadian rhythms has been known for centuries. Some people are born to be larks (to get up and go to bed early) while others are owls (late risers and late to bed). Larks are 'morning people' –
45 communicative from the time their eyes open – while owls are grouchy and groggy and find life impossible until midday. Research suggests that owls may pay a price for this in terms of health problems, because they tend to go to sleep at less regular times. While the temperature of the body should fall
50 at night (and does, whether or not we are asleep, reaching its lowest temperature at around 4 a.m.) it falls more in larks than in owls, giving larks a better quality of sleep.
Much of the damage that can be done by disrupting the biological clock has been seen in nightshift workers. The
55 fatigue and disorientation following nightshifts is similar to that of jet lag. As with jet lag, the body adjusts over time, but the wake-and-sleep cycle never seems to be totally reversed. As more of us push back our circadian clocks, going to bed later and later, the effects on our bodies will be similar to
60 those of nightshift workers, and that can't be good.

Vocabulary Collocations with *time*

4 Complete each sentence using an expression from the box in the appropriate form. Sometimes more than one answer is possible.

> find (the) time
> give someone time
> kill time
> pass the time
> run out of time
> spend the day/week
> spend (the) time
> take (the/your/his/her) time
> waste an hour / a day
> waste time / waste someone's time

1 We weren't able to finish the work on our nightshift because we had .... time.
2 Now I work at night I don't .... so much time stuck in traffic.
3 My alarm goes at six o'clock in the morning to .... me time to get ready for work.
4 .... your time. I can wait for you – there's no hurry.
5 How much of your time is .... worrying about not sleeping?
6 While I was waiting to see the doctor I .... the time reading a magazine.
7 I don't know how you .... the time to run two businesses.
8 Paola .... her time eating her lunch because she didn't want to rush.
9 Tom was early for the meeting so he .... time by having a coffee.
10 I always .... time in exams and never finish the paper.

5 With a partner, talk about the following.

1 What do you do to pass the time when you're waiting for a bus or train, or on a long journey?
2 What do you think are activities which waste time?
3 Do you give yourself enough time to do your homework?
4 Do you spend any time reading a newspaper?
5 Do you run out of time when you do a test?
6 If you didn't need to work, how would you spend your time?

17·2

1   Would you like to do nightshift work? Discuss this with a partner and
    list the advantages and disadvantages. This will help you to orientate
    yourself when you listen to the recording in exercise 2.

Listening

2   Listen to someone on the radio talking about
    nightshift working and answer the questions. The
    recording is in two parts: questions 1–5 and
    questions 6–8.

🎧 **Questions 1 and 2**
*Choose the correct letter **A, B** or **C**.*

1   The speaker says that compared to daytime workers,
    nightshift workers
    A   take longer to fall asleep.
    B   sleep more deeply.
    C   need more sleep.

2   People generally find it difficult to
    A   stay awake in the first part of the night.
    B   stay alert in the afternoon.
    C   stay asleep all day.

Questions 3–5
*List **THREE** things which the presenter says will help
nightshift workers fall asleep.*

*Write **NO MORE THAN THREE WORDS** for each
answer.*

3   ....

4   ....

5   ....

🎧 **Questions 6–8**
*Write **NO MORE THAN THREE WORDS AND/OR A
NUMBER** for each answer.*

6   How long should a nap last to be useful?

    ....

7   What should workers definitely not do if they are
    feeling tired?

    ....

8   At what time are nightshift workers the least alert?

    ....

Grammar

Modal verbs: obligation, lack of obligation and prohibition

3 You often need to use modal verbs in the Writing and Speaking Modules when you are asked to comment on a statement.

Look at these sentences, some of which are from the recording. Match sentences 1–6 with explanations a–f.

1 You mustn't operate machinery if you are feeling sleepy.
2 All workers must wear their identity badges at all times.
3 You must come to dinner sometime after work.
4 Nightshift workers don't have to travel to work in the rush hour.
5 You must try to have a regular sleep schedule, even at weekends.
6 Workers at our factory have to wear a special uniform.

a something that isn't necessary
b something that is strongly recommended, coming from the speaker
c something that is prohibited
d something that is a rule, imposed from outside and out of the speaker's control
e something that is a rule – possibly a notice in a public place
f something that is a casual invitation

4 With a partner, talk about the difference between sentences 1 and 2, and the difference between sentences 3 and 4.

1 We have to keep our work confidential.
2 We must try to get more sleep.

3 You don't have to wear a uniform now you're a manager.
4 You mustn't wear your uniform outside the factory.

G ···❖ page 142

5 Rewrite each sentence using a modal verb. Sometimes you are given the first word of the sentence in brackets.

EXAMPLE: Years ago, children were forced to work in mines.
 Years ago, children had to work in mines.

1 Smoking is forbidden in the factory. (*You ...*)
2 It's not necessary to leave home early to beat the rush hour now. (*You ...*)
3 The regulations state that the nightshift begins at 9.30. (*We ...*)
4 The notice says that it is vital that all workers wear a hard hat on the site.
5 'You aren't allowed to make personal calls,' said the manager to the staff.
6 I can stay in bed all day tomorrow.
7 When I work nights, I am forced to do my shopping on the Internet.
8 It isn't necessary for me to go to the bank in the daytime as I can ring them at any time now.

Writing extra

6 Do this IELTS Writing Task 2. Try to use some of the modal verbs you have learnt in this unit.

Write about the following topic:

In the last ten years, people have been finding they have to move away from a twelve-hour day to a twenty-four hour day. This can only have a negative effect on society, with people becoming less productive and being unable to enjoy a social life.

To what extent do you agree with this view?

Give reasons for your answer and include any relevant examples from your own knowledge or experience.

Write at least 250 words.

It is important to give your opinion, but also to consider both sides of the argument. Use the information from both the reading and listening passages to help you get ideas for your essay. Remember you need to have an introduction, two or three paragraphs giving reasons and examples, and a conclusion.

Useful language

Balancing your view
There is no doubt that ...
One of the main arguments in favour of / against ... is ...
On the one hand ... On the other hand ...
Another example of ...

Test folder 9

Speaking

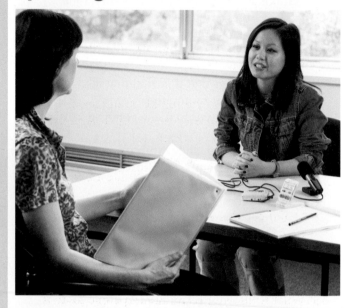

Advice

- The Speaking Module gives you the opportunity to show how well you can speak English. Show what you know. Make sure you use as wide a range of grammar and vocabulary as you can.
- It is in three parts, so don't worry if you feel you have done badly in one – you can make up for it in the other parts.
- Your English is being assessed, not your intelligence or imagination. So don't worry if you think your answers aren't very clever, or if you say something that isn't true.
- Try to behave in a friendly, relaxed way, as that will help you to do your best. Don't expect the examiner to comment on what you say: this isn't like a normal conversation.
- If you don't understand what the examiner asks you, ask him or her to repeat it, or say that you don't understand.
- Don't leave long silences, as they don't show how good your English is.

Part 1

The examiner will ask you some questions about yourself, your opinions and everyday topics.

Make sure your answers are of a reasonable length. Saying just a word or phrase doesn't show how good your English is, and a very long answer won't allow enough time to go through the whole Module.

1 🎧 Listen to these five questions and answers. Decide which comment from the box applies to each answer.

1 ....
2 ....
3 ....
4 ....
5 ....

> A The answer is too short.
> B The answer is appropriate, but the candidate leaves a long pause.
> C The answer is too long.
> D The answer is hard to understand.
> E The answer is the right length and appropriate.
> F The answer does not deal with the question.

2 Think of a suitable answer to each of these questions. Make sure you use a suitable tense. Practise asking and answering with a partner.

1 What part of your country do you come from?
2 Is that a good area for finding work?
3 Have you ever worked or studied at night?
4 Why do some people have to work at night?
5 How would you feel about working at night?

Part 2

You are given a topic to speak about for one to two minutes. The topic is based on your own experience. Quickly think of something that is relevant to the topic. If you can't remember anything suitable, invent something.

You have one minute to prepare. Write down three or four key words, to remind you of what you want to say. Don't write whole phrases or sentences: if you simply read out what you have written, you will get a low band score.

The first three points are usually quite factual. Speak about them in turn, fairly briefly. Allow yourself enough time to talk about the last line. This often asks for an explanation, so it gives you the opportunity to use a wider range of language.

Make sure you keep to the topic. Don't worry if the examiner stops you before you have finished. This won't affect your band score.

3 🎧 Look at this card. Then listen to a candidate giving a talk. Do you think it was a good talk? Why, or why not?

> **Describe an occasion when you did something for the first time.**
>
> **You should say:**
>
> **what you did**
> **why you did it**
> **why you hadn't done it before**
>
> **and explain how you felt about doing it.**

Notice that the examiner asks one or two questions after the talk. These should be answered very briefly.

4 Now read this topic card, and spend one to two minutes planning a talk. Make notes if you want to. Then, with a partner, speak for one to two minutes.

> **Describe a special occasion when you had an unforgettable time.**
>
> **You should say:**
>
> **what the occasion was**
> **what you did**
> **how you felt at the time**
>
> **and explain what made it unforgettable.**

When you have finished speaking, think of short answers to these questions.

- Do you prefer special occasions to be planned or to be a surprise?
- How often do you think people should celebrate special occasions?

Part 3

The examiner will ask you questions related to the topic of Part 2. The questions will use verbs like the ones in exercise 5 below.

Your answers should be at least one or two sentences long. Expand them, for example by considering both sides of an argument.

Speculate about possibilities; for example, *If shops weren't open late in the evening, it would be easier for shop workers to spend time with their families and friends.*

If you can't immediately think of an answer, say something to give yourself time to think; for example, *I haven't thought about that before.*

5 🎧 Look at these questions and make sure you understand them. Then listen to the answers and assess them.

1 Could you **describe** how society can benefit from people working at night?
2 Can you **compare** going to the cinema or other entertainments at night with going to the same entertainments by day?
3 What would you **recommend** people to do if they have to work at night?

Now answer these questions.

4 Can you **identify** ways in which attitudes towards working at night have changed?
5 Could you **outline** the effect on family life of people working at night?
6 How would you **evaluate** the importance of public transport operating all night?
7 Could you **speculate** on whether we will move even more towards a 24/7 society?
8 Can you **suggest** ways in which people could be encouraged to work at night?

18·1 The tourist boom

Speaking *Part 1*

1 With a partner, ask and answer the following questions.

- What are the advantages of a two-week holiday away from home?
- How many weeks' holiday do workers usually get in your country?
- What makes a good tourist?

Listening

2 You are going to hear a lecturer giving a talk about tourism. Read through the summary below carefully before you listen.

Questions 1–5
Complete the summary below.
*Write **NO MORE THAN TWO WORDS** for each answer.*

Both social factors and the development of **1** .... have been important in the growth of tourism. It would appear that how much **2** .... a country possesses is the main factor in whether its people will travel widely. Most tourists today are from the **3** .... world, but their populations are levelling off. Soon there will be an increase in the number of older tourists, who will be less likely to want to go **4** .... and will probably prefer alternatives such as trips to **5** ....

Questions 6–10
Complete the tables below.
*Write **NO MORE THAN TWO WORDS** for each answer.*

	Technological breakthrough
Modern tourism	Jet plane
First package tour	**6** ....
New booking method	**7** ....

Destination	Attraction
Ireland in the past	countryside
Ireland today	**8** ....
Crystal City, USA	broccoli (a vegetable)
Gilroy, USA	**9** ....
Stratford, Canada	**10** ....

Pronunciation

Pronouns as objects of phrasal verbs

3 🎧 Listen again to this extract from the recording in exercise 2.

Festivals are another way to bring them in.

When the object of a phrasal verb is a pronoun, it is normally unstressed.

Listen to these phrases and repeat each one.

1 give it up
2 cut them down
3 bring her round
4 work it out
5 pick him up
6 let me through
7 fill them in
8 ask us out

Now practise saying them with a partner.

4 Think of a sentence for each of the phrases in exercise 3 and tell your partner.

EXAMPLE: *I hate smoking. I'm going to give it up.*

Vocabulary   Collocations related to travel

5 Cross out the word on the left which *doesn't* collocate with the noun on the right

EXAMPLE: a ski, travel, ~~seaside~~   brochure

1 a long-haul, luxury, Caribbean   cruise
2 a ski, holiday, sightseeing   resort
3 a day, business, tour, skiing   trip
4 the high/low, skiing, student   season
5 a beach, travel, package, sightseeing   holiday
6 a/an short-haul, exotic, popular, far   destination

Now write six sentences to show you know how to use the vocabulary above.

EXAMPLE: I went to get a travel brochure so I could find out about skiing holidays in Switzerland.

Writing extra

Academic Task 1

6 The diagram below shows how much British households spent on holidays in the UK and abroad in 2002. Summarise the information by selecting and reporting the main features, and make comparisons where relevant. Write about 150 words.

Holidays by age of head of household (2002)

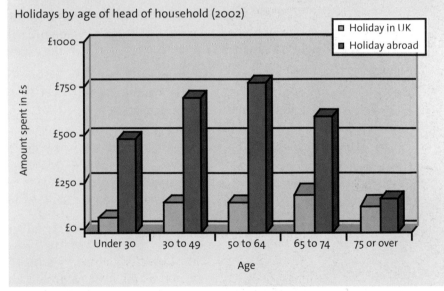

Useful language

Comparing and contrasting
Although all age groups spent money on holidays abroad, the 50 to 64 age group spent the most.
The 75 and over age group spent less than £250 of their annual budget on holidays abroad, **whereas/while** the 50 to 64 age group spent just over £750.
The 75 and over age group spent less than £250 of their annual budget on holidays abroad. **In contrast**, the 50 to 64 age group spent just over £750.
The 75 and over age group spent less than £250 of their annual budget on holidays abroad, **compared to** the 50 to 64 age group, who spent just over £750.

18·2

Grammar Phrasal verbs

A phrasal verb is a verb + a particle. Although phrasal verbs are more commonly used in spoken English, the *Cambridge Academic Corpus* shows us that many of the ones in this unit are used in academic English too.

These examples of phrasal verbs are from the recording in 18.1:

*the demand for holidays will **take off** there*
*as it **keeps down** their costs*
*the Irish Tourist Board **came up with** the idea of promoting*

1 A phrasal verb can have a number of meanings. Match the phrasal verbs in the box above with the meanings below.

  1 to suggest or think of a plan
  2 to become popular or successful
  3 to prevent something increasing

Some phrasal verbs take an object and some don't. Which of the phrasal verbs in the examples above *doesn't* take an object when it is used with the meaning it has here?

2 Which of the phrasal verbs in these sentences have an object?

  1 She made up her face before starting work at the travel agency.
  2 Tessa passed out after spending all afternoon in the hot sun.
  3 It's hard to make out her handwriting.
  4 We checked in two hours early for our flight to Dubai.

Phrasal verbs without an object

When a phrasal verb has no object, the verb and particle cannot be separated:

EXAMPLE: We say: *Trish turned up too late for her flight to Tenerife.* ✓

               We can't say: *Trish turned for her flight up too late to Tenerife.* ✗

Phrasal verbs with an object

When the particle is an adverb, the particle can go *before* or *after* a noun object but can only go *after* pronoun objects.

EXAMPLE: *The airlines would like to **cut down** the amount of airport tax they pay.*
           *The airlines would like to **cut** the amount of airport tax they pay **down**.*
           *The airlines would like to **cut** it **down**.*

3 Rewrite each sentence below twice using a phrasal verb from the box. First, separate the particle from the verb using the noun, and then write the sentence again, changing the noun to a pronoun, as in the examples above.

give out	make out	put forward
set up	take on	take over

  1 It was hard to see the cruise ship through the fog.
  2 A rival bought the student travel company when it went bankrupt.
  3 Can I suggest Maria as a suitable replacement for Lisa?
  4 My father started the holiday company in 1967.
  5 We'll have to employ extra staff when it's high season.
  6 Josh was asked to distribute free tickets to the guests.

Three-part phrasal verbs

Some phrasal verbs have three parts, consisting of the verb + adverb + preposition.

No separation is possible.

EXAMPLE: *Hotels can no longer **get away with** poor service nowadays.*

         *Hotels can no longer **get away with** it.*

4 Underline each phrasal verb in sentences 1–6 and match it with its meaning a–g opposite.

EXAMPLE: **0 f**

0 The local council <u>are looking forward to</u> receiving a grant to help increase tourism in their area.

1 Leila came up against some very difficult customers when she worked at the airport.

2 The whole ship's company went down with food poisoning during the trip.

3 The courier tried to make up for some of the problems the tourists had had by offering them a free meal.

4 It's time we woke up to the environmental damage caused by the increase in air travel.

5 Today we find it hard to put up with long queues and delays at airports.

6 Our company needs to face up to the fall in demand for package holidays.

a to compensate for something bad
b to accept
c become aware of
d to fall ill
e to have problems with
f to be pleased about something that is going to happen
g to tolerate

G ⋯⋗ page 143

Writing extra

5 Complete this letter to a local newspaper, using words from the box. There are some extra words which you will not need.

Dear Sir/Madam,

I am writing to object to the plan, **1** .... was reported in your newspaper on 9th June, to build a high-rise hotel next to the town beach. I believe that the plan is **2** .... to go ahead next summer. I have lived here **3** .... 2002 and feel that more consultation is needed **4** .... the work is started.

As you know, this town has a population of only 7,000, mainly made up of people **5** .... have retired here to enjoy the peace and quiet. We **6** .... have two small hotels and a number of guest houses and these have fulfilled our visitors' needs **7** .... many years. There are many old buildings in this town and its character would be totally destroyed **8** .... a ten-storey glass and steel hotel was built right in the middle of the sea front.

To sum up, I object strongly to this plan and I hope you will publish this letter in your paper.

Yours faithfully,

additionally	already	and	because
before	due	for	if	providing
since	still	unless	which	who

Plans for Ocean Hotel

Speaking *Part 2*

6 Spend one minute preparing the talk below. You can make brief notes if you like. Then give your talk to your partner. The talk should last one to two minutes. It's a good idea to try to record yourself so you can hear your own mistakes and improve your talk.

> **Describe a memorable trip.**
>
> **You should say:**
>
> **where you went**
> **who you went with**
> **what you did there**
>
> **and explain what made it memorable.**

Speaking *Parts 2 and 3*

1 What forms of transport do you prefer? How do you decide what transport to use for a particular journey?

2 Choose two different forms of transport, and compare their advantages and disadvantages. Remember to develop your comments. Consider convenience, safety, price and effect on the environment.

> EXAMPLE: *Although planes are much faster than helicopters, they need a much larger space to land in.*

3 Many city centres and major roads are congested. How can the problem be solved? Consider the advantages and disadvantages of these suggestions:

- banning non-essential traffic
- making driving very expensive
- improving public transport
- encouraging people to live near their work.

Vocabulary

4 Most of the words in the box occur in the listening passage. Use a dictionary to make sure you understand and know how to pronounce them. Then match each explanation 1–3 with the appropriate words. You should use all the words in the box.

1 an accident involving vehicles

....

2 the state of floating in the air

....

3 the act of preventing something from happening

....

collision	crash	disruption
disturbance	elevation	interruption
levitation	suspension	

Listening

5 You will hear three students giving a presentation about monorails. Have you seen or travelled on a monorail? What do you know about them?

6 🎧 Before you listen to the first part of the recording, look at the sentences, and think about what kind of information you need to listen for. Then answer the questions as you listen.

Questions 1–4
Complete the sentences.
Write **NO MORE THAN TWO WORDS AND/OR A NUMBER** for each answer.

What is a monorail?

Tracks are usually **1** ....
Most monorails are used for transporting
2 ....
The oldest monorail still in use opened in the year
3 ....
Shanghai monorail trains normally reach a speed of
4 .... kilometres an hour.

🎧 Now read and think about these notes as you did above. Then answer the questions as you listen.

Questions 5–9
Complete the notes.
*Write **NO MORE THAN TWO WORDS** for each answer.*

Safety:
• very rarely derailed
• no risk of **5** ....

Environment:
• produce relatively little **6** ....
• stations can be in **7** .... and other busy places

Economics:
• only installation takes place on site
• low operating costs
• very **8** .... compared with other forms of transport

Disadvantage:
• they use a **9** ....

Before listening to the third part of the recording, look at the diagram opposite, and for each number, write the appropriate word from the box. Use a dictionary if necessary. This will help you here, but note that in the test it normally isn't possible to label the diagram without listening to the recording.

balcony	beam	operating unit	pillar
vehicle	walkway		

10 ....
11 ....
12 ....
13 ....
14 ....

🎧 Now listen to the third part of the recording, and check your answers. You will hear them in the order of the questions. In some cases, the word in the recording is different from the one in the box, but has a similar meaning. This is often the case in the Listening Module. Beside your answers above, write the words that you hear.

Pronunciation *Rhythm*

7 Look at these sentences, where the stressed syllables are underlined.

I've <u>bought</u> a <u>ticket</u>.
I've <u>put</u> it in my <u>wallet</u>.

In the natural rhythm of English, the stressed syllables of key words come at roughly equal intervals. Other less important words, such as articles, pronouns, prepositions etc., are usually spoken more quickly and are 'weak'.

Read these sentences aloud, and try and say the stressed syllables at regular intervals.

1 I've <u>bought</u> a <u>ticket</u>.
2 I've <u>put</u> it in my <u>wallet</u>.
3 I'm <u>waiting</u> for the <u>train</u>.
4 I've been <u>waiting</u> for the <u>train</u> for <u>half</u> an <u>hour</u>.
5 I <u>seem</u> to spend my <u>life</u> <u>waiting</u> for the <u>train</u>.

🎧 Now listen to the sentences on the recording and repeat them.

ground level

Speaking *Part 3*

1 What impact have modern forms of transport had on our lives? Do you think there were any benefits when people could only travel on foot or by using animals? Consider, for example, where we live, work and spend our free time and holidays.

Reading

2 Read this passage quickly. As you read it, think of how to summarise it in one short sentence.

⏱ about 750 words

One way that transport has affected our lives

For many centuries, there was little need for time to be accurately measured. The transition from day to night, the movement of the moon and the changing of the seasons were enough to measure large units of time, and for most people, the passing of the sun through the sky was adequate to indicate sunrise, midday and sunset.

Those who needed to order their daily time more accurately, such as monks or scientists, used a combination of measuring devices, such as sand timers or candles, or, if the sun was shining, the shadow of a sundial. All these devices were unreliable. Until late into the 18th century, very few people could afford watches and clocks, which were themselves inaccurate.

The Earth rotates once every 24 hours, and so places to the east start their day sooner than places to the west. When it is night in one place, it is day in another. Across Britain there is a difference in time of approximately half an hour from the eastern to the western extremities.

When travel and communications were slow, these local time differences were of little importance, and most towns and cities in Britain used local time. By the 18th century, coaches – which were drawn by horses – were taking mail and passengers across Britain, and the guards on these coaches carried timepieces so that they could regulate the arrival and departure times. These timepieces were adjusted to gain about 15 minutes in every 24 hours when travelling from west to east, to compensate for the local time differences. And they were adjusted to lose 15 minutes in 24 hours when returning.

In the early part of the 19th century, communications started to be significantly improved, construction of the railways began, and telegraph by wires became common. Accurate time was becoming more and more essential for many aspects of life, and local time became a great inconvenience. A baby born in London early on Saturday morning might officially be a day younger than a baby born a few minutes later in Dublin – where it was still Friday evening. This could have quite serious legal implications for inheritances.

By the 1840s, there were at least three organisations which suffered inconveniences because of the use of local time – the railways, the telegraph companies and the Post Office – and it was the first of these that started the process of standardising time in Britain.

Trains travelling east to west appeared to be travelling more quickly than on the return journey from west to east, which caused many problems with timetabling. In November 1840, the Great Western Railway ordered that London time should be used in all its timetables and at all its stations, and by 1847 most of the railway companies had followed suit. It was usually referred to as 'railway time'. However, with a few companies keeping to local time, there could be all sorts of problems of missed trains and connections. In some places, there were even two minute hands on the public clocks, one showing local, and the other one London time.

By 1855 the great majority of public clocks in Britain were set to London time, which is in fact the time at the Greenwich Observatory, just outside London: hence the name Greenwich Mean Time, or GMT. The last major opposition to standardisation came from the legal profession, which operated by local time for many years.

In 1845 the Liverpool and Manchester Railway company petitioned Parliament to ask that the same time be used for all ordinary and commercial purposes. This attempt was unsuccessful, and it was not until 1880 that Parliament introduced a standard time across the whole of Britain and there was no more confusion caused by local time. Britain was in fact the first country to standardise the time throughout a region, although the clock on the tower of Christ Church Cathedral, in Oxford, still shows local time, five minutes behind the rest of the country.

Co-operation on setting the time around the world dates from the International Meridian Conference in 1884.

3 Questions 1–6

Complete the flow chart below.
Use NO MORE THAN THREE WORDS *from the passage for each answer.*

> Early scientists: only had **1** .... ways of measuring time (e.g. sundials)

↓

> Until late 18th century: **2** .... were very expensive

↓

> 18th century: timepieces used on **3** ....

↓

> 1840: **4** .... introduced by a railway company and called 'railway time'

↓

> 1880: **5** .... introduced

↓

> 1884: a **6** .... was held to co-ordinate time internationally

Questions 7–12

Complete each sentence with the correct ending **A–I** *from the box below.*

Write the correct letter **A–I** *by questions 1–6.*

7 The distance across Britain from east to west
8 The slow speed of travel
9 The direction of travel
10 An event that took place before another one
11 The railway companies
12 The legal profession

> **A** relied on unreliable devices to measure the time.
> **B** led the demand for standard time.
> **C** made accurate time-keeping unnecessary.
> **D** could legally occur on the following day.
> **E** varied, depending on the time of year.
> **F** meant that local time varied by up to half an hour.
> **G** resisted the adoption of standard time.
> **H** affected the rate at which time appeared to pass.
> **I** made London time compulsory.

Grammar Unreal present and future

4 🎧 Listen to the short talk about the attitudes of a particular car driver, and answer these questions.

1 Does Mr Smith have plenty of money?
2 Does he think the traffic problem is being solved?
3 Does he think trains are too crowded?
4 Does he need to earn a living?

5 🎧 Listen again, and complete the sentences.

1 If he .... plenty of money, he'd buy the car of his dreams.
2 It's high time the problem .... solved.
3 He would rather the money .... out of general taxation.
4 He sometimes travels by train, but he wishes they .... so crowded and .... at so many stations.
5 He often says to himself, 'If only I .... to earn a living.'

6 Now look at the verbs you have written in exercise 5, and complete this rule.

When the following structures introduce a statement about an unreal situation, the verb after them should be in a .... tense.

(I) wish ...   (I)'d / would rather ...
It's (about/high) time ...   If (only) ...

wish + would

Compare sentences A and B:

A *I wish the government would build some new roads.*

This means that
• I am complaining about the present situation.
• I want something to happen, but it seems unlikely.

B *I hope the government will build some new roads.*

Here I am not complaining, and I think that the government may construct some new roads.

G ⋯⟩ page 143

7 Make up sentences for each of these situations, beginning *I wish* ... .

EXAMPLE: You think people use their cars too much and should walk more often.
I wish people would use their cars less and walk more.

1 A friend of yours never phones you when she says she will.
   ....

2 Your friend keeps promising to return a book that you lent him a year ago, but he never does.
   ....

8 Can you think of situations where you might say something beginning *I wish* ... ?

Test folder 10

Labelling diagrams and maps

(Academic Reading, General Training Reading and Listening Modules)

In the Reading Modules, you may be asked to label a diagram with words from the passage.
In the Listening Module, you may be asked to label a diagram or map.

In the Reading Modules, you will be told the maximum number of words for each answer. The questions may not follow the same order as the information in the passage.

In the Listening Module the questions follow the order in which you will hear the relevant information on the recording. You may need to choose words from a box (as in 19.1 exercise 6, numbers 10–14), or choose parts of a drawing or map labelled alphabetically (as in exercise 1 below).

If you have to choose words from a box, there will be more words in the box than you need.

Words must be spelt correctly to gain marks.

Listening

1 🎧 This is similar to Section 1 of the Listening Module.

Label the plan below.
*Write the correct letter **A–L** next to questions 1–6.*

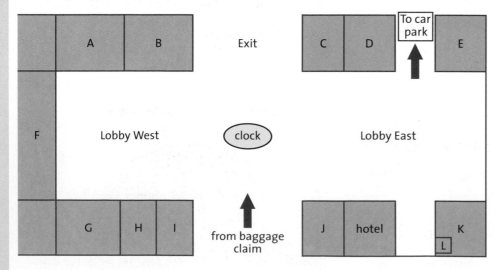

1 luggage lockers	....
2 the Coffee House	....
3 cash machines	....
4 art gallery	....
5 classical CDs	....
6 quiet lounge	....

Advice

Reading Modules

- Skim the whole passage before you start working on any of the tasks.
- Read the instructions carefully. Study the drawing, and the heading, if it has one. Try to work out what the drawing shows.
- Find the part of the passage that is relevant to the drawing – the heading will help you. Read this part carefully, and look for the first answer. Write your answer, making sure you spell it correctly and write no more than the maximum number of words.
- Look for the other answers in turn.
- Check your answers. Make sure that they make sense: for example, if you are giving the names of parts of a machine, they should all be nouns or noun phrases.

Reading

2 Read this passage. It is similar to those in the Academic Reading Module, but shorter, at about 250 words. The task is typical of both Reading Modules.

New tunnels under city centre

A new eight-kilometre road is under construction linking the port area with the motorway system. This is expected to carry 20,000 trucks and cars a day, significantly reducing congestion in the city centre. As part of the project, two four-kilometre road tunnels are being bored below the central area of the city, one for northbound traffic, the other for southbound. The two tunnels are approximately 20m below the surface and are nearly 12m wide, providing for two lanes of traffic in each direction.

In the upper part of the tunnel two ventilation ducts remove vehicle exhaust fumes and maintain the quality of air inside the tunnel. The lighting is at the top of the tunnel, virtually at its highest point. There will also be electronic signs at frequent intervals, indicating traffic conditions ahead, and clearly visible to drivers. The wall is made up of four main elements, including a waterproofing membrane and, on the inside of the tunnel, a concrete lining.

Each tunnel is roughly circular, with the lower part somewhat flattened. The road surface lies on the base slab, which is of concrete reinforced with steel. Mains drainage, just below the road surface on one side, removes any excess liquid, particularly water. In the event of fire, the fire main, which is made of steel, pipes water to numerous fire hydrant stations at regular intervals along the length of the tunnel. The fire main is at the side of the tunnel, at the level of the road surface. Other systems in the tunnel will include emergency phones.

Label the diagram below.
*Choose **NO MORE THAN TWO WORDS** from the passage for each answer.*

Example:

0 ....*ventilation ducts*........

1 ....

2 .... on the tunnel side of the wall

3 ....

4 ....

5 ....

Cross-section of proposed tunnel

road surface

Speaking *Part 3*

1 Discuss the following questions.

- Can you suggest reasons why people move to another country?
- Can you comment on the benefits for a country of receiving people who have moved from abroad?
- Can you speculate on possible future movements of people between different countries?

Reading

2 What do these words mean? Choose the best answers from the box.

1 migration
2 emigration
3 immigration
4 assimilation
5 settlement

---

a becoming similar to a country's native inhabitants
b moving from one country to another
c moving away from one's home country
d making a permanent home in a country
e moving into another country

---

3 Now read this passage. As in the Academic Reading Module, there are 13 questions. Try to read the passage and answer the questions in 20 minutes. You may find it helpful to write a few key words beside each paragraph. Think about question 1 as you read.

Question 1
Which of these statements best sums up the passage?
A The reasons for migration have changed significantly.
B Migration is caused by a combination of many factors.
D Governments have the most influence on migration.
C Migration is best explained in terms of personal choices.

⏱ about 725 words

IMMIGRATION: AN INTRODUCTION

A Migration takes many forms. People migrate as manual workers, highly qualified specialists, entrepreneurs, refugees or as family members of previous migrants. Whether the initial intention is
5 temporary or permanent movement, many migrants become settlers. Migration has been part of human history from the earliest times, but it has grown in volume and significance, and may be one of the most important factors in global change.

10 **B** No single cause can explain why people choose to leave their country and settle in another. It is hardly ever a simple individual action, in which a person decides to move in search of a better life, leaves the home country and quickly becomes
15 assimilated in the new country. Much more often, the process of migration and settlement stretches over a long period, affecting the rest of the migrant's life and also later generations. It is a collective action, caused by social change and
20 affecting the whole society of both countries.

C While some theories about migration emphasise individual choice, and others focus on the influence of governments and business, it is more realistic to understand migration in terms of a
25 complex interaction among all these elements. Large-scale institutional factors, such as international relations, political economy and government policies, play a part in any decision to emigrate, as do the informal social networks,
30 practices and beliefs of the migrants themselves.

D Migration generally arises from the existence of previous links between home and new countries, based on colonisation, political influence, trade, investment or cultural ties. For instance, migration
35 from some North and West African countries to France is linked to earlier French colonisation, leaving French as a major language of the countries concerned.

E Typically, migration is started by an external factor, such as a shortage of labour in the new country. Often the initial movement is by young people, usually men. Once a path has been established, relatives and friends follow, and are assisted by those already there. Social networks based on family or a common place of origin help to provide housing, work, assistance in coping with bureaucratic procedures and support in personal difficulties. These social networks make the process of migration safer and more manageable for the migrants and their families.

F Migrant groups develop their own social and economic infrastructure: places of worship, associations, shops, cafés, lawyers, doctors, and other services. This is linked to families being reunited: the longer the original migrants stay, the more likely they are to bring their partners and children in, or to start new families. People begin to see their life as being based in the new country. This is particularly true of migrants' children: once they go to school in the new country, learn the language and make friends, it becomes more and more difficult for the parents to return to their homelands.

G While the links between immigrant community and area of origin may sometimes be weakened, they are more likely to continue over generations. Family and cultural links remain, new business links may be developed.

H Although each migration has its specific historical patterns, certain generalisations can be made on the way migrations evolve. For example, most start with young, economically active people going abroad temporarily. They want to save enough in a higher-wage economy to improve conditions at home, to buy land, build a house, set up a business, or pay for education. After a period in the new country, some of these migrants return home, but others stay on.

I This may be because they find living and working conditions in the new country better than in their homeland. But it may also be because of relative failure: migrants may find it hard to save as much as they require, and stay on in the hope of succeeding eventually. As time passes, many of them are joined by their families, or find partners in the new country. With the birth of children, settlement takes on a more permanent character, whatever the original intentions.

J This can be summed up in a four-stage model. First, young workers move in order to work abroad temporarily, and send money home. Secondly, the stay is lengthened, and social networks are developed, providing mutual help. Thirdly, the original migrants' families join them, there is an increasing orientation towards the new country, and ethnic communities emerge with their own associations, shops, professions, and so on. And finally settlement becomes permanent.

Questions 2–8

*The passage has ten paragraphs labelled **A–J**.*
Which paragraph contains the following information?

Example: an outline of a pattern of migration

Answer: J (*This can be summed up in a four-stage model…*)

2 likely effects of being brought up in the new country
3 a reference to alternative, less likely, explanations of migration
4 how not achieving an objective may lengthen a stay abroad
5 some ways in which existing immigrants may help newcomers
6 'large-scale' reasons why migrants have moved from certain areas to a particular country
7 a description of a pattern of migration that rarely occurs
8 some reasons for sending money home

Questions 9–13

Complete the flow chart below using words from the box.

Model of migration process

temporary migration by young workers to increase **9** ....

↓

creation of **10** ....

↓

11 .... of families, growing sense of **12** ....

↓

permanent **13** ....

assistance	belonging	citizenship
earnings	employment	friendships
residence	reunion	

Listening

1 Can you answer these questions about Canada?

1 What is the capital?
2 What is the biggest city?
3 What are the two official languages?
4 What are the three oceans to the west, north and east of Canada?
5 Is the leaf on the Canadian flag from an oak, a maple or a redwood tree?

2 You are going to hear about two immigrants to Canada.

🎧 The first section is about Azim Lila, whose family moved from Tanzania to Canada when he was nine.

Questions 1–5

Complete the notes using words from the box.

Remember that the words in the notes may not be the ones you hear on the recording.

capital	challenges	coast	cultures
education	family	jobs	talents

Azim Lila

- place where brought up: **1** .... of Tanzania
- brought up to believe in value of **2** ....
- moving to Canada presented various **3** ....
- **4** .... helped to finance his studies
- believes life in Canada helps people develop their **5** ....

🎧 The second section is about a Russian woman, Tatyana Litvinova.

Questions 6–12

Answer the questions below.
Write **NO MORE THAN TWO WORDS** for each answer.

6 What is Tatyana's field?
7 What did she want money for?
8 Who did she miss most after moving to Canada?
9 What was she unable to help her children with at first?
10 What did she listen to, in order to improve her English?
11 What does she think is beautiful in Canada?
12 What does she particularly admire about Canadians?

3 Should immigrants want to become part of the community of the country they move to? Or should they still feel they belong to the country they came from?

Vocabulary Phrasal verbs

4 Read through this passage, and choose a different phrasal verb from the box for each space, putting it in the right form.

deal with	hold on to	live up to
look forward to	put up with	
turn out	work at	

Immigration and identity

The interviewees in this study, all immigrants to New Zealand, were attracted by the country's freedom and prosperity. For most of them, the country had fully **1** .... their expectations. For some, going there **2** .... to be the best move they had ever made.

However, many immigrants find that their new situation shakes their sense of cultural and personal identity. They might need to **3** .... difficult questions of how they define themselves, and how much of the new country's culture they are willing to accept into their lives.

The people we interviewed fall into three main groups. One group define themselves by their own, personal identities. They may maintain their original heritage, but at the same time they are open to New Zealand culture, and **4** .... their eventual assimilation into the community.

Another group maintain a strong sense of identity with their homeland, and tend to mix with others from that country living in New Zealand. They make the most of those aspects of the local culture that they can relate to, and **5** .... the rest.

The third group do all in their power to **6** .... their original cultural identity, and **7** .... recreating their own ethnic community inside New Zealand. They avoid contact with people from other cultures. Despite some tensions, all three groups have become important elements in the complexity and depth of New Zealand culture.

Grammar

Position of adverbs

5 When certain words are placed with the verb in a sentence – rather than at the beginning or end of the sentence – there are rules about their precise position. These words include *all, both*, adverbs of frequency like *always, often, hardly ever*, and some other adverbs, such as *also, almost, probably, soon* and *no longer*.

Look at these three examples, then match the situations 1–3 with the rules a–c.

*Azim's parents were **both** from Tanzania.*
*When Azim went to university he **soon** found a job.*
*Azim's family had **never** been rich.*

1 When there is only one verb, and it is *to be*, the adverb …
2 When there is only one verb, and it is **not** *to be*, the adverb …
3 When there is at least one auxiliary or modal verb, the adverb …

a goes after the first one.
b goes in front of the verb.
c follows the verb.

G ···⬧ page 143

6 Put a slash (/) in each sentence to indicate where the adverb in brackets should go, according to the rules above.

1 Tatyana Litvinova is working at the University of Alberta. (currently)
2 Before emigrating to Canada, Tatyana had been separated from her sister. (never)
3 Years after moving to Canada, she loves Russia. (still)
4 However, she is happy with her life in Canada. (still)
5 Some people have left their home before deciding to emigrate. (hardly ever)
6 Because of my new job, I changed my mind about emigrating. (almost)
7 Since moving inland, I go to the beach every day. (no longer)

7 The following sentences show errors made by IELTS candidates who have put the adverb in the wrong place. Write each sentence with the adverb in the right place. One sentence is correct.

1 We **also** can see from the chart that the number of immigrants rose sharply.
2 An immigrant who has **already** work experience will find it easier to get a job.
3 People who are living in a foreign country **still** can find happiness in their lives.
4 We must **always** look on the bright side.
5 **Particularly** I like meeting people.
6 Immigrants **sometimes** will miss people and things from their old home.
7 It will be **still** very cold next month.
8 The number of immigrants to Canada has been **also** affected by economic conditions in other parts of the world.

Quiz

8 And finally … here is a quiz about some other English-speaking countries.

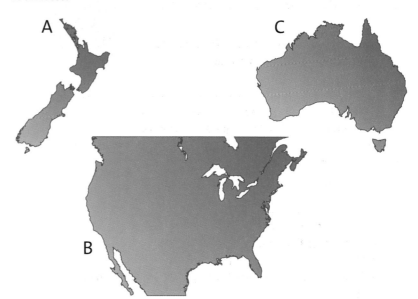

1 What are the three countries shown in the maps?
2 Is a didgeridoo a musical instrument, a poisonous snake or a type of plant?
3 What is the capital of Australia?
4 Which of these animals is native to Australia: a mongoose, a panda or a koala?
5 What are the names of New Zealand's two main islands?
6 Which bird is the symbol of New Zealand: the kakapo, the kiwi or the kookaburra?
7 Which of these are the most numerous in New Zealand: sheep, people or kangaroos?
8 After English, which language is spoken by the largest number of people living in the USA?
9 As well as being a plant, is 'bluegrass' an animal, a vehicle or a type of music?
10 What is the maximum time that a US president can hold office?

Writing folder 10

Preparing for the IELTS General Training and Academic Writing Modules

Advice

- Underline key words or phrases in the question.
- Take time to plan your answer.
- Quickly write down some ideas and then try to organise them into paragraphs.
- Leave a clear line between paragraphs.
- Write neatly.
- Cross words out in a neat way and not too often.

- Make sure your answer is the right length – that is at least 250 words but not more than about 290 words for Task 2 and at least 150 words for Task 1.
- Check your spelling and grammar carefully – that is, proofread your work!
- Make sure you answer all parts of the question.
- Check you have used appropriate language, especially in a formal letter or essay.

Proofreading

1 The following are sentences taken from essays written by IELTS candidates on the subject of immigration. Correct the common grammatical errors that they contain. All the sentences contain errors.

1 I am agree that people should be allowed to travel to find work.
2 If people have many experience, I think they can become citizens quite easy.
3 Young people what are new to a country have to learn many things about it.
4 There are many place, for example in factories, in where they can work.
5 In some countries people they can be stay there as long as they want to.
6 The families are not as close as they used to because widespread emigration.
7 It is known that every problems comes from poor communication.
8 You need many money for taxes, for clothes, for food, for everything in new country.

Using appropriate language

2 When writing a Task 2 essay in both the General Training and Academic Writing Modules it is important to use a formal style. Read this Task 2 question and answer, and circle the more academic of the words in italics.

There are more advantages to studying abroad than disadvantages.

To what extent do you agree with this statement?

Nowadays, there is a **1** *growing / big* tendency among some families to send their **2** *kids / children* abroad for a better education. **3** *First of all / In the first place*, some countries **4** *such as / e.g.* the USA, Canada, Britain, **5** *etc. / and so on* have very advanced **6** *schools / educational systems*. **7** *Kids / Children* studying there will **8** *receive / get* a very good education.
9 *Next / Secondly*, living abroad will also **10** *enrich / make better* their knowledge, broaden their minds and widen their horizons. It will help them in the understanding of other countries, both of the culture and the people.

11 *Admittedly / True*, studying abroad requires **12** *a considerable amount / a lot* of money. The tuition **13** *money / fees*, the living expenses and the **14** *flat / accommodation* all cost **15** *a great deal / a lot*. **16** *In addition, / And* a child living abroad alone may **17** *get lonely / suffer from loneliness*.

18 *However, / But* the advantages of sending a teenager abroad **19** *to get educated / for educational purposes* far outweigh the disadvantages. They can **20** *study / learn* advanced technology and science, they can learn to speak a language **21** *well / fluently* and their minds will be enriched. The **22** *problem / trouble* is, when is **23** *an appropriate / the right* age to send them abroad? **24** *If you have enough money / Money permitting*, I think the time after high school is the **25** *most suitable / best*. **26** *At this time / Then*, they can live **27** *by themselves / independently*, and therefore learn something new **28** *better / more effectively*.

Further practice

Task 1

You should spend about 20 minutes on this task.

The diagrams below give information about immigration to the United States.

Summarise the information by selecting and reporting the main features, and make comparisons where relevant.

Write at least 150 words.

Total number of immigrants to the USA in each decade: 1850s to 1930s

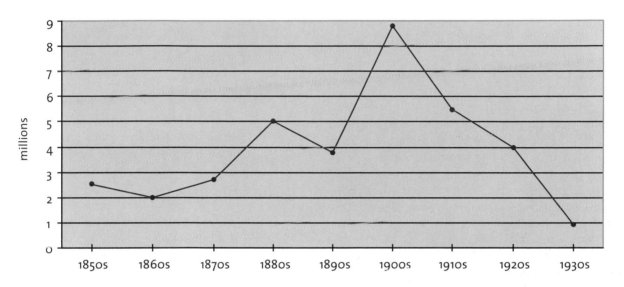

Immigration into the USA by country of origin 1882

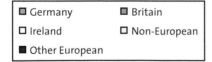

☐ Germany	☐ Britain
☐ Ireland	☐ Non-European
■ Other European	

Immigration into the USA by country of origin 1907

☐ Austria-Hungary	☐ Italy
☐ Russia	■ Other European
☐ Non-European	

Task 2

You should spend about 40 minutes on this task.

Write about the following topic:

A larger proportion of people live and work in other countries today than at any time in the past. It is very probable that in the future there will be no borders and people will be able to move freely between countries.

To what extent do you agree with this opinion?

Give reasons for your answer and include any relevant examples from your own knowledge or experience.

Write at least 250 words.

Units 17–20 Revision

Topic review

1 How far do you agree with these statements? Give reasons for your answers.

    1 Occasionally, it's a good idea to spend a day without a watch or clock.
    2 Entertainments should be planned for daytime or early evening, not late at night.
    3 Wasting time can be good for us.
    4 Society should be organised so that only emergency workers need to work at night.
    5 Working in the tourist industry has plenty of advantages.
    6 Children are unlikely to benefit from travelling to other countries.
    7 We should live close to our work rather than at a distance.
    8 Air travel is harmful for the environment, so people should be discouraged from flying.
    9 People should be able to live in any country they choose.
    10 Cities with communities from many countries are likely to be exciting places to live in.

Vocabulary Phrasal verbs

2 Complete these sentences with a phrasal verb consisting of a verb from the first column and a particle from the second. You will need to use one of the verbs twice. In number 6 the particle follows the object. All of these phrasal verbs are used in 18.2 and 20.2.

deal	down
keep	forward
put	on
set	over
take	up
	with

Since the factory where I work was **1** .... by one of its competitors, shift work has been introduced. The staff are unhappy about this, and want the company to **2** .... the problems faced by shift workers. They have **3** .... some suggestions for improving conditions. One is that the company should **4** .... a working party to find out what is known about the effects of working at night.

They also want the company to **5** .... additional staff and reduce working hours. The senior managers' aim, however, is to **6** .... the number of employees .... and improve productivity.

3 Complete the three-part phrasal verbs in these sentences. All of them are used in 18.2 and 20.2.

    1 I was very disappointed when I broke my leg and had to cancel my holiday, because I'd been looking .... it for months.
    2 People sometimes plan a long holiday, then come .... the problem that they can't get enough time off work.
    3 Nowadays we so often see famous places on television that they may not live .... our expectations if we visit them.
    4 Holiday companies are coming .... ideas for attracting new customers, such as targeting activity holidays at the elderly.
    5 I didn't much like the tour guide, but as we were in the middle of the rain forest I had to put .... him.
    6 Increasing competition means that package tour operators can't easily get .... selling holidays that are poor value for money.
    7 Holiday companies must face .... growing concern about the impact of travel on the environment.
    8 The experience that can be gained on an adventure holiday makes .... any lack of comfortable facilities.

Grammar

Phrasal verbs

4 Some of the phrasal verbs in **bold** need a pronoun. If they do, write the phrasal verb with the appropriate pronoun in the right position. Some sentences are correct.

EXAMPLES: The travel company was very successful, but lost its separate identity after a bigger rival **took over.**
took it over

In some holiday locations, insects can be irritating but you just have to **put up with.**
put up with them

1 I didn't have time to book my flight, so a friend offered to **deal with.** ....
2 The Tour Leader **came across** as being very intelligent. ....
3 Here's a very old boat ticket to Canada. I **came across** in a suitcase in the attic. ....
4 I've got some leaflets for the passengers. Could you help me to **give out**? ....
5 Understanding another country's culture takes time – you have to **work at.** ....
6 The cost of living has risen so much recently that more and more people are struggling to **get by.** ....
7 This poster has faded so much that I can hardly **make out.** ....
8 When there was an outbreak of flu, many people who were living in crowded conditions **went down with.** ....

Position of adverbs

5 Put a slash (/) to show where the adverb in brackets should go in the sections of the sentences in *italics*.

1 It is encouraging to know that *monorails are involved in accidents.* (hardly ever)
2 *I travel by public transport* if I can. (nearly always)
3 People who work at night *are able to sleep well during the day.* (rarely)
4 *The passengers were asleep* when the plane flew over Niagara Falls. (all)
5 *It has been said* that travel broadens the mind. (often)
6 *We can hope* that we aren't stuck in this traffic jam for much longer. (only)
7 I'm afraid *the special offer on tickets is available.* (no longer)
8 It took so long to say goodbye that *I missed the plane.* (almost)

Obligation, lack of obligation and prohibition

6 Complete this leaflet by choosing *must*, *mustn't*, or a form of *have to* or *don't have to* for each space.

Stamford Ecotours:
Information for potential Tour Leaders

We organise tours for small groups, each with a Tour Leader, to environments as varied as rain forests, deserts and the Arctic.

Some people fear that any form of tourism is harmful, but we believe that people **1** .... give up travelling altogether – responsible tourism (ecotourism) is the answer. We can explore other countries, but we **2** .... keep our impact on the local environment and community to a minimum.

To achieve that, at Stamford Ecotours we have established certain rules: our Tour Leaders and our customers

• **3** .... do their best to conserve the environment and preserve the well-being of local people
• **4** .... dispose of litter in a responsible manner
• **5** .... buy products that exploit wildlife or harm the environment.

Anyone wishing to become a Tour Leader **6** .... be sympathetic towards the concept of responsible tourism. However, he or she **7** .... have worked in the tourist industry, as we will provide training. Please note that as a Tour Leader, you will **8** .... spend up to six months at a time based abroad, before returning home.

Unreal present / future

7 Complete each sentence with a suitable verb. Make sure you use the correct tense. Some verbs need to be negative.

EXAMPLE: I'd rather you ...*didn't give*... me anything more to carry – I've already dropped your sunglasses.

1 Many people wish they .... enough time and money to travel around the world.
2 It's time the government .... more effort to reduce the use of private cars.
3 Drive if you really want to, but I'd rather you .... here by train.
4 It's a lovely day for walking along the beach. If only I .... so far from the coast!
5 I wish more shops .... open twenty-four hours a day.
6 You're obviously very tired – it's high time you .... to bed.
7 I'd rather you .... so much noise, as I'm trying to sleep.
8 It's about time you .... your own car instead of borrowing mine.

Grammar folder

Unit 1
The passive

The passive is used:

- when the action is more important than the person doing it
  The World Wide Web was invented by Tim Berners-Lee.
- when we don't know who did something
  Paper was invented in China.
- when reporting the news, and in academic and scientific writing where we are more interested in events and processes than in the person doing the action
  The conference on Internet marketing is held every year in September.

Formation of the passive

The passive is formed with *be* + past participle of a transitive verb. For modals it is formed with the modal + *be* + past participle.

present simple	*It is made*
present continuous	*It is being made*
present perfect	*It has been made*
past simple	*It was made*
past continuous	*It was being made*
future simple	*It will be made*

Compare these sentences:
A *Martin Cooper made the first public mobile phone call.*
B *The first public mobile phone call was made by Martin Cooper.*
Sentence **A** is active and follows the pattern of Subject (*Martin Cooper*), Verb (*made*) and Object (*the first public mobile phone call*).
Sentence **B** is passive and the pattern is Subject (*the first public mobile phone call*), Verb (*was made*) and Agent (*by Martin Cooper*).

The infinitive

Where the situation is in the present and an impersonal sentence is needed, we can use the passive form of the verb plus the infinitive.
The language is said to be dying out.
In the past, we use the passive plus the past infinitive.
Silbo is said to have come from Africa.

Unit 2
Comparison

Comparative and superlative adjectives

- Regular one-syllable adjectives have forms like these:

adjective	comparative	superlative
young	young**er**	(the) young**est**

If an adjective ends in a single vowel and consonant (not w), the final letter is doubled, as in *thin* to *thinner*.
Examples: *sad, big, fat, hot, wet*

- Two-syllable adjectives ending in a consonant followed by the letter *-y* have forms like these:

adjective	comparative	superlative
dirty	dirt**ier**	(the) dirt**iest**

Examples: *angry, busy, easy, funny, happy, heavy, silly, tiny*

- Most other two-syllable adjectives and all longer adjectives form their comparative and superlative like this:

adjective	comparative	superlative
careful	**more** careful	(the) **most** careful

- Some common two-syllable adjectives can use either of the forms above.

adjective	comparative	superlative
simple	simp**ler** OR **more** simple	(the) simp**lest** OR (the) **most** simple

Examples: *clever, cruel, gentle, likely, narrow*

- Irregular adjectives have the following forms:

adjective	comparative	superlative
good	better	(the) best
bad	worse	(the) worst
far	farther/further	(the) farthest/furthest
old	older/elder	(the) oldest/eldest

Negative comparatives and superlatives

- To make negative comparisons we use *not as ... as* or *less ... than*.
  We tend to use *not as ... as* with adjectives that have a positive meaning, e.g.
  Chips are not as good for you as baked potatoes.
  We tend to use *less ... than* with adjectives that have a negative meaning, e.g.
  Some types of fat are less harmful than others.
- To make negative superlative statements we use *the least*.
  He always chooses the least expensive dish on the menu.

adjective	negative comparative	negative superlative
heavy	less heavy (than) OR not as heavy as	(the) least heavy

Using adverbs of degree

- These adverbs of degree can be used in front of comparative adjectives: *a bit, a good deal, a great deal, a little, a lot, much, rather, slightly, considerably.*
  Bananas are a bit better for you than apples.
  There is a great deal more Vitamin C in a potato than in rice.
- These adverbs of degree can be used in front of superlative adjectives: *by far, easily*
  Chocolate is by far the nicest thing to eat!

Unit 3
Cause, purpose and result

Cause

Because and *because of* are used to express the cause of an event or state.

Because is a conjunction, so it must be followed by a finite clause:
Edinburgh attracts a lot of visitors during the summer because the festival is very popular.

Because of is a compound preposition ('compound' means that it consists of more than one word). It is most often followed by a noun phrase:
Many people prefer cities to the countryside because of the night life.

Because of can also be followed by a clause beginning with a *wh*-word, usually *what*.
I visited the museum because of what I'd been told about it.
A more formal alternative to *because of* is *on account of*.

Purpose

The purpose of an action (that is, what is hoped for as a result of the action) can be expressed by using *so that* (usually *so* in informal language). It is followed by a finite clause, often containing *could* or *would*.
I booked a hotel room in advance so (that) my friends could meet me there as soon as I arrived.
Notice that in this example, the two subjects (*I* and *my friends*) are different, and that we don't know whether my friends met me or not: all we know is that that was my purpose, or intention.

Result

Unlike a purpose, a result is something that actually happens. It can be expressed with *so* (**not** *so that*). *So* is a conjunction and is followed by a finite clause.
All the hotels seemed to be full, so I stayed in a youth hostel.

Be careful not to confuse the purpose and result meanings of *so*.
I booked a cheap hotel at a distance from the city centre so I could save money, but I spent a lot on taxis, so I didn't save anything.
The first *so* introduces a purpose; the second one – a result.

In formal language, results are usually expressed in other ways:
The city's advertising campaign led to / resulted in a big increase in the number of tourists.
The bridge was closed, with the result that traffic came to a standstill.

Unit 4
Review of present tenses

Present simple

This is the most common of the present tenses. It is used for certain meanings, and also when the meaning is not covered by one of the other tenses, so use it if you are not sure which present tense is right.

Main meanings:
- frequency (how often an action is carried out)
  In my college, prizes are given once a year.
- a general or permanent truth (not only now)
  Good teachers explain the subject in a way that their students can understand.
- This tense also has a future meaning: see page 140, Unit 8.

Present continuous

Main meanings:
- a temporary activity happening at this moment
  I won't interrupt Johnny now because he's writing an assignment.
- a temporary activity happening around now
  In music this year we're making our own instruments.
  Only verbs referring to an action, whether physical or mental, can be used in the continuous tenses. This sentence is grammatical because the verb refers to a temporary action:
  You're being very silly.
  However this sentence is ungrammatical, because *to believe* doesn't refer to an action:
  ~~I'm believing in the importance of studying with other people.~~
  This should be:
  I believe in the importance of studying with other people.
- This tense also has a future meaning: see page 140, Unit 8.

Present perfect simple

This tense connects the past with the present.
Main meanings:
- an action or situation that started in the past and continues to the present
  Schools of some sort have existed for well over two thousand years.
  I've never studied economics.
- an action or situation that finished at an unspecified time in the past
  The only foreign language I've studied is Spanish.

- an action or situation that started in the past, and may or may not have finished. The emphasis is on its result in the present.
  I've forgotten my password, so I can't access my emails.

The present perfect simple is generally used with *just*, *yet* and *the first/only time*.
I haven't finished reading this book yet.
That was a really good lecture – it's the first time I've understood the subject.

Present perfect continuous

This combines the meanings of the continuous and perfect tenses.
Main meanings:
- actions which have lasted for some time and are likely to continue. Often a length of time is given.
  I've been studying chemistry for three years and there's another year to go.
- actions which have lasted for some time and have just stopped. Usually no length of time is given.
  I've been reading about colleges in this area, and there are several that offer the qualification I want.
Like the present continuous, this tense can only be used with verbs referring to a physical or mental action.

Unit 5
Review of past tenses

Past simple

This is used to talk about events which:
- began and ended in the past
  The USA became independent in the late 1700s.
  This indicates a completed action in the past with a fixed time phrase.
- happened regularly
  The archaeologists returned to the site every summer.

Past continuous

This is used to talk about events which:
- were unfinished at a particular time in the past
  The islanders were fishing when the explorers first saw them.

Past perfect

This is used to talk about events which:
- happened before a particular time in the past
  Kim took some photos of the palace after he had taken ones of the temple.
Note that the past perfect needs to be used when it is important to show a time difference. Sometimes it is omitted if it is not important to the sense of the sentence.

Unit 6
Past simple or present perfect?

See Unit 4 for the present perfect and Unit 5 for the past simple.

Unit 7
Relative clauses

There are two types of relative clause:
Defining: gives essential information about the noun it relates to, making it clear what the noun refers to.
Many people of all ages enjoy TV commercials which rely on humour.
This means something different from *Many people of all ages enjoy TV commercials.*

Non-defining: gives additional, non-essential information. If this information is omitted, it is still clear what exactly the noun refers to.
In recent years, advertisers have had considerable success with viral marketing, which probably dates from 1996.

As the examples show, commas are used in non-defining clauses, but not in defining clauses. It is important to use punctuation correctly in relative clauses, as inaccurate use can change the meaning of the sentence.
A manufacturer of sports clothes has cancelled its advertisements which have been criticised by the public.
A manufacturer of sports clothes has cancelled its advertisements, which have been criticised by the public.
In the first example, only the advertisements which have been criticised have been cancelled, and the manufacturer's other advertisements will continue. In the second example, all the advertisements have been cancelled because they have all been criticised.

Relative pronouns

In **defining relative clauses**, you can use:
*   *who* or *that* when referring to people
    I'm going to a talk to be given by an athlete who/that appeared in a TV commercial for running shoes.
*   *which* or *that* when referring to things
    The event which/that Toby Young describes was intended to advertise his latest book.

The relative pronoun can be left out when it is the object of a clause, as in the second example above, where it is what Toby Young describes. It must be included when it is the subject, as in *who/that appeared in a TV commercial for running shoes.*

In **non-defining relative clauses**, you can use:
*   *who* when referring to people
    Gary Phillips, who set up his advertising agency ten years ago, has become very successful.
*   *which* when referring to things
    At yesterday's meeting, which was arranged to discuss the current campaign, the manufacturers agreed to extend their contract with the advertising agency.
*   *which* when referring to a whole clause
    In one particular commercial, <u>a man washes his hands in car oil</u>, which is intended to imply that the oil is also good for car engines.
    Here *which* refers to the whole of the underlined clause.

whose

Whose is used to refer to people and – less often – things.
Our next speaker is Sharon Cooper, whose book on the history of advertising was published last year.
A commercial whose strength lies in humour is more likely to be remembered than a more straightforward one.

whom

Whom is mostly used in fairly formal language. It can be the object in a clause, or follow a preposition.
The group whom the government wishes to protect from the effects of advertising is children.
To whom it may concern: Stephanie Allen has been employed at this advertising agency since September 2003.

where, when, why

These words can be used instead of a relative pronoun after appropriate nouns. It is possible to omit *when* and *why* in defining relative clauses, as in these examples:
The launch of a new product is the time (when) you see if all your hard work has been successful.
The brilliant advertising campaign for these running shoes is the reason (why) sales have rocketed.

Unit 8
Talking about the future

There are many ways of talking about the future, usually reflecting the speaker's attitude. These are the main ones:

shall/will/'ll
*   a decision or offer made at this moment
    If you want to sell some furniture, I'll put an ad in the local newspaper for you.
*   a prediction
    This poster will definitely attract people's attention.

going to
*   something already decided or (less often) arranged
    We're going to use Veronica's ideas for the banner, and that's why she's been put in charge of the project.
*   a future result of a present situation
    Our advertising campaign did nothing to improve sales, so this is going to be a very bad year for us.

present continuous
*   something already arranged or (less often) decided
    I'm being interviewed on the radio tomorrow about my new book.

present simple
*   time and conditional clauses introduced by *if, unless, when, as soon as*, etc.
    I'll show you my proposal for the advert as soon as I get to the office.
*   a timetable, usually not involving the speaker (this is much less common that the structures above)
    My train leaves in ten minutes.

future continuous
*   a temporary event in the future
    This time tomorrow I'll be working on my next commercial.
*   a future event that will happen as a matter of course, independently of the wishes or intention of anyone concerned
    I try to avoid Jeremy Matthews as much as possible, but I'll be seeing him at the marketing conference.

future perfect
*   an event or situation that will be finished before a particular time in the future
    I'll have finished this project by Friday.

Unit 9
Countable and uncountable nouns

A noun can either be countable or uncountable. Uncountable nouns cannot be made plural, and they only have one form. They take a singular verb. Uncountable nouns are often the names of things or substances or abstract ideas which cannot be counted. Examples of common uncountable nouns are:
accommodation, traffic, news, pollution, work, weather, information, advice, electricity

Singular countable nouns can use *a/an* and *the*.
A new project was started this morning.
The man next door is a government scientist.

Some nouns can be countable and uncountable and have a difference in meaning:
*Her **hair** is very long.* (uncountable noun meaning the hair on her head)
*There's **a hair** in this sandwich!* (countable noun)

***Coffee** grows in Brazil.* (uncountable noun for the product)
*Would you like to come round for a **coffee**?* (countable noun meaning 'a cup of coffee')

There is an important difference in meaning between *a few / few* and *a little / little*. For example:
*There were **few** people at the meeting.* (It was disappointing because not many people were there.)

*There were **a few** people at the meeting. (There weren't many people there, but there is no suggestion that more were expected.)*

I've seen little improvement in your work recently. (negative comment)
I've seen a little improvement in your work recently. (positive comment)

Unit 10
-ing forms and infinitives 1

-ing forms

-ing forms can be the subject or object of a clause or sentence:
***Analysing** the results took them all day.* (subject)
*I enjoy **working** with computers.* (object)

-ing forms are used:

- after certain verbs and expressions, especially those expressing liking/disliking
  I don't mind sharing a flat.
  Other examples are:

love	can't stand	miss
enjoy	dislike	imagine
adore	don't mind	finish
feel like	avoid	it's not worth
detest	suggest	it's/there's no use
hate	consider	there's no point

- after adjective and preposition combinations
  My landlady is fantastic at cooking.
  Other examples are: *good/bad at, pleased, worried about, afraid, terrified of, interested in, keen on*
- after verb and preposition combinations
  I don't approve of having parties every night.
  Other examples are: *look forward to, object to, insist on, believe in, succeed in, apologise for, accuse someone of, consist of, congratulate someone on*
- after phrasal verbs
  The college took over running the hostel from a private landlord.

The infinitive

The infinitive is used

- after certain verbs
  I can't afford to pay too much rent.
  Other examples are: *agree, hope, promise, ask, want, expect, choose, intend, prefer, help, pretend*
- after certain adjectives
  I was surprised to see him making his bed.
  Other examples are: *difficult, possible, happy, certain, simple*
- after verbs with the pattern: verb + someone + *to do* + something
  I asked her to open the window.
  Other examples are: *encourage, permit, allow, persuade, teach, force*
- to express purpose
  I went to Australia to study economics.

The infinitive without *to*

This is used after modal auxiliaries (*can, must*), after *let, had better* and *would rather*. *Make* has no *to* in the active, but adds *to* in the passive:
I made him go to school. / He was made to go to school.
Help is followed by the infinitive with or without *to. Let me help you (to) move into your new flat.*

Unit 11
Articles

There are three possibilities with articles: *a/an* (the indefinite article), *the* (the definite article) and no article (the zero article):
*We stopped near **a** lion and **a** tiger. **The** lion noticed us but **the** tiger didn't.*
Lions are fascinating animals.

The indefinite article, *a/an*, is used:
- before a singular, countable noun when it is used for the first time, as in the example above: *We stopped near a lion and a tiger.* Before plural countable nouns used for the first time we use *some*, and before uncountable nouns either *some* or no article:
  We stopped near some lions.
  I need some information.

The definite article, *the*, is used before singular and plural countable and uncountable nouns when it is clear what is being referred to, for one of these reasons.
- it has been referred to directly before, as in the example above:
  The lion noticed us but the tiger didn't.
- it has already been referred to indirectly:
  *I visited a zoo recently, and really enjoyed watching **the** animals.*
  The *zoo* implies that there were animals there.
- it is clear from the situation
  I took the children to the zoo yesterday.
  Here the speaker assumes that the listener knows which children I'm referring to (probably my own) and which zoo (probably the only one where I live).
- it is unique, or generally talked about as though it is unique
  the Earth, the sun

No article is used
- with uncountable nouns
  Zoology is a fairly popular subject.
- when something is referred to in general
  Lions are fascinating animals.

Unit 12
Should, had better, ought to

These are used to give advice, or say what we think would be a good thing to do now or in the future.
- *Should* and *ought to* mean the same, but *should* is used much more often.
  The team should spend / ought to spend less time chatting, and more time training.
- *Shouldn't* is used to give advice about what not to do. *Oughtn't to* is also possible, but is used less and less.
  The team shouldn't spend so much time chatting.
- *Had better* (usually shortened to *'d better*) normally refers to the present situation, rather than the future, and is more informal than the other two. It is used in speech more than in writing.
  We'd better do some more practice before the match.

Should have done and *ought to have done*

These refer to the past, and are often used for criticism because an action didn't happen.
We should have spent / ought to have spent longer practising.

Shouldn't have done and (occasionally) *oughtn't to have done*

These refer to the past, and are often used for criticism because an action happened.
We shouldn't have spent so long chatting. (We've missed our train.)

Unit 13
Conditionals

Conditional clauses state the condition which must be satisfied before the main clause may be true. There are four main types:

Zero conditional

If + present tense / present tense
Not a true conditional, as the events described both happen.
If I go shopping alone, I spend too much money.

First conditional

If + present tense / future tense with *will*
Used to talk about something that will probably happen in the future, if something else happens.
If I have enough money, I'll study abroad.
I'll go to the party on my own, if you don't make a decision soon.

Second conditional

If + past tense / *would, could, might*
Used to talk about unlikely or impossible situations. *Were* instead of *was* is often used after *if*. This is common in both formal and informal styles. Some people consider *were* is more correct, especially in American English.
If I inherited some money, I'd go on an expensive holiday.
I wouldn't watch TV if there was/were something better to do.

Third conditional

If + past perfect / *would have, could have, might have* + past participle
Used to speculate about what could have happened in the past.
If we had had a choice, we wouldn't have left school at 16.
If Marisa had caught the right train, she wouldn't have been late for class.

Other words with the same meaning as *if*.
- *Unless* has a similar meaning to *if not*, in the sense of *except if*.
  I never wear a suit unless it is absolutely necessary.
- *As/so long as, providing (that), provided (that), on condition that* are all used to make conditions.
  They were given permission to build the office block as long as they provided adequate parking facilities.

Unit 14
-*ing* forms and infinitives 2

Some verbs can be followed by both an -*ing* form and an infinitive. In some cases the meaning of the verb may change according to whether it is followed by the -*ing* form or the infinitive.

No change in meaning

Verbs such as *start, begin, continue, attempt, intend, can't bear*
The artist started to paint the man's portrait.
The artist started painting the man's portrait.

Slight change in meaning

Verbs such as *like, prefer, hate, love.*
Compare: *I like wearing blue.* (talking about something in general)
  I like to wear a black suit to work. (talking about a habit)

After *would like, would prefer, would hate* and *would love* an infinitive is used.
Would you like to choose a colour for the kitchen walls?

A change in meaning

Verbs such as *try, stop, regret, remember, forget, mean, go on*
*I **remembered / didn't forget to buy** a newspaper while I was out shopping.* (I remembered it and then I did it.)
*I **remember** / I'll **never forget going** to the Louvre Museum two years ago.* (I remember it after I did it.)
*I **mean to work** hard at university.* (this is my intention)
*It **will mean** going to the library more often.* (this will be the result)

Unit 15
Speculating about possibilities

May/might (not)

These refer to a present or future possibility. *May* is usually slightly more certain than *might*.
In England, unexpected guests may/might be offered some tea.
In future, people may/might not need to travel to business meetings.

May/might (not) have

The modal perfects refer to a past possibility.
Life when my parents were young may/might have been less demanding than it is now.

Must and can't

Look at the two clauses in this sentence:
Jackie has travelled a great deal, so she must know a lot about different countries.
In the first clause the speaker means 'it is a fact that Jackie has travelled a great deal'.
In the second clause the speaker means 'I am sure Jackie knows a lot about different countries because I have worked it out from the evidence (the fact that she has travelled a great deal).'

Can't is used to show that the speaker has considered the evidence and is sure that something isn't true:
Jackie has only spent a few days in Canada, so she can't know much about the country.

Must have done and *can't have done*

These are used to come to similar conclusions about the past:
Jackie must have been to South Africa because she's got a lot of photographs of Cape Town.
Jackie's told me about every country that she's visited, and she's never mentioned Egypt, so she can't have been there.

Unit 16
Non-finite clauses

Non-finite clauses contain an infinitive (e.g. *to do*), present participle (e.g. *doing*) or past participle (e.g. *done*). In these examples the non-finite clauses are underlined.
I hope to write a best-selling novel.
Using international road signs reduces the risks when people drive in another country.
Books printed in the early days of the printing press are very valuable.

These clauses are ungrammatical on their own: they have to be part of a larger sentence, where they can function in a number of ways. In the first sentence above, the non-finite clause is functioning as the object (what I hope); in the second it is the subject (what reduces the risks) and in the third it is a relative clause, describing *books* (shortened from *which were printed ...*).

The main difference in meaning is that the present participle generally has an active meaning (*people use road signs*), and the past participle generally has a passive meaning (*books are printed*).

When a non-finite clause functions as the subject of a sentence, it normally uses a present participle:
Writing in Chinese is difficult for foreign learners.
Alternatively, the clause can be replaced by *it* and moved to the end of the sentence. In this case it normally uses an infinitive:
It is difficult for foreign learners to write in Chinese.

Unit 17
Modal verbs: obligation, lack of obligation and prohibition

Strong obligation: *must, have to*, (informal) *have got to*

must

Must is used to talk about strong obligations in the present and future that are imposed by the speaker. It is also used to talk about laws and rules. To talk about the past we have to use *had to*.
I must arrange to have a telephone alarm call.
I had to take a taxi.

have to / have got to

Have to / have got to are used to talk about strong obligations in the present and future that are not imposed by the speaker.
I've got to work nights this week. (My boss says so.)
If in doubt whether to use *must* or *have to*, use *have to*.

had to

Had to is used to talk about past and reported obligations.
I had to help on the farm when I was young.
We were told we had to get a work permit before we started the job.

Lack of obligation: *doesn't/don't have to*

Don't have to is used to talk about things that aren't obligatory – they are optional.
She doesn't have to come to the meeting if she doesn't want to.
We didn't have to wear a uniform at our school.

Prohibition: *mustn't*

Mustn't is used when something is forbidden.
You mustn't use machinery when you are sleepy.

Unit 18
Phrasal verbs

Many English verbs can be followed by a preposition or an adverb particle. These particles join together with verbs to make two-word verbs, sometimes with different meanings. These are called phrasal verbs.

Adverb particles

Examples of phrasal verbs with adverb particles are:
put off – this can mean *postpone*
give up – this can mean *stop (doing something)*

- Adverb particles can go before or after noun objects:
  The agency took on extra staff for the summer.
  The agency took extra staff on for the summer.
- Adverb particles can only go after pronoun objects:
  The agency took them on for the summer.
- When used without an object, the verb and adverb particle of a phrasal verb cannot be separated.
  We sat up all night when our plane was delayed.

Preposition particles

Examples of phrasal verbs with preposition particles are:
fall off – *He fell off his bicycle on the way to work.*
look at – *Here are my holiday photos. Would you like to look at them?*

Prepositions normally go before the object and no separation is possible.
He listened to the safety talk on the plane.

Three-part phrasal verbs

For three-part phrasal verbs (these consist of a verb, adverb particle and preposition), no separation is possible:
I'm really looking forward to my holiday in Venice.

Unit 19
Unreal present and future

In certain structures that refer to a situation which doesn't exist, past tenses are used to refer to the present or future.

if (the second conditional)

If I lived closer to my work, I wouldn't have to spend so long in my car.
For more on the second conditional, see page 142, Unit 13.

it's time, it's high time, it's about time

It's (about/high) time we looked more seriously at alternatives to cars.
It's high time and *it's about time* are stronger than *it's time*, and generally express criticism.
No money has been invested in railways for years. It's high/about time the government did something about it.
These phrases are mostly used in informal English.

if only and *wish*

If only / I wish people drove more carefully.
I wish this bus weren't/wasn't so full.
These are mostly used with a past tense when the speaker (or the subject of the sentence) would like a present situation to be different from what it is. The structures are most common in informal English.

if only and *wish* + *would*

These are used when the speaker (or the subject of the sentence, e.g. John) is complaining about the present situation, and wants something to happen in future, but thinks it unlikely. The structures are most common in informal English.
If only / John wishes you would keep your eyes on the road.
Many people wish the government would spend more on education.

would rather

This means the same as *prefer* and is mostly used in informal English.
I'd rather you didn't go by car.

Unit 20
Position of adverbs

Normally at the end of the sentence

The most common position for adverbs (including adverbial phrases) is at the end of the sentence. This sentence contains two adverbial phrases:
A large number of immigrants arrived <u>in Canada</u> <u>at the end of the nineteenth century</u>.
Some adverbs can be placed at the beginning of the sentence, for emphasis.
<u>At the end of the nineteenth century</u> a large number of immigrants arrived in Canada.

Normally at the beginning of the sentence

A few adverbs normally go at the beginning of the sentence. Most of them add a comment, rather than being part of the main meaning of the sentence. See also page 95.
***Perhaps** I'll go to Scotland to study.*
***To everyone's surprise**, the climate turned out to be very good.*
***Frankly**, the multicultural festival was poorly organised.*

Normally in the middle

Certain adverbs are placed with the verb. The most common ones include, *also, almost, probably, soon, no longer*, adverbs of frequency like *always, often, hardly ever* and other words like *all* and *both*.

Their exact position depends on the verb.
- Where there is only one verb, and it is *to be*, the words listed above follow it:
  *My grandparents **were all** immigrants from Sweden.*
- Where there is only one verb, and it is **not** *to be*, the words listed above go in front of it:
  *Immigrants **generally went** to places where there was plenty of work.*
- Where there is at least one auxiliary or modal verb, the words listed above go after the first one:
  *A high level of immigration **would probably** have been welcomed by the Canadian government at the end of the nineteenth century.*

Self-study folder

The following pages contain the answers to the exercises, with additional notes where relevant, the recording scripts and sample answers for the writing tasks. The Map of *Objective IELTS Intermediate Student's Book* on pages 3–5 gives full details of the language and test skills covered in each unit. The *Content of the IELTS Test* on pages 6 and 7 provides information about the test, with links to the relevant Test folder or Writing folder.

Unit 1

1.1 pages 8–9

1 The pictures show the following types of communication:

a mobile phone call	e face to face
b email	f a text message
c a postcard	g whistling
d a letter	

2 You will probably need to improve your reading speed so that you can cope with the 2,000 to 2,750 words you will have to read in the test. The passage in this unit is about 500 words long, much shorter than the ones you will have in the test, apart from General Training Part 1. Read it as quickly as possible and time how long it takes you. A native speaker would take about a minute and a half. While you are reading, you should think about what type of text this is: for example, would you find it in a novel, a textbook or a newspaper? Give a reason for your answer.

> **Answer**
> This is a newspaper report about something that is happening around now. It also contains quotes from the different people involved.

3 Take only a couple of minutes to scan the passage for the answers.

> **Answers**
> 1 1999
> 2 Venezuela, Cuba and Texas
> 3 Atlas Mountains of North Africa

4 This exercise is similar to the ones found in the Reading Modules. In the test, each reading passage will have a mixture of task types. In the first few units of the Student's Book, there are shorter reading passages with only one task type. Candidates often find the *Not given* questions the most difficult to do. For advice on how to tackle this type of question, see Test folder 1, page 12.

The answer section gives line numbers in the text to help you to find where the answers are.

> **Answers**
> 1 TRUE — *With the opening of the island to tourism and the arrival of the telephone, Silbo Gomero had started to die out.* (lines 9–10)
> 2 NOT GIVEN — No mention is made of how the children feel about learning Silbo Gomero.
> 3 FALSE — *students spend 25 minutes a week learning it* (lines 14–15)
> 4 NOT GIVEN — The text doesn't tell us how well Darias teaches.
> 5 TRUE — *An important step towards saving the language was the First International Congress of Whistled Languages, which was held in La Gomera in 2003.* (lines 29–31)
> 6 FALSE — *If we spoke English, we'd use an English structure for whistling.* (lines 57–58)

5

> **Answers**
> 1 peak 2 to die out 3 the basics 4 is made up of
> 5 traces of 6 settlers 7 originated in
> 8 was adapted (to) 9 relies on 10 disjointed

6 Try to expand your answers to the questions and not just give short answers. The Speaking Module is your opportunity to show what you know – use it well. Try to record your answers and listen to check that you give reasons for your answers and that you don't keep repeating the same vocabulary and grammatical structure.

> **Possible answers**
> 1 I come from a large/small family. We are very close.
> 2 I prefer to confide in my brother as he really understands me best.
> 3 I find it easy/difficult to say what I want in another language.

1.2 pages 10–11

1 Look at sentences **a** and **b**. Sentence **a**, in the passive, is more impersonal and formal than sentence **b**. You will often need to use the passive in the Writing Modules, especially for describing processes. Many Academic writing tasks need to be both formal and impersonal.

2 Look at the examples from the reading passage. Refer to the Grammar folder if you are unsure about how the passive is formed and used.

Answers
Other passives in the passage are:
is made up of (present simple passive, line 19)
was held (past simple passive, line 32)
will ... be carried out (future simple passive, line 36)
to be transmitted (passive infinitive, line 49)
was adapted (past simple passive, line 52)
are whistled (present simple passive, line 55)

3

Answers
1 The telephone was invented in 1876 by Alexander Graham Bell.
2 The World Wide Web was invented in 1994 by Tim Berners-Lee.
3 The photocopier was invented in 1951 by Chester Carlson.
4 The fax machine was invented in 1966 by Xerox.
5 The typewriter was invented in 1714 by Henry Mill.

4 Read through the text first to get an idea of what it is about before attempting to do the exercise.

Answers
1 was made   2 walked / was walking   3 looked
4 used / was using   5 was introduced   6 cost
7 are   8 weigh   9 can be bought   10 are used
11 will be used   12 don't / do not seem

5 This exercise gives practice in forming the passive.

Answers
1 is/was thought; are/were sent   2 is said   3 is stolen
4 should be switched off   5 was told
6 were first designed   7 is often used
8 have just been called   9 will be carried   10 were taken

6 These words come from the *Cambridge Learner Corpus*, a database of candidates' scripts from past sessions of Cambridge exams, including IELTS. While writing this course, we have made extensive use of both this and the *Cambridge International Corpus*. Reference to the scripts in the *Learner Corpus* has given us a much fuller picture of what IELTS candidates can and cannot do. The following are words that IELTS candidates often spell wrongly.

Answers
1 government   2 countries   3 because
4 advertisement   5 achieve   6 which   7 should
8 environment   9 through   10 beginning

7 Names which are spelt out in the Listening Module must be spelt correctly. Spell out the names of the inventors and then listen to the recording to check pronunciation.

8 Listen to the recording and write down the numbers you hear. Notice that 0 can be said in a number of ways, depending on how it is used.

Recording script and answers
1 01993 548333
   oh, one, double nine three – five, four, eight, treble three
2 0 degrees centigrade
   zero degrees centigrade
3 14th March 2004
   the fourteenth of March, two thousand and four
4 30th November 1918
   the thirtieth of November, nineteen eighteen
5 5,432 kilos
   five thousand, four hundred and thirty-two kilos
6 £1,500
   fifteen hundred pounds or one thousand, five hundred pounds
7 £3.12
   three pounds and twelve p or three pounds and twelve pence
8 £4.50
   four pounds fifty
9 2.5 centimetres
   two point five centimetres
10 70 metres
   seventy metres

9 Write down and then record yourself saying numbers and dates which are important to you. Give reasons why they are important.

10 This listening passage is similar to what is heard in Part 1 of the Listening Module. Read through the task and decide what sort of information could go in the spaces. In the test, the recording is only heard once. At this stage it is up to you how many times you need to hear it played.

Answers (relevant parts of the recording script are underlined)
1 home (and) office
2 (from) 80 (to) 250 (pounds)
3 i/I 860 (eight sixty)
4 8.30 / eight thirty / half past eight
5 Park Lane
6 opposite (the) cinema
7 supermarket
8 cash (only)
9 Stanway
10 (on the) third/3rd

Recording script

Man: Good morning. Computer Solutions.
Woman: Oh, hello. My printer's broken and I need to get a new one. Someone gave me your number, and I was wondering whether you could help me.
Man: No problem. We stock printers suitable for both <u>home and office</u>.
Woman: Well, I'm a student. I just need one for my coursework. How much do they cost?

Man: An inkjet printer will probably be good enough for what you want – it'll do text and pictures. They start at £80 and go up to £250.

Woman: Mm. Quite a good price range, then. I can spend about £150. Can I get a good one for that?

Man: Yes. I'd go for the Trion i860. It's had good reviews and we've had no complaints about it.

Woman: The i860. I'll come in and have a look. What time are you open to?

Man: Normally we close at 5.30, but today, being Saturday, it's 8.30.

Woman: And where exactly are you?

Man: In Hollowridge – 15 Park Lane.

Woman: 15 Park Lane, got that. Is that in the town centre?

Man: Yes, opposite the cinema.

Woman: OK, and is it easy to park? If I buy the printer, I'd want to take it home with me today.

Man: No problem. There's a car park quite near, just at the back of the supermarket.

Woman: OK. Oh, one more thing – do you take credit cards?

Man: Cash only, I'm afraid. Will that be all right?

Woman: Yes, but I mustn't forget to go to the bank before I come! Oh, by the way, what's your name?

Man: Jack Stanway. That's S-T-A-N-W-A-Y. There are two Jacks here, so when you ask for me, give my surname too.

Woman: OK, I will.

Man: I work in the office, but you need to go to the third floor, where the printers are. Just ask for me there and I'll come out and see what I can do to help. See you later.

Woman: The third floor. Great – thanks for your help. Bye.

Test folder 1

pages 12–13

Make sure you fully understand the notes and advice. Evidence for the answers is given below, but this is not part of the answer. You should only write *YES / NO / NOT GIVEN*.

Answers

1	YES	*the answer that most of us would give … this must surely be the most widely recognized function of language* (paragraph 2)
2	NO	*There are several other functions where the communication of ideas is irrelevant* (paragraph 2)
3	YES	*It cannot be 'communication of ideas', for there is no one else in the room* (paragraph 3)
4	NOT GIVEN	*Here we have one of the commonest uses of language.* (paragraph 4) The writer doesn't say that we are becoming more aware of it.
5	NOT GIVEN	In paragraph 5 the writer refers to *the semi-linguistic noises often called interjections (such as 'Wow' and 'Ouch')*, but not to languages other than English.
6	NOT GIVEN	In paragraph 6 the writer refers to *the use of such phrases as 'Good morning'* to maintain a comfortable relationship between people, but doesn't mention other feelings the phrases might express.

7	NO	*The weather is not as universal a conversation-filler as English people might like to think!* (paragraph 8)
8	YES	*the enjoyment … applies to all age groups* (paragraph 9)

Unit 2

2.1 pages 14–15

1 The illustrations are of two food pyramids which show the basic diets of people in Asia and people in Latin America. *Staple foods* are ones that the people eat every day.

Possible answers
- The staples for Asia are based on cereals. The staples for Latin America are grains, beans, nuts and tubers, together with fruit and vegetables.
- Latin Americans eat more meat than Asians. Both diets are rich in fruit and vegetables. Asians drink more tea than Latin Americans. They both eat the same amount of sweets and eggs.
- Fruit and vegetables are better for you than sweets and too much meat.
- a carbohydrate: rice, wheat, potatoes, corn
  b protein: meat, fish, beans, eggs, poultry
  c fat: dairy, plant/vegetable oils

2 Read the information in the Test spot. More information on this type of question can be found in Test folder 3. It is always a good idea to read through the questions before listening to the recording so that you can get an idea of what you are going to listen for.

Answers (relevant parts of the recording script are underlined)
1 5,000 2 550 million 3 103 4 clothes 5 March 1994
6 Tuesday 7 first/1st 8 adverts/advertisements/ads
9 8/eight 10 45 minutes

Recording script

Presenter: Today on the food programme I'm going to be telling you about two interesting websites which give you information about two very important foods – rice and noodles. First of all, let's look at the Pagewise website. This site will tell you all about the history of rice, about the rice harvest, the different types of rice, how to cook it and what else you can do with it. For example, did you know that rice belongs to the grass family and was first grown about 5,000 years ago in India? It was introduced into Europe about 700 years ago and arrived in the USA in 1726. Nowadays, more than 550 million tonnes is produced around the world each year, 92% of that being produced in Asia.

Rice is the staple food for the majority of the world's population – that is, far more meals are based on rice than on anything else. It is naturally fat and sodium free and one serving has only 103 calories – so it's very good for you. Interestingly, although rice isn't as rich in vitamin C as the potato, for example – it is less fattening. Now I always find rice difficult to cook, but the best way, apparently, is to keep the lid on the pan when you boil it – this will keep the steam in and produce perfect rice every time. One interesting thing to note is that European and American rice, which is grown in dry fields, absorbs a lot more water than Asian rice, which is grown in flooded fields. Now, other things you can do with rice besides eat it – you can make drinks from it, glue to stick paper together with, and also – <u>you can make clothes from it</u>!

Moving on now to the Japanese Food page. There you can find out about the history of the noodle at the Yokohama Noodle Museum site. Noodles can be made from rice or wheat and are the fast food of Japan. There are more noodle shops in Japan than any other kind of restaurant. According to this website, noodles make one of the quickest and least expensive meals – much quicker than a rice dish, for example.

The museum, <u>which opened in March 1994,</u> sounds like it's well worth a visit if you go to Japan. It's more than just an ordinary museum – it's part theme park and part restaurant. And it stays open later than most museums – from 11.00 a.m. to 11.00 p.m., with the last admission being 10.00 p.m. The museum is <u>open every day except for Tuesday,</u> with Sunday being the busiest day and Thursday being the least busy.

<u>The first floor of the museum</u> has a souvenir shop and you can buy noodle-related objects online as well. It sells bowls for eating noodles out of, equipment for making noodles – even curtains with pictures of noodles on them! There are empty noodle packets on the walls for decoration, and <u>overhead</u> <u>TVs show adverts</u> for noodles from the past 25 years. You can see a display showing how noodles are made and also one giving the history of the noodle.

On two underground levels there is a historical theme park with shops, houses and restaurants from the year 1958. <u>There are also eight different noodle shops</u> serving ten different types of noodle. If you want to go, you can get there by train. The museum is only a three-minute walk from JR Shin-Yokohama railway station. <u>Shin-Yokohama is about 45 minutes from Tokyo.</u>

On the programme next week …

3   Look at the menu and check you understand the vocabulary items. Use an English–English dictionary to help you. Then listen to the conversation and think about which words are stressed.

Answers
Content words such as nouns and main verbs are stressed. Grammatical words, such as prepositions, articles, pronouns and modal or auxiliary verbs are usually not stressed.

---

4   Sometimes it is necessary to stress the short words. Usually this happens when the word

- ends a sequence of words – *How much is it?*
- contrasts with another word – *I sent it to her, not him.*

Listen to the example so you can hear the second stressed *and*. Then look at the conversations 1–4 and say whether the underlined words are weak or strong. Listen to the recording to check your answers.

Answers and recording script
Listen to the example: I ordered raspberries and cream <u>and</u> ice cream.
Now do the exercise.
1   A: <u>Do</u> you like chocolate? *weak*
     B: Yes, I <u>do</u>. *strong*
2   A: Where's <u>the</u> waiter? *weak*
     B: <u>That's</u> him, by the bar. *strong*
3   A: What <u>do you</u> want with the raspberries, cream or ice cream? *weak*
     B: I'd like cream <u>and</u> ice cream – they're lovely together! *strong*
4   A: I'm eating <u>at the</u> Savoy Hotel tonight. *weak*
     B: Not <u>the</u> Savoy Hotel in London? *strong*

5

Answers
1 rotten   2 spicy   3 ripe   4 sour   5 stale   6 bland
7 burnt   8 fresh

---

6   Refer to the Useful language box. This will enable you to vary your responses to the questions.

Possible answers
1   I really like noodles and any type of fish.
2   I can't stand meat – I'm a vegetarian.
3   Well, to start with, I'm very keen on melon or prawns. Then, for the main course I like steak and salad. For dessert, I like any type of fruit or cheese.
4   I like to go out to eat on special occasions. I like French and Italian food.
5   I can only cook pasta, but I'm really good at making lasagne.

2.2 pages 16–17

1   You should make sure that you really understand how to compare and contrast, as you will have to do this fairly often in the IELTS Test, especially in the Speaking and Writing Modules.

Answers
1 -er   2 i   3 -er   4 more   5 -est   6 i   7 -est
8 (the) most   9 as   10 than   11 (the) least

2

Answers
1 the best   2 worse   3 the most expensive   4 easiest
5 sweeter   6 cheaper   7 nicer   8 healthier
9 not as expensive   10 the least expensive

---

3   Refer to the box containing information about adverbs of degree. You should look at the chart which compares the consumption of rice, sugar and tea in five different countries. Read through the examples about rice and then write down six sentences about both sugar and tea.

> **Possible answers**
> India consumes by far the most sugar.
> China consumes nearly as much sugar as Brazil.
> Japan consumes the least sugar.
> Brazil consumes considerably / a lot / much / a good deal more sugar than Indonesia.
> Brazil consumes slightly / a little / a bit more sugar than China.
> India consumes the most tea.
> Japan consumes by far the least tea.
> Japan consumes considerably/far/much less tea than China (does).
> India consumes considerably / a good deal / a great deal / a lot / much more tea than Japan (does).

4   Check that you understand the difference between the formal and informal examples. Refer to the Writing extra box, which gives more information on writing academic English.

5   The exercise gives examples from the *Cambridge Learner Corpus* of inappropriate language.

> **Answers**
> 1   Some people **become angry** when they find that they do not have enough water to grow their crops.
> 2   **Children** are the ones who suffer most during food shortages.
> 3   Many children eat junk food **because** they see their **friends** buying it.
> 4   The **manager** of the supermarket told us to put the **goods** on the shelves.
> 5   There were some **men** planting rice in the field.
> 6   Men eat **a great deal** more meat than **women**. (*A lot more* is also acceptable, but *a great deal more* is more appropriate in a formal report, for example.)
> 7   **Regarding** the food you ordered for your party, could you please confirm the date on which it is required?
> 8   Many **people** in the world do not have enough to eat.

6   Refer to the Test spot and Useful language box.

> **Possible answers**
> 1   I think that factory farming should be banned, because it is cruel and unnatural. I always try to buy organic food, even if it is sometimes more expensive.
> 2   In my opinion, all children should be taught to cook at school. The second point I'd like to make is that, if children learned what a healthy diet is at school, then there wouldn't be as much obesity as there is now.
> 3   I believe that fast food plays too great a role in my country. Let me explain. Fifty years ago, everyone used to sit down as a family to eat dinner. Nowadays, they prefer to sit in front of the TV, eating a hamburger.

Writing folder 1
pages 18–19

Refer to the Advice box and check you understand the information. It gives useful advice on how to approach the task.

1   It is important that any answer to a Task 1 question begins with a summary sentence. This should never be copied from the question on the Test paper, but should still give the main details of what the diagram or table shows. One way of doing this is to paraphrase the question.

Read through summary sentences **a**, **b** and **c** and then look carefully at the diagram. Check you understand the vocabulary.

> **Answer**
> a

2   You will receive more marks in the test if you make appropriate use of sequencing words and also make sure the information you give is in the right sequence.

> **Answers**
> The correct order is
> **c**   First of all
> **a**   then
> **f**   Next
> **g**
> **e**
> **b**   After
> **d**   Finally

3   Both the present simple active and passive are used in this description. The present simple is used to describe a process.
See the underlined verbs in the suggested answer to exercise 4 below (**bold** = active; *italic* = passive).

4   Paragraphing is very important in both Task 1 and Task 2 and you should do a plan before you start writing your answer.

> **Suggested answer**
> The diagram **shows** the human digestive process.
>
> First of all, food in the mouth *is broken down* by the process of chewing with the back teeth and then by the action of enzymes. The resulting mass *is* then *swallowed* and *is passed* through the throat into the oesophagus. The oesophagus **is** a long tube which **connects** the throat with the stomach. It **uses** muscle action to send the food mass to the stomach.
>
> Next, the food mass **mixes** in the stomach with gastric acid, which **breaks down** the food further and helps digestion. From the stomach, the partly digested food **goes** into the small intestine. Here it *is mixed* with a chemical called bile, which *is produced* in the liver.
>
> After passing through the small intestine, the food **enters** the large intestine, where water *is removed* and there **are** bacteria to help in the digestion process. Finally, waste material *is excreted*.

5 Look at the diagram, which shows how chocolate is made, and check that you understand the vocabulary.

6

> **Sample answer**
>
> The diagram shows the stages in the process of making chocolate.
>
> Chocolate comes from the cacao tree, which is grown in parts of South America, Africa and Indonesia. The tree produces large red pods which contain white cocoa beans. Firstly, when the pods are ripe, they are harvested, the beans are removed and they are fermented for several days in large wooden boxes. During the fermenting process, the beans turn brown.
>
> Next, the brown beans are spread in the sun to dry. They are then put in large sacks and transported by train or lorry. After this, the beans are taken to a chocolate factory where they are roasted in an oven at temperatures of between 250 and 350 degrees Celsius.
>
> After being roasted, the beans are crushed and the outer shell is removed. This part is not needed for making chocolate. Finally, the inner part of the bean is pressed and liquid chocolate is produced.
>
> (156 words)

Unit 3

3.1 pages 20–21

1 Think about answers to the questions. They are similar to questions in Part 1 of the Speaking Module.

2 This will help you to pick out important points from the passage.

> **Possible answers**
> **Edinburgh Castle** appeals to people who are interested in history. It's also a good place to go if you want to see the whole city.
> **Our Dynamic Earth** attracts people who want to learn about the planet.
> **The Forth Railway Bridge** is an unusual engineering structure, so it particularly appeals to engineers.
> **Deep Sea World** is a good place to go if you want to see sharks, piranhas and other fish face to face. And if you're in good health, you can go scuba diving among the sharks!

3 This type of matching task (matching information to part of a passage) is used in GT Reading, and is similar to matching in Academic Reading. The statements normally *paraphrase* the passage.

> **Answers** (evidence from the passage is given, but this is not part of the answer)
> 1 C *This was very time-consuming. The solution was to construct the Forth Railway Bridge*
> 2 B *a striking, purpose-built tented structure*
> 3 D *You must be at least 16*
> 4 C *It was opened in 1890, and has been in continuous use ever since.*

> 5 A *The Military Tattoo ... takes place at Edinburgh Castle every August*
> 6 D *we can help the children in your class to improve their scientific skills*
> 7 B *explores the extremes of our planet Earth*

4 It is often necessary to explain cause, purpose or result, both in academic and everyday English. Note that purpose is the hoped-for outcome of an action. It may not actually happen. If you have problems, refer to the Grammar folder on page 138.

> **Answers**
> 1 d 2 b 3 f 4 g 5 c 6 e

5 Working out the rules will help you to remember them. Then you can use them in future, to make your English more accurate.

> **Answers**
> 1 *Because of* is used to introduce a cause. It is followed by a noun phrase.
> 2 *So that* is used to introduce a purpose. It is followed by a clause.

6 Again, you should work out the rules.

> **Answers**
> 1 *So* gives the purpose, or intention. *So that* is also possible.
> 2 *So* gives the result, the actual outcome of the situation. It may not have been intended. *So that* isn't possible.
> 3 purpose (*so that* is possible)
> 4 result (*so that* isn't possible)
> 5 either purpose or result
> 6 result (*so that* isn't possible)
> 7 either purpose or result
> (The picture shows an exhibit at Our Dynamic Earth.)

7

> **Possible answers**
> Living in a city is good for young people because of the wide range of facilities. However, it can be bad because of the pollution.
> A lot of people move to cities so that they can get a well-paid job.
> Cities can be exciting because there is so much to do.

3.2 pages 22–23

1 The subjects of the pictures are talked about in the recording.

> **Answers**
> top left: Sydney Opera House and Sydney Harbour Bridge
> bottom left: a dragon boat
> right: the Rocks area of Sydney

2   The notes follow the order of the passage, and words must be spelt correctly. You mustn't write more than the maximum number of words – three in this case.

(NB: Robin is a girl's name in Australia and the USA, and a boy's name in the UK.)

> **What kind of information is needed**
> 1   noun phrase: a building, structure or area (e.g. *road, harbour*)
> 2   noun phrase: a building, structure or area (e.g. *tower*)
> 3   noun phrase: a period of time (e.g. *two hours*)
> 4   noun phrase: an area that could be part of the Opera House (e.g. *reception area, car park*)
> 5   adjective, possibly a superlative, or noun used adjectivally (e.g. *most popular, tourist, business*)
> 6   noun phrases: things in a district (e.g. *shops, cinemas*)
> 7   number (e.g. *500*)
> 8   noun phrases: activities (e.g. *swimming, music*)

> **Answers** (relevant parts of the recording script are underlined)
> 1   bridge   2   observation area   3   an/1/one hour
> 4   Guided-Tours office / Guided Tours office   5   oldest
> 6   cafés/cafes; restaurants (*in either order*)
> 7   2000/2,000   8   drums; dancing (*in either order*)

Recording script

Robin: Hello?

Jerry: Hi Robin, it's Jerry.

Robin: Jerry! Nice to hear from you. How're you doing?

Jerry: Fine, thanks. Guess what? I'm going on holiday to Australia next month!

Robin: Wow, that's great!

Jerry: I thought you might be able to give me some ideas about what to do while I'm in Sydney. That's where you come from, isn't it?

Robin: That's right. And I wish I was there now, instead of here in the cold.

Jerry: What's the temperature likely to be there?

Robin: Oh, next month it'll be around <u>25</u> degrees. If you went during the British summer, and the Australian winter, it would only be about 16 degrees.

Jerry: I'm looking forward to some warm weather.

Robin: So how long are you staying in Sydney?

Jerry: Only a couple of days. I'm going to spend a month touring Australia.

Robin: Sounds good. Well, you'll need at least a morning exploring the harbour area – it's fascinating. I really like the Pylon Lookout: <u>the entrance is on the bridge</u>. It's got an interesting display on how the bridge was built, and <u>the panorama of the harbour from the observation area is spectacular</u>.

Jerry: Right, I'll do that.

Robin: And of course you can see the Opera House – that and the bridge are Sydney's most famous sights.

Jerry: Do you know if there are any tours of the Opera House?

Robin: Yes, there are. As far as I remember there's one every 30 minutes, and <u>you spend around an hour</u> exploring different parts of the building, depending which tour it is.

Jerry: Uh-huh. Do I need to book tickets in advance?

Robin: No, <u>just buy them at the Opera House, from the Guided-Tours office</u>. You'll see the signs to point you in the right direction.

Jerry: Right, I'll do that. It'll be interesting to find out how the Opera House is run.

Robin: Then I reckon you should walk around the Rocks. <u>It's the oldest part of the city</u>, and always crowded with tourists of all nationalities, as well as local people. <u>The cafés and restaurants keep very busy</u>. Whenever I go back to Sydney I enjoy sitting outdoors with a cup of coffee, watching the people passing by.

Jerry: Yes, that sounds like a good idea.

Robin: Oh, and I almost forgot – it's the Dragon Festival next month. You should arrange to be in Sydney that weekend. You'll have a great time.

Jerry: What is it?

Robin: You don't know the Dragon Festival? It's to celebrate the Chinese New Year. There are races between lots of traditional wooden boats, decorated with dragons' heads and tails. Each boat has something like 20 people rowing it, and <u>over 2,000 people take part</u> altogether.

Jerry: Mm.

Robin: Crowds of people go to watch. <u>The opening ceremony is pretty exciting, too, with drums and dancing</u>. Why don't you check the dates on the Internet?

Jerry: I will. It sounds great. Well thanks for the suggestions, Robin. I'm looking forward to my holiday.

Robin: Have a good trip, and call me when you get back to the UK. Bye.

Jerry: Bye.

3   This exercise focuses on adjectives that you can use to describe buildings, towns and events.

> **Answers**
> 1   massive   2   thrilling   3   striking   4   spectacular
> 5   famous   6   beautiful   7   fascinating   8   terrifying
>
> The word from the box that isn't used is *crowded*, as in *The beach was so crowded there was nowhere to sit.*

4   This exercise focuses on adjectives that are related to verbs. Make sure you understand the difference in meaning between the *-ing* adjectives and the *-ed* adjectives. Make sure you spell the words correctly.

> **Answers**
> 1   amazed   2   astonishing   3   exciting   4   fascinating
> 5   frightened   6   interesting   7   surprising   8   terrified
> 9   thrilled

5   This will help you to check that you have understood the difference between the two adjective endings.

> **Answers**
> 1   fascinating   2   interesting   3   astonished   4   fascinated
> 5   interested   6   amazing

6 This will give you practice in talking about places and using adjectives to describe them.

> **Possible answers**
> 1 I think Sydney is a very exciting city, because there are people from all over the world.
> 2 Some visitors to Shanghai are amazed that there are so many tall buildings.
> 3 It's surprising that Oslo doesn't have more visitors in the winter, because it has lots of indoor activities.
> 4 Most people who visit Cape Town for the first time are thrilled when they see Table Mountain.
> 5 It's astonishing that Cairo is so crowded.

7 It is very important to stress words in the right place, as it can be very difficult to recognise words that are stressed wrongly. **NB** Every syllable must have a vowel sound; consonants are less important, so *Au'stralia*, *Aus'tralia*, *Aust'ralia* and *Austr'alia* are all acceptable.

> **Recording script and answers**
> 1 in'form   in.for'ma.tion
> 2 ob'serve   ob.ser'va.tion
> 3 solve   so'lu.tion
> 4 'ac.tive   ac'ti.vi.ty
> 5 'lo.cal   lo'ca.li.ty
> 6 'na.tion   na.tion'al.i.ty
> 7 a'ca.demy   a.ca'de.mic
> 8 'sci.ence   sci.en'ti.fic

8 Working out this rule will help you to put the stress in the right place in a large number of words.

> **Answer**
> When a word ends in *-tion, -ity* or *-ic,* the stressed syllable is always the one immediately before that ending.
> Some other examples:
> ex'plain – expla'nation   ob'jective – objec'tivity
> 'curious – curi'osity   'allergy – a'llergic

9 When pronunciation is shown, each symbol always represents the same sound. If you use the symbols in a dictionary, it will help you to pronounce words correctly.

> **Answers**
> 1 famous   2 attractive   3 striking   4 historical
> 5 beautiful   6 magnificent

Look up new words in an English–English dictionary that shows pronunciation and stress (e.g. *Cambridge Advanced Learner's Dictionary*). It's useful to write new words in a notebook, marking stress, and saying the word aloud a few times, to help you remember it.

Test folder 2

pages 24–25

Make sure you understand the information and advice.

1 The picture shows Manhattan, New York.

> **Answers** (relevant parts of the recording script are underlined)
> 1 E   2 F   3 H   4 D   5 J

Recording script

You will hear the leader of a study programme about New York City talking to the participants. First you have some time to look at questions 1 to 5. (pause)

Now listen carefully and answer questions 1 to 5.

Leader: Well, good morning, ladies and gentlemen, and welcome to New York City and our study programme about the city. I know that for some of you, this is your very first visit to the United States, so I'd particularly like to welcome you, and say I just know you're gonna have a great time. First, let me outline this week's programme of activities.

Tomorrow morning, Monday, we'll take the Circle Line cruise along the Hudson, East and Harlem rivers, so you can orientate yourselves. It's a fantastic way to see Manhattan Island, the heart of New York, and to bring the map to life. The cruise lasts three hours, and along the way you'll see some of the famous and most impressive sites of the city, like the Statue of Liberty, Battery Park and Brooklyn Bridge.

Then on Tuesday, I want to give you some insight into New York City's fascinating history, created by the millions of immigrants who have come here by sea or by land from all corners of the world, in the hope of finding a better life. But many of them arrived only to live in poverty and terrible, crowded conditions. We'll visit the Lower East Side Tenement Museum, located in a building where 7,000 people were resident between 1863 and 1935, with large families crammed into one- or two-room apartments.

On Wednesday morning we'll go to Grand Central Terminal for a tour of the very impressive station, and a speaker will tell us how New York City's mass transit system has developed, including its subways, railroads, buses and ferries. Over 150,000 people commute to Grand Central daily from their homes outside the city, and the subway system alone carries over seven million passengers each day.

And that takes us to Thursday. I'm sure many of you will visit the city's major museums and art galleries, like the Metropolitan Museum of Art, with its hundreds of world-famous masterpieces. But you need to take your own time in places like those, so instead, I'll show you something rather different, a small but very interesting museum dedicated to the fairgrounds of Coney Island, where millions of New Yorkers used to go for a day out, to enjoy rides like the Cyclone Rollercoaster, the Wonder Wheel and the Parachute Jump.

Friday's outing is to somewhere you might not expect to find within the limits of New York City – an area in and around Jamaica Bay that's been set aside as a refuge for a wide range of <u>birds, butterflies, reptiles and rare flowers</u>. Its <u>habitats</u> include <u>salt marsh, fields and woods, several ponds and an open expanse of bay and islands</u>. Although it's close to JFK Airport, this is a good place to escape from the crowds and noise of the city.

OK, now the next thing we need to do …

2

> **Answers** (evidence from the passage is given, but this is not part of the answer)
> 1 B *streets with familiar names like Savile Row, famous for its men's suits*
> 2 A *listen as we recite parts of his novels*
> 3 D *the former power generating station has been transformed into Tate Modern art gallery*
> 4 C *the original termination of the New River, constructed to bring water to London*
> 5 E *buildings, some of which can only be visited by special arrangement*
> 6 D *Borough Market, where you'll find it hard to choose among all the fine food and other goods on sale.*
> 7 B *Mayfair has been the most upmarket district in London*
> 8 D *the new Globe, a replica of Shakespeare's theatre*
> 9 E *you'll discover how Stinking Lane and Turnagain Lane got their names*

Unit 4

4.1 pages 26–27

1   The pictures show a young woman being taught by her mother at home and a class of students in a school or college. Talking about different ways of studying will help you to understand the recording, and will also help you to speak in the test. Try to give reasons for your answers. If you don't have an opinion, talk about possibilities, for example *Maybe it's better to study in a class because you can help each other.*

> **Possible answers**
> *Possible advantages of one-to-one lessons:* having the teacher's attention all the time, studying at a speed that suits you, having to think for yourself.
>
> *Possible disadvantages:* not being able to learn from other students, not having the possibility of developing ideas together, not having a chance to relax

2   This recording is fairly similar to Section 3 of the Listening Module. *Morag* is a traditional Scottish girl's name.

> **Answers** (relevant parts of the recording script are underlined)
> 1 C   2 A   3 B   4 A
> 5 B, D, E (*in any order*) NB: Here there is only one mark for all three answers. When there is one mark for each answer, each question is numbered separately.
> 6 B, E (*in either order*)

Recording script

Example

Interviewer: Good morning. Now in this programme we've been looking at different forms of education for children up to the age of 16. And this week, I've invited Morag to come and tell us what it's like having lessons at home. Morag, have you ever been to school?

Morag: Oh yes, I started at infants' school when I was four, and when I turned seven, I went on to junior school. <u>I left when I was eight</u>, and my mother's been teaching me at home ever since – she's a qualified teacher.

Questions 1–4

Interviewer: Why did you leave?

Morag: Well, my family moved to a remote island in Scotland, and <u>there wasn't a school nearby</u>. My parents thought I was quick at learning, and could cope with being taught at home instead – the alternative was to live away from home. I enjoyed school, so at first I was quite unhappy about leaving, and I missed my friends. But now I prefer it.

Interviewer: Is there anything you don't like about having lessons at home?

Morag: Most of the time it's great. We start around 9 o'clock, five days a week, and work for about six hours a day, which I enjoy. The only difficulty is that <u>I'm the centre of attention – if I feel bored, or don't understand something, I can't hide it, as I'm the only student!</u> Some people think I must be lonely, but I enjoy doing things on my own, and anyway I spend most weekends with other people.

Interviewer: Do you work with your mother all day long?

Morag: No, I do a lot of projects on particular topics, and after we've planned one, I do most of the work on my own. So I sometimes spend quite a long time finding information on the Internet, or in books. At the moment, I'm doing research into the island where we live. I've talked to a lot of the people who live there, and that was very interesting. <u>I really learn a lot from projects</u>, because you have to look at the topic from different angles, and try to make sense of it all.

Interviewer: What do you think is the hardest part of doing projects?

Morag: Mmm, the first stage isn't too difficult. That's when my mother and I talk about what exactly the project should cover. With the one about the island, we decided that I should focus on what jobs were available and why. Then I have to search for material, which is why I use the Internet a lot. Though with most projects, I also interview people or do experiments. <u>After that I have to write a report on what I've found out and I find that quite hard.</u>

Questions 5 and 6

Interviewer: Apart from working on projects, what subjects do you study?

Morag: Well, there's history – I'm not very keen on that, though – it seems to be mostly about fighting. Um, <u>geography's much more fun</u>, because you learn about the world and how things like mountains or the climate affect the way we live. And I know English is necessary, but I don't really look forward to the lessons. Then there's <u>biology, which is one of my favourite subjects. Um, I didn't like economics at first, but after a while I really took to it.</u> We're going to start Spanish soon, but I don't know how much I'll enjoy that – I find the pronunciation of foreign languages quite difficult, and I can't seem to remember the vocabulary!

Interviewer: And what about when you finish your education? Have you thought much about that?

Morag: I haven't really made up my mind yet. I used to want to be a tennis player, but I'm not good enough to be professional, so I'll go on playing just for pleasure. I think photography is fascinating, because there are so many things you can do when you take photographs. So, I might go into film-making – I'd like to do something creative. My father wants me to become a musician, like him, but it really doesn't appeal to me. And of course my mother's a teacher, though I think one in the family is enough! I'm thinking seriously about becoming a doctor, even though it would mean a lot of studying.

Interviewer: OK, well, good luck ...

3 Here you should give your own opinion.

4 Exercises 4 and 5 will help you with reading in the test. They will also help you to read more effectively – both in English and in your own language.

Possible answers

1 Yes: *why* you're reading affects *how* you read it.
2 No: if you're looking for specific information, such as the time that a TV programme starts, you can stop reading as soon as you've found it.
3 Yes: the title may indicate whether the text contains the information you want.
4 Maybe, depending on what the topic is, why you're reading about it, and who you ask. It's likely to be more useful *after* you've read a text, though.
5 No: the main information is much more likely to come near the beginning of each paragraph.
6 No: if you need to remember important parts of the text, it's more effective to summarise them in your own words.

---

5 This is similar to a True/False task.

Answers

1 ✓ (lines 3–4) 2 ✗ 3 ✓ (line 12) 4 ✗ 5 ✗ 6 ✗

---

6 When you're learning words, try and find out if they are mostly used in formal or informal language. In the Academic Writing Module, and Part 2 of the GT Writing Module, you need to write in a more formal style.

Answers

1 comprehension (title)
2 purpose (line 4)
3 method (line 5)
4 specific (line 6)
5 relevant (lines 8, 17)
6 title (line 12)
7 relates (line 21)

---

7 Using words is the best way to remember them!

Answers

1 method 2 title 3 specific 4 purpose
5 comprehension

---

8 This will help you to develop your answers in the Speaking Module.

Possible answers

- It's usually easier to learn effectively in a group of four or five than in a group of 40 or 50.
- Some teachers are good at motivating students. Some know a lot about their subject, but can't explain it clearly.
- Lessons are more interesting if the activities are varied.
- Equipment like CD players and language labs can be helpful, because they add to the variety of activities.
- Explaining something to someone who knows less than you can help you to understand better.

4.2 pages 28–29

The picture shows a young woman studying in a park.

1 Thinking about answers to these questions will help you with Part 1 of the Speaking Module.

2 Verb tenses are complicated in English, but it is important to use them correctly, because they express a lot of meaning. If you have difficulty, refer to the Grammar folder on page 139.

Answers

1 b 2 a (*'m doing*); c (*live*) 3 b 4 c 5 a 6 c
a present continuous b present simple
c present simple

Remember how these tenses are formed:

- Present simple: one word only, the same as the form used in dictionaries (except *to be*), but the third person singular ends in *-s*.
- Present continuous: present simple of *to be* + present participle (*-ing* form) of main verb.

The present continuous has specific meanings, and is used less than the present simple.

3 This will help you to use what you have practised in exercise 2.

Answers

1 are studying (a)
2 understand (c)
3 am having (a)
4 do you work (b)
5 is thinking (a)
6 think (c)
7 never spend (b)

---

4 This will help you to apply the information in the tinted boxes.

Answers

1 How much time I spend doing homework **depends** on what else I want to do. (relationship verb)
2 Please stop talking – I**'m listening** to the teacher. ((a) in excercise 2)
3 Most people **feel** tired when they've worked hard all day. ((c) in excercise 2)
4 This week we**'re having** lessons in the library because our classroom is being decorated. ((a) in excercise 2)

---

5 This will help you to know when to use the present perfect tense. Remember how the present perfect is formed: present tense of *to have* + past participle of the main verb.

Answers
1 a 2 c 3 b 4 b 5 c 6 a

6 The present perfect continuous generally emphasises a *length* of time. Remember how it is formed: present perfect tense of *to be* + present participle (*-ing* form) of the main verb.

Answers
1 b 2 a 3 b 4 a

7 Here you practise using the two present perfect tenses.

8 In words of two or more syllables, it's important to stress the correct one – otherwise people may have difficulty understanding. The sentences are from the recording.

Answers
1 pre.'fer 2 'di.ffi.cul.ty 3 re.'port 4 'stu.dy
5 par.'ti.cu.lar 6 'cli.mate 7 pro.nun.ci.'a.tion
8 vo.'ca.bu.la.ry 9 pho.'to.gra.phy 10 'pho.to.graphs

9 The most useful stress patterns to remember are these:
   a words with certain suffixes always have the stress immediately before the suffix (pattern 1)
   b two-syllable words generally stress the first syllable (pattern 3)
   c longer words generally have two unstressed syllables after the stressed one (pattern 4)

Answers
(You should mark the stress, but you don't have to divide the syllables.)
1 pro.nun.ci.'a.tion, pho.'to.gra.phy (also e.du.'ca.tion)
2 pre.'fer, re.'port
3 'stu.dy, 'cli.mate
4 par.'ti.cu.lar, 'pho.to.graphs
5 'di.ffi.cul.ty, vo.'ca.bu.la.ry

Writing folder 2
pages 30–31

Read the Advice box.

1 Line graphs compare two variables. Each variable is plotted along an axis. A line graph has a vertical axis (y) and a horizontal axis (x). Line graphs are good at showing
   • specific values of data
   • trends in data.

Answer
b This is both more informative and a more precise summary.

2

Answers
1 slight fluctuation
2 gradual/steady rise/increase
3 sharp/steep fall/decline
4 gradual/steady fall/decline
5 went up / rose / increased sharply/steeply
6 reached a peak
7 remained/held steady *or* was stable *or* remained constant *or* levelled off
8 reached a peak
9 fell/decreased/declined steeply/sharply
10 went up / rose / increased slightly/gradually

3 Each question has a clue as to the type of word(s) needed.

Answers
1 between 2 From 3 increase/rise 4 had risen to
5 fall/decrease/decline 6 rose gradually/steadily
7 sharp/steep/dramatic rise/increase
8 rise/increase 9 rise

Units 1–4 Revision
pages 32–33

The aim of this revision unit is to focus on the language covered in Units 1–4.

1 You can practise this section by recording your answers and listening to see whether you have made mistakes or used the same structures and vocabulary instead of trying to vary the words you use.

2

Answers
1 originated 2 have been found 3 was always made
4 blew 5 made 6 became 7 was praised
8 were forbidden 9 gave 10 are usually made
11 are mixed 12 is heated 13 melts 14 becomes
15 is removed 16 is blown

3

Answers
1 have been living / have lived 2 believes 3 *correct*
4 *correct* 5 never understands 6 has been waiting
7 I've been / I went 8 *correct*
9 I've known 10 freezes 11 has known
12 are you doing; I'm reading 13 *correct* 14 *correct*

4 The photograph is of high-rise buildings in Hong Kong.

Possible answers
1 Las Vegas has a smaller number of high-rise buildings than Osaka, even though it has a slightly larger area.
2 São Paolo has the largest population of the seven cities.
3 Beijing has a much larger area than Durban.
4 Las Vegas has the smallest population.
5 Although New York has a smaller area than Hong Kong, it has fewer high-rise buildings.
6 Osaka has nearly the same area as Las Vegas.

5

Answers
1 of   2 on   3 on   4 on; by   5 at   6 to   7 at   8 on

6

Answers
1 boring   2 surprised   3 exciting   4 astonished
5 interesting

7

Answers
1 crowded – all the others are positive adjectives
2 spectacular – all the others are negative feelings
3 fresh – all the others are negative ways of describing food
4 spicy – all the others are negative ways of describing food

Unit 5

5.1 pages 34–35

1

Answers
1	B	The Great Wall, China	a system of defence
2	A	The Moai, Easter Island	sculptures
3	D	The Parthenon, Greece	a temple
4	C	The Pyramids, Egypt	tombs or burial chambers

2 The article gives background information on the Moai. Scan the text to find the answers to questions 1 and 2. It is important that you do not worry about the five missing words or any words you are unsure of. Try not to use a dictionary at this stage. You should take about three minutes to read the article.

Answers
1 In the Pacific Ocean between Chile and Tahiti.
2 They were built by the Rapa Nui people for religious reasons.

3 Match the words with their meanings. These words are all nouns and are quite specialised. If you find this exercise difficult, use a dictionary.

Answers
a 5 b 3 c 4 d 1 e 2

Now try to find where the words go in the text.

Answers
1 e extinct   2 c remains   3 d field   4 b sites
5 a clan

4 Refer to the Test spot. Up to now, there have been reading passages with only one task type. The passage in this unit has three different types of task and as a result is similar to one of the reading passages you will meet in the actual test. Work through the questions. Avoid using a dictionary, as one will not be allowed in the test.

Answers (evidence from the passage is given, but this is not part of the answer)
1	TRUE	He co-ordinated a team of experts (line 16)
2	FALSE	Scientists once believed … in the 5th century. (lines 21–25)
3	NOT GIVEN	We know that the number and size of the Moai varied from clan to clan, but not the burial chambers themselves.
4	NOT GIVEN	There is no mention of how long the Moai took to build.
5	TRUE	The building of Moai … until the 16th century. (lines 53–54)
6	FALSE	they weren't spending … were hunted to extinction (lines 59–60)

7 A (line 25) and E (line 67)
8 (Rano Raraku) volcano (lines 44–45)
9 33m (tall) (line 45)
10 rollers (line 61)

5 The collocations in this exercise are all common in academic English. 'Collocations' are words which are often found together. There are many collocations, and being aware of which words go together will enable you to show the examiner that you have a wide range of vocabulary, which will gain you higher marks. In this exercise you need to decide which verb *can't* be used with the specified noun.

Answers
1 to get   2 to find   3 to do   4 to make

6 The aim of this exercise is to make you aware that you have to expand your answers during the Speaking Module.

Answers
a Too short and doesn't show the examiner what the candidate knows
b A good answer, relevant and showing a range of language
c An expanded answer, but fails to answer the question and includes irrelevancy

Possible answers

1 Personally, I think that it is a subject that really needs a teacher who is imaginative and has a real interest in history. Let me give you an example of how *not* to teach history – if a teacher just reads out a list of dates, then it can become very boring and the class will be totally unmotivated.

2 For one thing, a teacher could take you to places of historical interest and really make you understand what was happening at the time. For another, he or she could show you films of famous people or battles to make the subject more alive.

3 Yes, there are so many periods of history that are interesting – for example, the Egyptian civilisation or the Romans; the Ming dynasty in China or the history of the Ottoman Empire. I think I would choose to study more modern history – American Independence for example.

5.2 pages 36–37

1

Answers
PS – **c** – 1 (*invited*), 2 (*believed*), 4 (*found*)
PC – **a** – 3 (*were building, weren't spending*), 4 (*were carrying out*)
PPS – **b** – 2 (*had come*), 4 (*had occurred*)

2

Answers
1 When did the Berlin Wall fall? It fell in 1989.
2 When did the Pharaohs build the Pyramids? They built the Pyramids around 2600 BC.
3 When did cavemen do the wall paintings at Lascaux? They did the wall paintings at Lascaux approximately 15,000 years ago.
4 When did Mao Zedong govern China? He governed China from 1949 to 1976.
5 When did the USA become independent? It became independent in the late 1700s.

3

Answers
1 was digging; I saw   2 was giving; went off
3 were looking; heard   4 dropped; was putting

4

Answers
1 The people had built large sculptures called Moai.
2 They had used volcanic rock to build them.
3 They had carved pictures on some of the Moai.
4 They had cut down the forest.
5 They had stopped fishing.

---

5 Sometimes it is not necessary to use the past perfect unless you want to emphasise the fact that an event actually happened before another event. If this isn't the case, and the narrative is simply about something that happened in the past, the past simple is used.

Answers
1 was working   2 discovered   3 contained   4 had spent
5 hadn't /had not had   6 was   7 began / had begun
8 were digging   9 found / had found   10 led / had led
11 had broken into   12 were

7 Look at the task for this exercise. You are going to listen to a guide talking about a museum and describing where things are in the museum. Make sure you understand *right* and *left, middle, back, opposite*, etc. You should write the letter(s) next to questions 1–5. You should try to get used to hearing the recording only once, as in the test.

Answers
1 AA   2 L   3 B   4 ER   5 GS

Recording script

Guide: Good morning, ladies and gentlemen. Now, before I tell you a little bit about the history of the museum, let's make sure you can find your way around. There are three floors to the museum, and we have a lot of very interesting things for you to see. You are now standing in the hall after entering through the Main Entrance.

I know you are all particularly interested in <u>Australian art, and you'll find examples of this if you go up the steps in front of you and go through the door immediately on your left.</u> There are also other displays of Australian and Native American objects on the second floor – you'll find the <u>lift in the corner of the room off the Australian art gallery.</u>

You may find it useful to go into the <u>bookshop before you begin the tour of the museum. It's here, as you can see, straight ahead of you up the main steps.</u> The cloakroom, and toilets are both in the basement – you can take the stairs next to the main entrance or use the lift.

If you would like to become a member of the museum you can apply at the museum office. Membership is £30 a year, and this entitles you to free entry. The museum office is on this floor, up the steps and to your right. And opposite the museum office, also on your right, is the <u>Egyptian room</u>. There you'll find a selection of mummies and wall paintings – some over 3,000 years old. At present, I'm sorry to tell you there are two galleries which are closed. The first one – <u>to your right between the main steps and the steps to the basement – is our Greek sculpture gallery.</u> The other one, the African paintings gallery, is on the first floor and is undergoing decoration. Both will be re-opening in March. Now, if you'd like to follow me up the main ...

8 This exercise is to give practice in the use of prepositions of location, which is useful for in Task 1 of both AC and GT Writing.

Test folder 3

pages 38–39

Make sure you fully understand the notes and advice.

1 Before listening, read the rubric and questions, and think about what might fit each space.

Answers (relevant parts of the recording script are underlined)
1 capital   2 houses of rock   3 12th/twelfth   4 royal
5 Agriculture   6 Gold   7 trading centre/center   8 salt
9 1600

Recording script

You will hear part of a lecture about the ancient African city of Great Zimbabwe.
First you have some time to look at questions 1 to 9. (pause)
Now listen carefully and answer questions 1 to 9.

Lecturer: One of the most impressive structures of southern Africa is Great Zimbabwe, a ruined city surrounded by a massive stone wall reaching a height of ten metres. This wall and the stone buildings within the city have survived, but unfortunately not the houses of the majority of people, which were of mud. Great Zimbabwe was part of a state which covered much of the interior of south-east Africa, and may well have been the capital. There's disagreement over the precise meaning of the name 'Zimbabwe': one interpretation is 'houses of rock', as this material was used for the most important buildings. Because of the historical significance of the Great Zimbabwe site, the name was adopted by the present country on independence in 1980.

Not very much is known about the people who constructed Great Zimbabwe, as they had no written language, and their oral traditions haven't survived. They were probably Shona-speaking people who moved into the area around the sixth century, and began building the stone walls – using granite quarried from nearby hills – in the twelfth. The walls were followed by the stone structures within them. One of these, the Great Enclosure, is likely to have been a royal residence, and it's the largest ancient structure south of the Sahara.

It's unclear why that particular site was chosen for Great Zimbabwe. Although the grasslands of the area were ideal for cattle grazing, the soil may not have supported agriculture to the extent required to feed so many people. Grain and other staples may have had to be brought in from elsewhere. It used to be thought that the site was chosen for the city because of the gold found in the district, but it now seems that this wasn't exploited until a century after Great Zimbabwe was founded. At least for part of the time that the city existed, its wealth seems to have come from its role as a trading centre. Ivory and, later, gold, were traded through east African ports for cloth and other goods from Arabia and further east. This was probably the main source of Great Zimbabwe's power and wealth.

By the middle of the 15th century, however, the city was in decline. Trade had moved further north. Local resources had apparently been overused, and salt was scarce. Possibly for these reasons, although we may never know for certain, Great Zimbabwe was abandoned by about 1600. At the height of its prosperity, the city was probably home to 18,000 people, perhaps more, but now it simply consists of ruins.

2 Words in boxes usually paraphrase words or phrases in listening and reading passages. A *cross-reference* is a note in a book or other document that tells you to look somewhere else in the same document for more information. A *source document* is a book, letter or other written text that information has been taken from.

Answers (relevant parts of the recording script are underlined)
1 books   2 aim   3 record   4 questions
5 source documents (NB: three sections are underlined)
6 daily life   7 software   8 cross-references   9 society

Recording script

You will hear two friends discussing how to carry out research into family history.
First you have some time to look at questions 1 to 9. (pause)
Now listen carefully and answer questions 1 to 9.

Martin: Jo, you're doing research into your family history, aren't you? Can you give me some advice?

Jo: I'd be glad to. Are you thinking of doing the same?

Martin: Yes, I might. My grandfather has just given me a box of old family photos, and I'd like to find out about the people in them. But I need to know more about how to set about it, before I make up my mind.

Jo: Well, the first thing is to find out more about the different things you could do. It's worth going to the library and reading one or two introductions to the subject. It'll give you an idea of what the possibilities are and what's involved.

Martin: Right.

Jo: Then you should work out what you're trying to get out of it. I mean, do you just want to discover the direct line of your ancestors, or all your relations, for instance. You can't really carry out the research efficiently unless you've decided that.

Martin: Uh-huh.

Jo: Then you should sit down at your computer and get down all the information you already have. Start with yourself, then your parents, then work through all the members of your family that you're interested in. Anything you can think of concerning names, dates, where they lived, and so on. And you need a system to keep track of anything you're not sure of, so you can try and find out later.

Martin: Right.

Jo: Once you've got that far, you should think about all your living relations, and maybe close friends of theirs, and arrange to talk to them. It's a good idea to put down a list of things you want to ask them first, but don't limit yourself to those. Encourage your relatives to talk about the family in a more unstructured way, too. You never know what might come up.

Martin: What about things like, um, birth certificates, photographs, and so on? How useful are they?

Jo: Oh, they're essential. They're the primary evidence that you need. Ask your relations if they've got anything that would be useful. There might be some real treasures tucked away somewhere.

Martin: At the back of a drawer, maybe.

Jo: Right. They can give you a real opening into history, particularly if there are any old letters or diaries. Just a casual mention of visiting Auntie Mary, for example, can tell you about people you hadn't heard of, or where someone lived. I think that what you'll enjoy most is finding out as much as possible about your ancestors – where they lived and worked, how much money they had, how they spent their free time – all that sort of thing. That's much more interesting than simply knowing a person's name and when they were born and died.

Martin: Yeah, I agree. How should I organise all the material, do you think?

Jo: Well, there are special computer programmes available for doing family history. It's easiest if you use one of those. I can give you details of what I used – it was very good.

Martin: Thanks.

Jo: One way it helps is by making it easy to group information together in various ways. For instance, if you've got a file about a person, you need to be able to see that some of the information there also relates to a different file, say about a particular year.

Martin: It must have been hard to keep track of everything in the days before computers.

Jo: Yes. I think I'd have given up pretty soon! And it's worth becoming a member of a family history organisation – I got so many good ideas from the other members, and it was very helpful to be able to talk about what I was doing with people doing the same thing.

Martin: Mm, good idea. OK, well, thanks, Jo. That's given me a lot to think about.

Jo: Let me know how it goes.

Martin: Oh, don't worry – I'll be on the phone asking you for help!

3 This is a difficult passage and task. Remember that questions 1–5 follow the order of the passage.

> **Answers** (evidence from the passage is given, but this is not part of the answer)
> 1 G *the history of a nation (or other group) is a story that gives meaning to the members of that nation living today.* (paragraph 1)
> 2 C *Historians try to combine an understanding of social, economic, political and cultural activity into a general story, explaining how these have affected each other to shape the general course of human events.* (paragraph 2)

> 3 E *the historian must develop a theory ... the more evidence it can satisfactorily account for, the better the theory.* (paragraph 3)
> 4 A *historians largely rely on developing new methods of analysis ... that show the relevance of evidence that was previously ignored.* (paragraph 4)
> 5 F *No historical theory can be proved beyond all doubt, because there is room for interpretation in any human activity.* (paragraph 5)

Unit 6

6.1 pages 40–41

1 The photos are of a man working hard in the office and a woman playing with some paper clips. Look at the photos and describe how you think the people are feeling. Suggested adjectives:

motivated, interested, ambitious, driven, challenged unmotivated, bored, fed up, tired, apathetic, uninterested, unchallenged

Look at the two charts. What conclusions can be drawn from the charts?

> **Suggested answers**
> UK workers are working longer hours than in the past.
> People who work long hours are more likely to do so because they are inspired by their bosses.
> People who work shorter hours probably do not feel inspired by their bosses.

2

> **Possible answer**
> I think the most motivating thing for me would be an excellent salary, followed by good holidays, promotion prospects, flexible working hours, responsibility, being part of a team, and an inspirational boss. I'm not really bothered about staff facilities because I probably wouldn't use them – it's good to get away from people at work sometimes.

3 Look at the Test spot. Stop the recording after each group of questions so you can read through the next set of questions carefully. In the test itself the recording is played all the way through without stopping, but it includes pauses to give you time to read the questions. Make sure that you write no more than two words and or a number for each answer.

> **Answers** (relevant parts of the recording script are underlined)
> 1 behaviour   2 job satisfaction   3 19th/nineteenth
> 4 money   5 in teams   6 basic/Basic   7 status/Status
> 8 55%   9 40%   10 B

Recording script

Questions 1 and 2

Lecturer: My lecture today is on motivation at work. If managers are to improve the running of their organisation, it's important for them to understand what motivates the workforce – to know how to satisfy both the high flyers and those who have lower ambitions or ability.

First of all, let's look at the model of how motivation works. You will see that every member of the workforce has needs or expectations, and these needs and expectations <u>will affect each person's behaviour</u>. For example, they will work harder if they know that they will be rewarded – that is, if they can achieve their goals of higher pay or promotion. <u>The achievement of these goals will, in turn, lead to job satisfaction</u>. This then feeds back into the worker's needs or expectations.

Questions 3–5

Lecturer: Over the years the development of different theories of management and different approaches to organisation has affected the way we view motivation. <u>In the nineteenth century</u>, the writer Frederick <u>Taylor put forward the theory that workers were only interested in making money</u>. In contrast, in the early twentieth century, researchers found that people went to work to satisfy a *range* of different needs, and not simply for financial reward. One need, in particular, was emphasised – the social need. An early study done on a coal-mining company, for instance, showed that <u>people generally were happier and worked more productively if they were able to work in teams</u>.

Questions 6 and 7

Lecturer: One important twentieth-century theory of motivation was that put forward by Maslow in 1943. Maslow identified five important needs which he placed in a triangle: <u>at the bottom of the triangle he put what he called 'basic needs':</u> good pay and pleasant working conditions. Then, above the basic needs, he put 'security needs' – safe working conditions and job security. His third need he called 'social' – the need to have friends at work and get on with the boss. <u>Fourth were 'status' needs</u> – a job title and social recognition. Finally, at the top of the triangle, Maslow identified the need for advancement – to have a challenging job with opportunities for promotion. His theory isn't perfect, but it's a convenient framework for viewing the different needs and expectations of work that people have, and, what's more, I believe it's still valid today.

Questions 8–10

Lecturer: During an early twenty-first century survey of full-time employees, when asked what gave them job satisfaction, 72% said having an inspirational leader. <u>55% of those questioned found satisfaction in the challenging nature of their work</u>, 50% – by being paid well, and <u>40% said flexible working hours</u>. Consequently, we can see that this indicates that today, an employee's opinion of the quality of the leadership in their workplace is an important factor influencing belief in the company as a good place to work.

Motivation varies over a person's working life and also according to where they live. Studies show that people have different goals in different countries. For example, a good lifestyle would appear to be more important in Spain than it is in Sweden. Financial security is more important in the US than in the UK. Social contact at work is important to workers in both Germany and Australia, <u>but not of top importance in Britain</u> and Italy. As to high status – this is more important in the USA than to Europeans. These results indicate clear differences between countries, but I think they shouldn't be taken too seriously.

There have been many theories which have attempted to explain the nature of motivation. These theories are all partially true, and by and large all help to explain the behaviour of certain people at certain times. However, none really provide all the answers. The best a company can do is to provide people with the right environment to be self-motivated. If they are self-motivated, they will perform well.

4 Remember to use an English–English dictionary.

> **Answers**
> **1** waste **2** left **3** spent / has spent / spends **4** change
> **5** pay **6** lend **7** gave **8** invest
> **9** saved / has saved / saves **10** made / has made / makes

5

> **Possible answers**
> 1 No, I always keep to my budget. I don't like the idea of being in debt.
> 2 I think it's to run your own business. You will never be rich if you work for someone else.
> 3 Yes, I often buy things second-hand. I can't afford to buy new things all the time.
> 4 No, I think it is better to be independent and not owe anyone anything.
> 5 I'm not really sure about that, as I have no experience of it.

6.2 pages 42–43

1 Units 4 and 5 have covered both past and present tenses, so you should be familiar with the form and function of these tenses. Work through this exercise.

> **Answers**
> **1** PS **2** PP **3** PS **4** PP

2

> **Answers**
> **1** grew up **2** went **3** started **4** left **5** went
> **6** didn't graduate **7** founded **8** opened
> **9** have expanded **10** started **11** founded **12** exceeded
> **13** has spent **14** hasn't only spent **15** has tried
> **16** crossed **17** broke

3 Decide which is the correct tense for the questions.

> **Answers**
> 1 Have you ever had/taken
> 2 Did you learn/take/have
> 3 Have you ever thought
> 4 Have you ever spent / Did you spend (... when you were at school)
> 5 Did you want
> 6 Have you ever had
> 7 Did you take
> 8 Have you ever seen

4 Writing a job application letter requires specialised, formulaic language.

> **Answers**
> 1 post 2 manager 3 Department 4 experience
> 5 qualified 6 CV 7 skills 8 salary 9 closing
> 10 interview

5 Look at the mind map – it will help you to prepare a talk. Match the points in the task with the points on the mind map. The last point is usually the one which is expanded on the most.

> **Suggested answers**
> - *Who they are:* A teacher at my secondary school
> - *What was special about this person:* Had worked in advertising. Knew about the business world.
> - *What other people say about this person:* Liked by most students. Not traditional enough, said parents.
> - *Why this person has motivated you:* Friendly, gave me confidence, extra help with exams. Helped with university application. Made me interested in business studies.

Do the task for yourself, using a mind map. Time yourself and, if possible, record your talk.

Writing folder 3

pages 44–45

1 Look at the Advice box. It is a good idea to use a highlighter pen to highlight the important parts of the question.

You will need to practise writing 250 words so you have some idea of what that number of words looks like on the page. This will help you to stop worrying in the test about how much you have written. You should always time yourself when you start writing, so you can see how long it takes.

Work through the questions.

> **Answers**
> 1 appropriate
> 2 may be appropriate – if this is your only knowledge and experience and you make that clear
> 3 probably irrelevant
> 4 appropriate
> 5 appropriate
> 6 appropriate if it's relevant – for example if your argument is that managers are paid more and therefore are expected to work longer
> 7 inappropriate – irrelevant
> 8 appropriate if it is relevant
> 9 inappropriate – irrelevant
> 10 may be appropriate if your arguments in the main body of the essay support this

2 Read through introductions A, B and C.

> **Suggested answers**
> A is inappropriate because …
> … it is lifting the question. Never just repeat the question.
> … it is too strongly worded for an introduction. These are usually more general.
> … it contains irrelevant personal information
>
> B is fine – general but to the point.
>
> C would probably be better as a paragraph after the introduction. It is going on to talk about different situations in different countries, and this would make a good paragraph for the body of the essay.

3 Refer to the Useful language boxes and read the example carefully.

4

> **Answers**
> Part 1 – Working hours today are too long.
> Part 2 – People are not spending as much time as they should with their families or on leisure activities.

> **Sample answer**
> In the 20th century, people believed that life in the future would be easier and that they would have more leisure time and spend less time at work. However, now we are in the 21st century, we can see that this is not the case. In fact, people in most countries need to work even harder today than they did in the past.
>
> This can affect families particularly badly. It is often necessary for both parents to work in order to earn enough money to pay the bills. Not only that, it is very unusual for them to work just nine to five. My parents are both professional people. My father is a lawyer, and my mother is a marketing manager. Both of them leave the house well before eight o'clock in the morning and usually get home about seven thirty.
>
> As a consequence, our family, consisting of three children, has always had a nanny or au pair to look after us. However, my family is still a close family, despite my parents going out to work. I do not think it is a big problem if my parents are not constantly at home with us. I think it is more important if they spend quality time with us – that is, time when we are all happy together.
>
> In conclusion, I would like to say that working long hours nowadays is a fact of life. It is up to the individual to try to work out a credible work-life balance so that they can spend quality time with their family and still pursue their work goals.
>
> (266 words)

Unit 7

7.1 pages 46–47

The pictures show advertising, including people providing free advertising for companies.

1 This activity will help you to develop your answers in the Speaking Module, particularly Parts 1 and 3. Read the exercise, and expand answers 1–3 by choosing among **a–e**.

> **Answers**
> 1 a, e   2 c   3 b, d

Think about what you could say about the three bulleted questions, using the phrases in bold in **a–e**.

> **Possible answers**
> - I do occasionally, for instance if I've bought something and been very disappointed with it.
> - I'm not sure. Maybe it does, because wherever you go, you see or hear ads.
> - I suppose it does, occasionally. I once bought a very expensive mobile phone because I thought it looked good in the ads. I didn't need it, since I already had a mobile.

2 This activity will help you with both multiple-choice and headings tasks in the Reading Modules. If you don't know what a *viral* is, you will find out when you read the passage. The passage is typical of Section 3 of General Training Reading. Multiple-choice and headings tasks are used in both Reading Modules.

Work through the example and questions 1 and 2. These three questions focus on the main point of each paragraph, as preparation for the headings task.

> **Answers** (evidence from the passage is given, but this is not part of the answer)
> 1 C   *the Viral Factory was making a 20-second film to promote my recently published book.*
> 2 A   *Viral marketing ... probably dates back to 1996, when it was used to advertise a free email service. Every time a customer used the service, the company's website address was automatically included at the end.*

Read the Test spot, then the paragraphs labelled 3–6, and choose the best heading for each one from **A–F**.

> **Answers** (evidence from the passage is given, but this is not part of the answer)
> 3 E   *Today, viral marketing is a lot more sophisticated.*
> 4 B   *But if a viral arrives in your email inbox from a friend, you'll be curious and click on it.*
> 5 C   *if the clip is too obviously designed to advertise a particular product, people won't pass it on ... On the other hand, nobody will buy the product if they don't know what it is.*
> 6 F   *traffic to my website increased dramatically*

3 Complete the table, making sure you understand all the words. Use an English–English dictionary if necessary. When you learn new words, write down related words as well, marking the stressed syllables. This will expand your vocabulary, familiarise you with suffixes for different parts of speech, and help you stress words correctly. Notice the change in stressed syllable between 'curious and curi'osity.

> **Answers**
>
> | verbs | nouns | adjectives |
> |---|---|---|
> | | 'virus *and* 'viral *when referring to a viral advertisement* | 'viral |
> | pro'mote | pro'motion, pro'moter | pro'motional |
> | 'advertise | 'advertising, 'advertiser, ad'vertisement (UK), adver'tisement (USA), 'advert, ad | |
> | 'memorise | 'memory | 'memorable |
> | a'ttend | a'ttention | a'ttentive |
> | | curi'osity | 'curious |
> | suc'ceed | suc'cess | suc'cessful |

4 Using the words will help you to remember them.

> **Answers**
> 1 curious   2 successful   3 Promotional   4 Memorable
> 5 attentive

5 Think about what you would say in answer to these questions. Remember to expand your answers.

7.2 pages 48–49

1 Think about what these three opinions mean, and whether you agree with them.

> **Possible answers**
> *Telling lies does not work in advertising.*
> This suggests that ads tell the truth, because people will soon find out if they claim something that isn't true, and that would be bad for business.
>
> *If the advertising budget is big enough, you can make people believe anything.*
> This suggests that by spending a lot of money on a very impressive and memorable TV commercial, for example, advertisers can make viewers believe that the product is also very impressive.
>
> *In our factory, we make lipstick. In our advertising we sell hope.*
> This is attributed to Charles Revson, who co-founded the US cosmetics company Revlon in 1932. It means that the advertising doesn't give factual information about the product; it creates an image, for example of a beautiful woman, and consumers buy the product because they hope the product will make them look beautiful.

2 Play the first part of the recording and answer questions 1–6 as you listen. (An *advertising agency* is a company that plans and designs advertising campaigns on behalf of other companies.) Then study questions 7–11 and answer them as you listen to the second part of the recording. (*Celebrity endorsement* is when a well-known person is used to advertise a product by saying that he or she thinks the product is good.) Remember that the words in the box may not be used in the recording.

Answers (relevant parts of the recording script are underlined)
1 information **2** demand **3** profit **4** competition
5 emotions **6** benefits
7 F **8** G **9** B **10** E **11** C

Recording script

Questions 1–6

Interviewer: My guest this evening is advertising expert Gary Phillips, who's going to tell us how advertising works. Welcome to the programme.

Gary Phillips: Thank you.

Interviewer: How did it all start?

Gary Phillips: When everyone lived in small communities, and knew the local farmer who grew and sold vegetables, advertising was unnecessary. But in a larger community it's a different situation. In fact, advertising dates back well over 2,000 years, and <u>for centuries, adverts simply gave information</u>: one of the earliest surviving ones is a sign painted on a wall in ancient Rome showing property to let. Later they announce that books, say, are available, and where they can be bought.

Interviewer: So, when did advertising become more persuasive?

Gary Phillips: The big change occurred in the late nineteenth century. Technological developments had made mass production possible, which meant firms could make products in large numbers, of roughly the same quality, and at roughly the same price. <u>Companies then found they had to stimulate demand in order to sell these products.</u> At the same time, in some countries, there were plenty of people with money to spend on <u>luxuries and other inessential goods. This created opportunities for companies to make and sell these at a much greater profit.</u> So a lot of advertising focused on luxury goods.

Another reason for the change in the nature of advertising was that more and more businesses were set up, making similar products, and <u>in the face of this competition, manufacturers needed to advertise in order to survive.</u> This was really the beginning of advertising designed to *persuade* people to buy. And when Freud's theories about our subconscious began to be applied in the advertising industry in the 1920s, advertising became very effective.

Interviewer: How does persuasive advertising work?

Gary Phillips: It tries to make people want a certain item, let's say a car. If we only bought goods for practical reasons, manufacturers would soon go out of business. <u>So they appeal to our emotions</u> in their advertising, to make us believe that if we buy that particular car, we'll feel good, we'll be in the fashion, people will admire us. Instead of focusing on the car's mechanical properties, the <u>advertising is about the benefits</u> that we hope to gain.

Questions 7–11

Interviewer: Gary, tell us about some of the techniques that manufacturers use to persuade us.

Gary Phillips: Let's start with one of the most important aspects of advertising, the name given to a product. Sometimes there's a symbol, too. Imagine a company which makes children's clothing. <u>It can spend a fortune on making the name well-known, and giving it a particular image, so that when consumers see the name, or the logo, they associate it with particular qualities</u> – style, value for money, fun, fashion, whatever. And they're more likely to buy that particular make.

Another very powerful, and very old, technique is to make it almost impossible for consumers to avoid the advertising. <u>You keep seeing a TV commercial for running shoes, perhaps several times in an evening, see adverts for them in newspapers and magazines, you see posters in the street.</u> That helps to fix the product in your mind, so next time you buy some running shoes, and you see a whole row of different products, the chances are you'll buy the shoes whose name you remember.

Of course with many products, <u>furniture for instance, advertisers attract us with special offers, or the chance of winning a holiday. And words like *bargain* and *sale* are used very frequently</u> to encourage shoppers to buy.

Interviewer: But surely consumers realise that advertisements are simply trying to sell products?

Gary Phillips: They do, of course. So agencies often produce advertisements that are entertaining. <u>A certain washing powder used to run an advertising campaign that appeared to be saying to the consumer, 'Look, *you* know and *we* know that we're trying to get you to buy our product, but at least we'll give you a laugh.'</u> It was very effective, because the manufacturer seemed to be on the same side as the consumer.

Another technique is <u>to use a famous person to promote a product, even if there's no real connection, like showing an athlete eating snacks.</u> This can work because we learn by imitating people who are important to us. So advertisers use film stars, pop singers – even cartoon characters, particularly if the product is targeted at children.

Language is an important aspect of advertising, and here's just one example. <u>A TV commercial for engine oil</u> showed a man washing his hands in the oil. Of course car engines and hands are made of different materials, so he can't tell us the oil will work equally well in an engine. Instead <u>he tries to get the viewer to reach that conclusion without stating any facts:</u> he says, 'Think how it'll work in your car.' He's *implied* the oil is good for car engines without *saying* so.

Interviewer: OK, now if we go on to another question ...

3 This exercise is concerned with which words in a sentence are likely to be stressed. Read the sentence aloud, as marked. Play the recording, then repeat it with the stress on the correct words.

Words that are stressed tend to be 'content' words, that is, those that convey most meaning: mostly nouns and main verbs. 'Grammatical' words, such as pronouns and auxiliary verbs, are not usually stressed.

4 Underline the content words, then play the recording.

5 If you are not sure of the different word classes, some examples are given here.

Answers (with possible examples)
Content words: adjectives (e.g. *local, larger*), adverbs (e.g. *locally, largely*), nouns (e.g. *farmer, vegetable*), main verbs (e.g. *start, lived*)
Grammatical words: auxiliary verbs (e.g. *will, have*), conjunctions (e.g. *when, and*), prepositions (e.g. *in, by*)

6

Answers
1 *Larger* needs extra stress because it forms a contrast with *small*.
2 *Persuade* needs extra stress because it contrasts with *gave information*.
3 *Advertising* is not heavily stressed because the word has already been used, so it doesn't provide new information.
4 The words *inessential goods* wouldn't be given much stress, as the meaning is included under *luxuries*, so it is not new information.

Play the recording and read the four sentences aloud, paying particular attention to stress.

7 Relative clauses add information about the noun or noun phrase preceding them (*Gary Phillips, a company*). Essential information is given in defining relative clauses, and extra information in non-defining relative clauses.

Answers
1 Non-defining: *Gary Phillips* is enough to identify who is being talked about, so the relative clause gives extra information.
2 Defining: the relative clause is essential, because the writer is referring to a particular type of company – one that makes children's clothing.

8

Answers
1 A great deal of advertising is about the benefits that we hope to gain. *defining*
2 Ordinary people who appear in advertisements are usually intended to make the viewer or reader identify with them. *defining*
3 Jewellery and perfume, which are luxury goods, are usually very profitable for the manufacturer. *non-defining*
4 Consumers that see the same advertisements many times are likely to remember the name of the product. *defining*

	defining	non-defining
people	*who* or *that*	*who*
things	*which* or *that*	*which*

Non-defining relative clauses need commas.

9

Answers
1 e 2 f 3 b 4 a 5 d 6 c

Test folder 4

pages 50–51

Make sure you fully understand the notes and advice.

1 Read the instructions, example and paragraph A. Make sure you understand why **x** is the best heading. Then complete the exercise.

Answers (evidence from the passage is given, but this is not part of the answer)
Example x *that's what more and more retailers are giving us*
1 vii *In between news clips, recipe tips and beauty advice, the screens show advertisements*
2 iii *the early years of in-store TV ... sometimes left a lot to be desired. This has been changing, though, as advertisers get more sophisticated at using in-store TV.*
3 xi *In-store ads have to be particularly attention-grabbing*
4 viii *Ads that communicate facts ... work better than the more emotional ... Shoppers ... want the ad to tell them specifically about a brand and what it is going to do for them.*
5 xii *content is tightly tailored to particular store areas*
6 iv *A minority of customers feel that, rather than wasting money on in-store TV, the retailer should lower prices, or at least invest in more useful services. The biggest turn-off, though, for both customers and staff on the shop floor, is noise.*
7 v *it has become more difficult for manufacturers and others to reach a mass audience on regular television. Through in-store TV they can reach the large numbers of people*
8 i *the majority of customers feel that in-store TV improves their overall shopping experience.*

2 In this exercise you have to consider a large number of options, all of which relate in some way to the paragraph.

Answer
v *a healthy buyer–seller relationship results in interdependencies between the two parties.*

Unit 8

8.1 pages 52–53

1 The pictures show people enjoying their leisure time in different ways: dancing, playing the electric guitar, and pottery.

Possible answers
I think it's a good idea to spend your leisure time actively, particularly if you don't get much exercise while you're studying or working.
Sometimes you need to relax and use your brain, rather than do anything active.

2 Think about any arts centres you know that organise a variety of cultural activities.

Completing a table is very similar to note taking. Note the headings of the table, and read about Jake Duff in the text. Make sure you understand why 'comedy' is the answer to the example. Complete the table.

Answers
1 rural life 2 best newcomer 3 talk 4 booklet
5 play 6 growing up 7 actors
8 photographic exhibition 9 everyday objects
10 polished metal

3 There are a number of ways of talking about the future in English, and usually the speaker or writer has a choice of more than one: it isn't the case that one is right and all others are wrong. Five ways are listed in **a–e**. Make sure you know what they mean.

Answers
1 c 2 e 3 c 4 d 5 a 6 b 7 a 8 d
a *will*
b *will*
c *present continuous / be going to*
d *be going to*
e *present simple*

For more information about the future, turn to the Grammar folder, page 140.

4 Often, when talking about a future event, the speaker or writer gives their opinion of how likely it is to happen. This grammatical exercise is in the form of an IELTS classifying task.

Answers
1 a 2 c 3 a 4 a 5 b 6 c 7 b 8 a 9 a 10 b

5 Think about what you might say in each situation, using the phrases given.

Possible answers
1 I'm convinced I'll enjoy the show, because I've always wanted to see her perform.
2 I may enjoy myself, but there's a chance the audience will be disappointed.
3 I'm sure I'll hate the film just as much the second time.
4 Maybe I'll be able to learn the rules quickly, but there's a chance I'll spoil the game for the other players.

8.2 pages 54–55

1 Think about why people choose to do the activities shown (paragliding, mountaineering and painting). Make sure you understand the five categories ('relaxation', etc.) and the activities given. *Paragliding* is the sport of jumping out of an aircraft with a special parachute that allows you to travel a long horizontal distance before you land. *Scuba diving* is the sport of swimming under water with special breathing apparatus. 'Scuba' is an acronym, formed from the initial letters of *self-contained underwater breathing apparatus*.

Possible answers
relaxation: yoga, collecting stamps
excitement: watching or playing football, dancing
communion with nature: walking in the countryside, angling
companionship: playing in an orchestra, going out with friends
creative expression: painting, singing in a choir

2 Read the Test spot, example and questions 1–9 for the listing task, then play the relevant part of the recording. Then do the same for questions 10–14.

Answers (relevant parts of the recording script are underlined)
1–3 rock climbing, paragliding, chess (*in any order*)
4–5 music, football (*in either order*)
6–7 surfing, bird-watching (*in either order*)
8–9 painting, drama (*in either order*)
10 (a) full experience 11 (to) socialise/socialize
12 retail therapy 13 entertainment 14 life

Recording script

Example

Lecturer: Leisure activities are as varied as crossing the Arctic, or collecting foreign coins, or a visit to a museum. Research into people's experience of leisure has revealed that people get a number of different kinds of enjoyment from leisure, some of which I'll briefly talk about now. But bear in mind that most activities will provide several types of experience.

We often talk about leisure as giving the opportunity for relaxation. Yoga is generally relaxing, both physically and mentally, as is stamp collecting. Relaxation tends to be associated with undemanding activities, but many leisure activities are far from relaxing.

Questions 1–9

Lecturer: At the opposite end of the spectrum is 'flow', the name given to a very intense experience, where you're completely absorbed in what you're doing and lose track of time. This often comes from activities where people set themselves challenges to test and improve their skills, as in rock climbing. Many activities that provide flow carry a considerable physical risk, which is likely to add to the experience – paragliding is just one example. But the same intensely emotional experience may occur in a very different activity, like chess. It isn't the activity alone which provides the experience, but also what the participant brings to it.

Another feature of many leisure activities is the introduction to a whole new social network, providing companionship with other like-minded people. New friends can be made through joining a music club, for instance. And social relationships can be strengthened through a shared interest in football. The media open up this experience to everyone who wants to participate, even if they don't play.

Then there's the pleasure that some people get from being in communion with nature, either alone or with companions. Surfing, for example, is likely to focus your entire attention on the sea, while one of the more relaxing ways of relating to the natural world is bird-watching.

Leisure activities can also provide an opportunity to express creativity. Again, these can be solitary or companionable. Painting is often done alone, although many people join a club that can give them encouragement and tips for improvement, while drama is normally a combined effort, with a performance as its goal.

Questions 10–14

Lecturer: An essential aspect of leisure is that we can pick hobbies to suit our personality, our needs and our wallet, and we can drop them at any time. This control is crucial, as people benefit from feeling that they're making their own decisions. That's one reason why children need to choose their own hobbies, instead of having them imposed by their parents.

With large numbers of people wishing to spend time on leisure activities, there's a growing demand for the organiser – whether it's a cinema or a dance class – to ensure that participants have a full experience. It isn't enough just to show a film: customers want to be able to find out in advance what's on, travel to the cinema easily, feel welcome when they arrive, and have the chance to buy popcorn to eat during the film.

People may enjoy an activity – a dance class, for instance – but drop it because these other parts of the experience have been overlooked. They're likely to enjoy themselves much more if they're made to feel welcome and there's an opportunity to socialise when the dancing ends.

Like cinemas, the retail sector is making efforts to package a variety of experiences. Many people go shopping for pleasure, and spend far longer comparing and discussing products than they do actually buying. This has even gained a name in recent years – 'retail therapy' – reflecting the view that it makes people feel better.

Shopping used to be purely practical: we bought what we needed. But that's no longer enough. Many shopping centres now ensure shoppers are provided with entertainment as well. This is good for business, as it attracts more customers, who stay longer and spend more.

And is leisure good for us, or simply a waste of time? According to psychologists, participating in leisure activities makes us healthier, both physically and mentally, and increases the pleasure we gain from life. So we've got good reason to carry on with our hobbies!

3   Vowel sounds fall into three main categories: short, long and diphthongs. Remember that spelling is not a helpful guide to pronunciation.

   NB The name of each vowel, *a, e, i, o* and *u*, is the same as its main long or diphthong pronunciation.

Answers

short vowels:	full /ʊ/, instead /e/, skills /ɪ/, study /ʌ/, hobby /ɒ/
long vowels:	far /ɑː/, more /ɔː/, music /uː/, bird /ɜː/, people /iː/
diphthongs:	about /aʊ/, goal /əʊ/, time /aɪ/, there /eə/, year /ɪə/

Play the recording and repeat each word. The words are in the order they are in above the table.

4   This activity will help you think about the types of questions you might be asked in Part 3 of the Speaking Module. Complete the sets of four questions about the four activities.

Writing folder 4
pages 56–57

Read the introduction and advice. This writing folder aims to go through the expressions and layout required in a letter. Look carefully at the Useful language box on page 57. Students often find it hard to know how to begin a letter and the Useful language box contains suggestions for letter purpose, which should be of help.

1

Answer
The letter is to the local council.

2

Answer
C is correct here because you don't know the name of the person you are writing to. **A** is informal to a friend and **B** is to someone you have met or know the name of and is semi-formal.

3

Answer
A is better, as there is an explanation of who is writing and a clear reason for writing is given.
B is too abrupt and gives the reader no idea of who is writing. It is also very rude – implying something about the council which may or may not be true, but which in any case is unlikely to receive a positive response.

4

Answer
It only deals with one suggestion – the question asked for 'suggestions'. Also it talks about how to find money for the facility, which was not asked for. And it contains some further irrelevancy towards the end. The reader wouldn't be interested in the personal information given.

5

Answer
This is too informal. A better ending would be something like:
I do hope you will consider my suggestions and ideas. Please get in touch with me if you would like to discuss them further. I look forward to hearing from you in the near future.

6

Suggested answers
1 Too abrupt: *I would like to work in your cinema if you have a vacancy in the near future.*
2 Too informal: *I hope that you will consider my application favourably.*
3 Too flowery: *I saw your job advertisement in the paper last week.*
4 Too rude: *I would appreciate it if you could reply as soon as possible.*
5 Too rude: *I'm afraid that I will be unable to attend the interview next week. I hope it will be possible to arrange another date.*
6 Too rude: *I'm afraid that I haven't yet received an application form.*
7 Too formal: *I'm sorry to say that I do not think you have adequately answered my question.*
8 Too informal: *I enclose my CV.*
9 Too informal: *Please do not hesitate to get in touch if you have any questions about my application.*
10 Too formal: *You will see from my CV that I am very well qualified for the position.*

7 This letter is not an exact correction of the one in the Student's Book but is politer and more agreeable in tone.

Possible answer
Dear Sir/Madam,

I am a twenty-year-old student and I am studying physical education at Pulteney College. I have been studying there for the past two years. I am writing to ask if there are any part-time job vacancies at your sports centre.

I really enjoy sport and my areas of particular interest and expertise are running, tennis, judo and basketball. I have had some experience of coaching for these sports during the time I have been at the college. Last year I worked in the holidays at a sports centre in my own country. I will be able to provide references from this summer job and also from my teachers at the college. I qualify as a sports teacher in two years' time.

I would prefer to work in the evenings and at weekends, as I have classes during the daytime, and I can start from the beginning of October.

I look forward to hearing from you in the near future.

Yours faithfully,

(159 words, not including opening and closing phrases)

Units 5–8 Revision
pages 58–59

The aim of this revision unit is to focus on the language covered in Units 5–8.

Exercises 2–6 can be done as a test.

1 Give your own answers.

2

Answers
1 levelled off   2 has dropped back   3 has changed
4 declined   5 was   6 was   7 experienced   8 continued

3

Answers
1 My colleague is always late for work, which makes my boss really angry.
2 The archaeologists have found the tomb of the king who/that ruled the country in 4500 BC.
3 We went to see the film which/that won an Oscar this year.
4 I am writing a book review which/that might upset the author.
5 Archaeologists are people who often have to work in difficult conditions.
6 I don't like advertisements which/that don't tell the truth.
7 What was the name of the company which/that gave all its workers a bonus last year?

4

Answers
1 My wife, who lives in New York, works in advertising.
2 The Dorchester Hotel, which is near Hyde Park, is very comfortable.
3 I know a lot of people who are archaeologists.
4 The boy who played the part of Peter in the play goes to my college.
5 The people who built the Pyramids must have worked long and hard.
6 My manager, who is very strict about punctuality, has been with the company for years.

5

Answers
1 site   2 research   3 tomb   4 salary   5 promotion
6 motivation   7 manager   8 earn   9 spend   10 waste
11 save   12 pay   13 play   14 exhibition   15 dancing
16 performance   17 relaxation   18 activity

a manager   b earn   c performance   d research
e exhibition

6

Answers
a carries out / does   b reached   c analysed   d support
e doing / carrying out; lead

Unit 9
9.1 pages 60–61

1 The photograph is from the film *The Day after Tomorrow*, which is about what might happen in New York if the climate changes.

Doing this quiz will help you prepare for reading the article on the opposite page.

Answers
1 A 2 C 3 A 4 B

2   Scan the article to find out the answer to the question. The article is about 700 words long and should take you about two and a half minutes to read.

Answer
Ronald Stouffer

3   Read through sentences 1–5 carefully and then read the article again to match the right heading to each paragraph **A–E**.

Answers (evidence from the passage is given, but this is not part of the answer)
1   C   *impact on ecosystems, agriculture* (line 47); *placing animals like polar bears at risk* (line 56)
2   E   *'You can't say …' says Stouffer* (lines 74–75); *'Is society aware …' says Marianne Douglas* (lines 79–81)
3   A   This paragraph talks about now and in the future.
4   D   *Greenland's ice sheet* (line 58); *the Maldives* (lines 65–66); *the Nile Delta* (line 67); *Bangladesh* (line 68); *the eastern seaboard of the USA* (line 70)
5   B   *Most scientists believe … But some scientists also point to …* (lines 29–33)

4   Look at the Test spot. This explains the summary task. For more information go to Test folder 5. For this summary, you must only use words which are in the article.

Answers
1 average 2 (coral) reefs 3 heat 4 habitats
5 ice sheet/cap 6 populated 7 7/seven 8 fossil fuels
9 sources of energy

9.2 pages 62–63

1   Countable and uncountable nouns often cause problems in the Writing Module. It is important that you learn to recognise whether a noun is countable or uncountable, so that you can make appropriate changes to the grammar in the rest of the sentence. Use a dictionary such as the *Cambridge Advanced Learner's Dictionary* which shows symbols for countable and uncoutable nouns. Read through the four sentences and, using the information contained in them, fill in the rules in **a** and **b**.

Answers
a   *research; information; much; amount;* singular
b   *scientists; countries; many; number*

Look at the table giving a list of which words can be used with which type of noun.

2

Answers

countable	uncountable
activity	pollution
university	knowledge
country	news
job	work
meal	accommodation
scientist	research
	advice
	information
	climate
	weather

3   Some nouns, for example ones which refer to groups of people like *company, family, staff, government,* can be used with either singular or plural verbs and pronouns.

Suggested answers
1   Global warming is happening / happens faster than (many/most) people think.
2   Information about ecology courses at universities is hard to find.
3   A lot of people are studying mathematics at my college this year.
4   Are/Is the company going to put new equipment in the computer lab next year?
5   The news this morning isn't good.
6   My work on climate change is being / is going to be published next week.

4   You can improve your writing skills by using more formal words in essays.

Suggested answers
1   **A number of / Many** people **think** that **much of** the information about climate change **has** been wrong. **Much / A great/good deal of** research **has** taken place into whether it has been more influenced by natural occurrences such as volcanoes.
2   **Many / A number of** gases trap the sun's heat in the atmosphere and **cause** a gradual warming of the Earth.
3   **A good/great deal of** research **has** found that all people **need** to do **is** use **less** fossil fuel.
4   There is evidence that a car **emits** as **much** carbon dioxide a year as an entire house. **Much / A large amount of** energy can be saved by driving more smoothly and keeping the tyres inflated.

5   This exercise is similar to Part 3 of the Speaking Module. It also acts as a warm-up to the listening in exercise 6. The pictures show someone taking a shower, cycling to work and a computer which has been unplugged. Try to use language from the Useful language box.

6   Read through the notes and predict what sort of answer is required for each space. Play the recording as many times as is necessary, but remember that it is heard only once in the test.

Answers
1 ($)2,000   2 conserving energy   3 light bulb(s)
4 refrigerator/fridge   5 (the) water   6 8/eight minutes
7 TV/television   8 ($)24   9 beef   10 bulk

Recording script

Presenter: Good morning and welcome to the programme. Did you know that today is Earth Day? Well, in case you didn't, I'm here to tell you what you can do to save the planet. According to a new book published recently, called *51 Easy Ways to Save the Planet*, each household in the USA could save as much as $2,000 on annual bills and help the Earth at the same time. Most people seem to think that there's nothing they can do on a local level – that it's something for governments to tackle. Well, according to the authors of this book, they couldn't be more wrong. And those of you who don't live in the USA – stay with us, there's plenty you can do too!

The book focuses on conserving energy, and the authors say that if 35 percent of the US population can be persuaded to follow their suggestions, US carbon-dioxide emissions can be reduced to the level targeted in the Kyoto Protocol, signed by a number of countries, but not the USA, in 2001.

Did you know, for example, that making a contribution to reducing the use of fossil fuels can be as simple as changing the type of light bulb you use? The new kind of bulb lasts ten times longer, uses one-fourth of the energy and produces more light per watt than the old type. Although they initially cost more they quickly pay for themselves and will save you money in the long term.

Another way the authors suggest you can save the planet is to place your refrigerator somewhere out of the sun and away from the oven or radiator. So simple! Now, do you leave the water running when you clean your teeth? Well, many of us do and it's wasting precious resources. Apparently, if your faucet is leaky and drips every three seconds, it can waste 29 gallons or 110 litres of water a month. Scary or what? Also, if you take an eight-minute shower instead of a ten-minute one, you will save about 290 gallons, or 1,100 litres, of water a month, so start timing yourself today!

Now, do you use the remote control for your TV? Do you realise that, according to the book, one-fourth of the energy consumed each year by the TV is used when it's actually turned off? Most people don't know about this, but the only way to stop wasting energy is to unplug it, not leave it on standby.

Your car is the next target. Your car is responsible for emitting as much carbon dioxide per year as your whole house. So choose your car with care. Tuning your engine will improve its efficiency by 15 to 50% and just pumping up the tyres regularly will save you $24 in gas.

Food next. The average American eats 265 pounds, or 120 kilos, of beef per year. By reducing your intake by just one pound, or half a kilo, each week, you can save $109 over the year. Did you know that the electricity used to water, feed and package just a pound of beef is the equivalent of burning one gallon of gas in your car's engine?

Now, finally, when you go shopping, why don't you buy your groceries in bulk rather than in small sizes? This will result in annual savings of up to $293, but, of course the problem is: where to put all those bulk buys? Would you need to build an extra room, buy extra refrigerators and use more electricity, thus

defeating the object of saving energy? Well, that's a question I can't answer, but I do think there are some good ideas in this book. Why don't you try some out and let me know how you get on? There'll be a prize for the best email on the subject. So, …

7

Answers
1 f   2 g   3 a   4 e   5 b   6 c   7 d

8   Read through the diagram, checking to make sure you understand the process (see WF 1). Note the numbering of the different parts of the process.

Sample answer
The diagram shows what might happen to the Earth if people continue to burn fossil fuels and cut down forests. The cycle begins when factories use fossil fuels such as coal, gas or wood as a source of energy in manufacturing. These factories emit huge clouds of smoke, which pollute the atmosphere. The smoke is composed of carbon dioxide and other gases. These gases trap heat which would normally escape into space, thus producing the 'greenhouse effect'.

The warming increases water vapour in the air, and more heat is absorbed into the atmosphere. If carbon dioxide and other greenhouse gases continue to pour into the atmosphere unchecked, the world will warm rapidly. Rising temperatures will melt snow and ice, and sea levels will rise. Many of the Earth's towns and villages are built on the coast, and a rise in sea level will spell disaster for them. (147 words)

Test folder 5
pages 64–65

Make sure you fully understand the notes and advice.

1   Skim the passage, then read the summary. Then read the passage more carefully and complete the summary.

Answers
1 ice melt   2 flooding   3 hail   4 glaciers
5 growing season   6 crops   7 seeds   8 harvests
9 famines   10 malnutrition   11 fungus

2   Read the summary, then complete it as you listen to the recording.

Answers (relevant parts of the recording script are underlined)
1 13   2 400   3 rotation   4 sub-tropical/subtropical
5 pilots   6 time and fuel   7 navigation   8 storms
9 showers   10 north   11 dry/drier

Recording script

You will hear part of a talk about winds high above the earth.
First you have some time to look at questions 1 to 11. (pause)
Now listen carefully and answer questions 1 to 11.

Lecturer: Today I'm going to talk about one of the major influences on the weather – jet streams – and one in particular. Basically, a jet stream is a wind, although it blows much more regularly than most of the winds we experience. It may help to think of it as a narrow, fast-flowing 'river' of air.

The Polar Front Jet Stream, which affects the weather of North America and the British Isles, is between 9 and 13 kilometres above sea level. It flows right round the globe, in sections thousands of kilometres long, and moves much faster than winds at ground level, reaching a maximum during the winter. Then the normal speed is about 400 kilometres an hour, though speeds of over 600 kilometres an hour have been recorded. The stream moves from west to east, because of the rotation of the earth.

The jet stream is formed on the boundary between two blocks of air of different temperatures. To the north, there's the cold air of the North Pole region, and to the south, the sub-tropical air closer to the equator. This of course is much warmer. The difference in temperature results in a difference in pressure, and this in turn forces the air to move.

Unlike rain or snow, which we've always known about, jet streams are a relatively recent discovery. In the 1940s, during the Second World War, pilots flying high-altitude planes noticed that they travelled faster when they were going eastwards, helped by strong tailwinds. Modern planes are affected, too. A flight from London to New York takes about $7\frac{1}{2}$ hours, but travelling in the opposite direction takes an hour less. This of course means a considerable saving in time and fuel. The drawback is that when planes enter and leave a jet stream, they meet considerable turbulence. So even for highly sophisticated modern aircraft, navigation isn't as easy as you might expect.

As I mentioned, jet streams affect the weather, so weather forecasters need to include them in their calculations. Data about the jet stream and other high-level conditions is fed into computers, making it possible to pick out the areas where depressions may form. In the British Isles, forecasters then calculate whether these depressions are likely to develop into storms, which may cause structural damage as they rush in from the Atlantic, or whether there'll be nothing more serious than showers. In fact, the jet stream has a major influence on the Atlantic depressions that bring rainfall to the British Isles all year round. This is actually a very beneficial climate, although not everyone would agree!

If global warming really starts to accelerate in the second half of this century, as many scientists expect, the area of warm air will be much larger during the summer than it is now. The impact on the jet stream will be that it will be located further north. The British Isles will then become dry, with an almost complete lack of summer rain. So there's a pretty unpleasant change in prospect.

3 Check that you know the meanings of the words in the box. Read the summary. Remember that the words may be paraphrases of the listening passage. Play the recording and complete the summary.

> **Answers** (relevant parts of the recording script are underlined)
> **1** dust **2** sunlight **3** snow **4** storms **5** hunger
> **6** riots **7** migration

Recording script

You will hear a university teacher talking about the effects of a volcanic eruption on the weather.
First you have some time to look at questions 1 to 7. (pause)
Now listen carefully and answer questions 1 to 7.

Lecturer: One of the most powerful volcanic eruptions ever recorded took place in 1815. In April of that year, Mount Tambora, in what's now Indonesia, erupted with catastrophic violence, ejecting over a million and a half tonnes of ash, which darkened the sky over a radius of 500 kilometres. Much of it reached the upper atmosphere and remained there for the next two years. To a considerable extent, this blocked solar radiation from reaching the earth, significantly lowering temperatures, particularly in the northern hemisphere.

The following year, 1816, became known as 'the year without a summer'. Southern Italy had the unusual experience of seeing snowflakes, and the sun was masked by a cloud of what looked like smoke. During the spring growing season, temperatures were abnormally low, and crops were ruined by hail and rain.

The resulting shortages made food very expensive across Europe, and thousands of people died of starvation. There was social unrest, as the poor took to the streets, and high levels of violence.

In the north-eastern United States, the spring of 1816 arrived late and was exceptionally cold, with rain, frost and snow continuing into June. Crops were destroyed, animals died, and tens of thousands of people were forced to move to the richer soil and better growing conditions of the Midwest. So, indirectly, the volcanic eruption contributed to the rapid settlement of this region.

Another side-effect of the eruption was that Mary Shelley wrote her novel *Frankenstein* when the bad weather forced her to stay indoors during a holiday in Switzerland.

Unit 10

10.1 pages 66–67

1 The pictures show different types of student accommodation – a shared flat and a study bedroom in a hall of residence.

> **Possible answers**
> - I'm living in a hall of residence at the moment. I don't mind staying in a hall of residence because it's my first year and it enables me to meet people.
> - It's quite new and very comfortable, although the study bedroom I have is small and I haven't a lot of room for my things.
> - What I would like most is to have a very large, sunny room in a flat with a good view of a park or countryside.
> - I'd like to share with someone who is honest, of course, and also easy-going and fairly tidy. I can't stand people who leave the dishes in the sink without washing them up or who never clean the bath.

Unit 12

12.1 pages 78–79

Think about the pictures. Have you have ever tried, or would you like to try, those sports? Zorbing, is explained in the listening passage.

1   Think about possible answers to the questions. Develop your answers, particularly in speculating about why the sports are popular.

> **Possible answers**
> Although not many people watch baseball, quite a lot play it so that they can keep fit.
> A lot of people watch football on TV. Maybe it's because football is fashionable and there are plenty of articles about it in the media.

2   Check that you understand the words in the box, then complete the sentences and define the extra word.

> **Answers**
> 1   event
> 2   record (notice the stress: 'record [noun], re'cord [verb])
> 3   spectator
> 4   Extreme
> 5   competitors; runner-up
> 6   team; score
> 7   tie
> 8   amateurs (amateur is both an adjective and a noun)
> Extra word: referee – a person who is in charge of a game and who makes certain that the rules are followed

3   Complete the table with the most common words related to those given.

> **Answers**
>
> | verb | noun (person) | noun (activity) | adjective |
> |------|------|------|------|
> | -------- | athlete | athletics | athletic |
> | to compete | competitor | competition | competitive |
> | to score | scorer | score, scoring | -------- |
> | to win | winner | win, winning | winning |

4   Decide which verb collocates with each activity. Which verb is often used before an -ing form?

> **Answers**
> 1 play   2 go   3 play   4 do   5 do   6 go/do   7 do
> 8 go   9 go   10 play
> Before an -ing form we often use go (numbers 2, 6, 8, 9; also go running/jogging/shopping).

5   Check that you understand the six headings.
   team sports: sports in which a number of people work together in a group

winter sports: sports that are done on snow or ice
spectator sports: sports that people go to watch
extreme sports: sports that are dangerous and exciting
athletics: a group of specific competitive sports, including running, jumping and throwing (in USA called track and field)
contact sports: sports in which competitors are allowed to touch each other, e.g. to get the ball

Complete the table with sports from the box, and with any others you can think of.

> **Answers** (with some additions to those given in the box)
> team sports: basketball, baseball, ice hockey, rugby, soccer (+ American football, cricket)
> winter sports: ice hockey, skiing, snowboarding (+ bobsleigh)
> spectator sports: basketball, baseball, boxing, horseracing, ice hockey, rugby, soccer, sumo wrestling (+ tennis and many others)
> extreme sports: bungee jumping, parachuting, snowboarding, white-water rafting (+ rock climbing)
> athletics: cross-country running, discus, the high jump, triathlon (+ pole vault, hurdling)
> contact sports: boxing, rugby, sumo wrestling (+ wrestling, American football)

6   Read the instructions and table, and think about possible answers, considering both grammar and meaning.

> **Possible answers**
> 1   adjective: a type of jump
> 2   number
> 3   noun: a person or institution capable of supplying documents
> 4   number
> 5   noun: some form of container, capable of rolling
> 6   adjective or past participle
> 7   noun or adverb: days of week, or frequency
> 8   number
> 9   number

Play the recording and complete the table.

> **Answers** (relevant parts of the recording script are underlined)
> 1   backward(s)   2   120   3   doctor   4   (£)97   5   ball
> 6   attached   7   weekends   8   110   9   (£)65

Recording script

Man: Hello, Grayson's Adventure Days. How can I help you?
Woman: Oh, good morning. I want to book an activity day as a birthday present for my father, so could you give me an idea of the sorts of things you organise, please?
Man: What a great present! Do you want the activity to take place in a particular location?
Woman: No, anywhere in the country would be OK.
Man: Right. Well how about bungee jumping? That's our most popular activity.

Woman: Uh-huh?

Man: After a safety briefing, you're securely fastened to the correct bungee rope for your weight. Then the crane takes you up to a height of 50 metres <u>in a cage</u>, and you jump from it.

Woman: You make it sound so easy!

Man: In fact, some people change their minds at the last moment. But for the really brave, <u>you can also book our special, which is one normal bungee jump and then a backwards one</u>. It's quite an experience!

Woman: I can imagine! Is it available every day?

Man: We do bungee jumping <u>all year round, on over 120 dates</u>, and in various locations, but you should try to book about four weeks in advance, if possible, as it's very popular.

Woman: OK. And are there any age restrictions? It'll be my father's fiftieth birthday, so I hope he isn't too old.

Man: No, he certainly isn't too old, but <u>we'll require a certificate from a doctor</u>, to confirm that he's in good health.

Woman: Oh, he's very fit, so that won't be a problem. How much is it?

Man: It costs £57 per person for the standard jump, and <u>97 for the special.</u>

Woman: Right. Now I've heard of something called 'zorbing'. Do you do that, too?

Man: Yes, we do. That's another very popular activity.

Woman: What exactly is it?

Man: Well, you're securely attached in the centre of a zorb, either alone or with another person. <u>A zorb is over three metres high, and it consists of one ball inside another,</u> both made of clear plastic, so you can see out through them.

Woman: And what happens next?

Man: You roll down a hill, at speeds of up to 50 kilometres an hour. You can also choose the hydrozorb experience, where 25 litres of water is thrown inside with you, and <u>you aren't attached</u>, so you slide around in the water while you're rolling.

Woman: Wow! I'm sure my father would enjoy that. What about the dates?

Man: The zorb rides take place <u>between April and October, but just at weekends.</u>

Woman: Are there any restrictions, I mean, for height or weight?

Man: Your father needs to be at least 160 cm tall, and <u>weigh no more than 110 kilos.</u>

Woman: Oh, that's fine. How much does it cost?

Man: Zorbing is £50 per person.

Woman: And is hydrozorbing the same price?

Man: <u>No, that's £65.</u>

Woman: Right, I'd better give my father details of both the bungee jumping and zorbing, and let him choose, and then I'll get back to you.

Man: Fine. We tend to get fully booked, especially at this time of year, so you ought to book well in advance.

Woman: OK, I'll get back to you in the next few days. Thanks very much for your help.

Man: No problem. Bye.

Woman: Bye.

7 Read the questions and Useful language box. Think about how you could answer the questions.

> **Possible answers**
> 1 For lots of people, sport is all about winning, but in my opinion it's more important to get plenty of exercise. So trying to win is good if it encourages you to run faster.

2 It seems to me that stadiums and equipment are useful because they make sport seem glamorous, and that means more people take part. Ideally, people would play even if there weren't any stadiums or expensive equipment, to develop their skills and keep fit.

3 I think the media create celebrities. There's so much in the papers and on TV about David Beckham and other sportspeople that the general public focus on individuals rather than on sports themselves. I think this makes people believe they can be stars, too, so it encourages them to try, and that's good.

4 There are so many everyday risks, for instance crossing a road or boiling water. You can't ban everything, so I don't think sports should be banned, either. It's more important to encourage people to be careful.

12.2 pages 80–81

1 Think about possible answers. Remember ways of expressing a purpose (*to, in order to, so, so that*) and a reason (*because, because of*).

> **Possible answers**
> A lot of people do sports … to keep fit / so that they can meet people with similar interests / in order to develop their physical skills / because they find sport exciting.

2

> **Suggested answers**
> to develop basic human skills (lines 3–4)
> to increase mastery of the environment (lines 7–8)
> connections with entertainment and work (lines 30–31)
> to develop fighting skills (lines 35–37)
> for food and survival (line 40)
> for pleasure or competition (line 41)
> escapism from the routines of life (lines 47–48)

3 Read the task carefully, find the relevant parts of the text (i.e. references to Ancient Greece, etc.) and find the answers. Remember to answer only according to what is stated in the passage.

> **Answers**
> 1 B *the military culture of Greece was an influence on the development of its sports.* (lines 35–37)
> 2 E *The Industrial Revolution and mass production brought increased leisure in the 19th and particularly the 20th centuries. This led to a major growth in spectator sports, and made it possible for far more people to play and watch.* (lines 41–45)
> 3 C *The existence of art is evidence of there being leisure time available. It is therefore possible that there was some activity at these times resembling sport.* (lines 13–16)
> 4 G *These activities seem to have developed as a form of entertainment, as well as serving a practical function in making people fit for work.* (lines 29–31)
> 5 D *Native Americans played games and sports before the coming of Europeans.* (lines 19–21)

4 Read the four sentences and answer questions 1 and 2.

> **Answers**
> **1** advising **2** *had better*

Notice that *to* is used with *ought* but not with *should* or *had better*, and notice the position of *not* in *you'd better not*.

5 Read the statement and the five pieces of advice that could be given in response. Answer questions 1–3.

> **Answers**
> **1** a, b, c: they advise 'Stop playing now.'
> **2** d, e: they advise 'As a general rule, three hours is too long to play.'
> **3** *had better* (*You'd better not play for so long* is an unlikely sentence.)

Read the notes. *Ought to* is rather old-fashioned.

6

> **Possible answers**
> **1** I think you ought to try zorbing.
> **2** You should take a wetsuit, a towel and some dry clothes to change into afterwards.
> **3** You'd better give up football and take up something less energetic, like chess.
> **4** You ought to try white-water rafting – it's much more exciting than swimming.
> **5** You shouldn't do it if you don't want to, but you should go and watch your friends do their jump.

7 In exercises 4–6, *should* is used to give advice. In exercise 7 it is used to talk about the future.

> **Answers**
> **1** It would be good to go skiing this week, because the weather should stay fine.
> **2** The two runners are both so good that the result should be a tie.
> **3** I've got a slight injury to my arm, but it shouldn't stop me playing football next week.
> **4** I've gone riding before, so I should manage to stay on the horse.
> **5** This sentence can't be changed. *Should* wouldn't be appropriate here because falling off is seen as something bad.
> **6** The team has just missed a goal, but it shouldn't make much difference to the final score.

8 Think about how you could answer the question.

Writing folder 6
pages 82–83

1 Examiners give higher marks to students who use connecting words appropriately. You may be aware of *and*, *but* and *so*, but you also need to realise the importance of variety in your writing. Decide which column to put the connecting words into.

> **Answers**
>
> | and | but | so |
> |---|---|---|
> | in addition (to) | though | consequently |
> | in fact | unfortunately | therefore |
> | also | despite (the fact that) | as a result (of) |
> | what is more | however | this means/meant that |
> | | although | |

The words aren't all used in the same way. Read through the examples to see whether the connector links two clauses or begins a new sentence.

2

> **Answers**
> **1** a In addition / Also / What is more / In fact
> b What is more / In addition / In fact
> **2** a Though / Although / Despite the fact that
> b though / although
> c However / Unfortunately
> d Despite
> e Despite
> **3** a consequently / therefore / as a result
> b As a result of
> c This means that / Consequently, / Therefore, / As a result,

4

> **Answers**
> **1** A **2** C **3** B **4** A **5** B **6** A **7** B **8** B **9** C

5

> **Possible answers**
> **1** … I think it's a hard profession; they have to work hard.
> **2** … are very dangerous.
> **3** … are invaluable for maintaining high standards.
> **4** … it is a fairly expensive sport.
> **5** … will be deciding which of the national competitions to enter.
> **6** … didn't win the national league.
> **7** … were then allowed to compete in a higher league.
> **8** … celebrated with a party.
> **9** … they have won cups for playing football.
> **10** … are advised to eat well.

Units 9–12 Revision
pages 84–85

The aim of this revision unit is to focus on the language covered in Units 9–12.

Exercises 2–6 can be done as a test.

1 Give your own answers.

2

Answers (letters refer to the rules in 11.2)
1 – (d)   2 – (d)   3 – (c)   4 – (d)   5 a (a)   6 – (d)
7 a (a)   8 The (b)   9 – (d)   10 The (b)   11 the (b)
12 – (d)   13 – (c)   14 – (d)

3

Answers
1 have   2 to move   3 to keep   4 writing   5 studying
6 to be   7 (to) improve   8 having   9 to believe
10 adapting

4

Answers
1 much time	6 many animals
2 many countries	7 much pollution
3 many universities	8 much work
4 much accommodation	9 Many people
5 much research	10 much news

5

Answers
1 recycling   2 endangered   3 extend   4 extended
5 workshop   6 referee   7 spectators   8 extreme
9 bungalow

6

Answers
1 effects of   2 melting of   3 effect on   4 increase in
5 threat to   6 loss of   7 causes of   8 dependency on

Unit 13

13.1 pages 86–87

1 You are going to read about a man who believes that more choice is not always a good thing. Read through the statements in the questionnaire. There is no right answer and you shouldn't take it seriously. The words 'maximiser' and 'satisficer' have been made up by Barry Schwartz, the writer of the article.

2 Remember to time yourself reading the text. It should take you a couple of minutes. Don't worry about words you don't know at this stage.

3 Questions 1–7 are testing Locating information (Test folder 7) and questions 8–9 are testing Multiple choice (Test folder 6). Use a highlighter pen to underline where in the text you think the answer is.

Answers (evidence from the passage is given, but this is not part of the answer)
1 A *But recently I was asked ... more and more dissatisfied.* (lines 6–9)
2 G *But no one wants to hear this ...* (lines 71–72)

3 C *psychologists and economists are puzzled by the fact that ...* (lines 34–35)
4 D *people are then upset by ...* (line 43)
5 B *Schwartz designed a questionnaire ...* (lines 18–19)
6 E *If there are few options ...* (line 53)
7 B *between what he termed 'maximisers' and 'satisficers'* (lines 19–20)
8 D
9 B

4 You will come across adverb–verb collocations very often in academic writing. You should make sure you have a section in your vocabulary notebooks for this very important group of words.

Answers
1 highly   2 firmly   3 hugely / (highly/totally)
4 anxiously   5 totally   6 widely   7 justly / (hugely)
8 hardly

13.2 pages 88–89

1 Read through 1–4 and then play the recording. Each speaker uses a different type of conditional. Refer to the Grammar folder if you are unsure of the form.

Answers
1 Speaker D   2 Speaker B   3 Speaker C   4 Speaker A

Recording script

Speaker A: When my grandfather was young, he had the chance to go to Paris to study the violin. I remember him telling me how excited he was – the only one in the family to win a scholarship. Then, overnight, great-grandfather lost all his money. My grandpa had to decide – he could still go to Paris, as it was fully funded, or he could stay at home and get a job to help the family. Well, you know the rest. But <u>if he had gone to Paris, who knows what would have happened – we might have had a famous musician in the family.</u>

Speaker B: I need to decide which college to apply to, but I'm finding it very difficult. My family want me to study something they think is useful, like medicine, and my tutor says that <u>if I train to be a doctor, I'll get a job fairly easily,</u> but the thing is, well, what I really want to do is Media Studies. I'm really into films – *making* them, not being *in* them, and, well everything about the film industry, and I'd like to learn more. So, what do I do? Upset my family or toe the line?

Speaker C: My sister works for a large multi-national in London. It's a really good job – most people would kill to have it – lots of money, but she does have to work 24/7. She wants to give it all up and go travelling – you know the thing – surfing in Hawaii, climbing Mt Kilimanjaro. I keep telling her not to be so stupid. After all, even she says <u>if she went on holiday for six months, they wouldn't keep her job open for when she returns.</u> You can't spend your life just hopping from plane to plane. She's mad.

Speaker D: How do I make choices? Well, I don't usually have any problem. <u>If I see something I like, I buy it.</u> Take last week. I was shopping with a friend and I saw the most gorgeous coat. It was a bit pricey, even for me, but I just had to have it, so out came the credit card again. I'll have to pay it off sometime, of course.

2

> **Answers**
> A *If he had gone to Paris, who knows what would have happened – we might have had a famous musician in the family.* (third conditional)
> B *If I train to be a doctor, I'll get a job fairly easily.* (first conditional)
> C *If she went on holiday for six months, they wouldn't keep her job open for when she returns.* (second conditional)
> D *If I see something I like, I buy it.* (zero conditional)

3

> **Answers**
> 1 i 2 j 3 d 4 b 5 a 6 c 7 e 8 g 9 f 10 h

4

> **Possible answers**
> 1 Unless you wear something smart, you won't get a job.
> 2 I would have bought a new CD if I hadn't run out of money.
> 3 If I were you, I'd get a job rather than go to college.
> 4 If I had had the chance, I would have chosen a different course.
> 5 As long as you let me choose the film, I'll go to the cinema with you.
> 6 If I had to choose between studying at home and studying abroad, I'd choose the latter.
> 7 I won't go shopping unless you treat me to lunch.
> 8 I'll buy you a new jacket if you like.

5 The expressions in 7 and 8 are commonly found in letters. They feature the polite *would* in both sides of the sentence.

> **Answers**
> 1 It **would** be best if the children were in bed when we go out tonight.
> It is best if the children **are** in bed when we go out tonight.
> 2 You will not go wrong if you **choose** her for your secretary.
> You **would** not go wrong if you chose her for your secretary.
> 3 If I ever **have** money, I **will spend** it wisely.
> If I ever **had** money, I **would spend** it wisely.
> 4 What would happen if the cheque **went** missing?
> What would **have happened** if the cheque **had gone** missing?
> 5 If you choose to live in the town centre, **you'll need** to pay more.
> If you **chose** to live in the town centre, you'd need to pay more.
> 6 Unless we ~~will~~ hurry, we will be late.
> 7 I would appreciate it if you **would write** back to me.
> 8 I would be grateful if you **would/could** reply as soon as possible.

6 The pictures show two different types of shopping experience – one very impersonal in a large supermarket and the other in a small shop with personal service.

7 There are four people speaking – Pete, Tom and Lucy, who are students, and their tutor. This should not make a difference to understanding, as it is very clear who is who. Part 3 of the Speaking Module often has up to four speakers, but two usually dominate.

8 Read through questions 1–3 and then answer them as you listen to the first part of the recording. Then study questions 4–10 and answer them as you listen to the second part of the recording.

> **Answers** (relevant parts of of the recording script are underlined)
> 1 A 2 C 3 B
> 4 CDs 5 confusion marketing
> 6 price; taste 7 first impression
> 8 (your/their) parents 9 trend setter
> 10 designer clothes

Recording script

Questions 1–3

Tutor: Good morning. So, in our tutorial today we're looking at the nature of choice. Now, last week we were saying that compared with 50 years ago, today we're totally surrounded by choice. We have it in the shops at a level which we've never previously had. But <u>if choice were to disappear, I mean if we were to live in an economy where we only had one type of biscuit on offer or one clothes shop in the vicinity, do you think we would really be worse off as a result?</u>

Pete: Oh, I think so, most definitely. It'd be so boring.

Tutor: Yes, I would argue that the very idea which <u>economics is based on is that people have different preferences</u>, and forcing people to buy a particular brand would make most people worse off. Unless we lived in a world where people happened to be identical and agree, which of course, happily, we don't.

Tom: But having too many choices can lead to problems – not having enough time, for example.

Tutor: Mm, <u>I read somewhere that in the US the average number of TV channels is about 55, and the average number that is viewed in a week in a typical American home is about 13, and if there are 99 channels, it is still about 13.</u> I think this is telling us something – it shows us the amount of time people are prepared to spend finding a programme.

Questions 4–10

Tutor: So, is the same true for washing powder or toothpaste, do you think?

Lucy: Certainly, as far as I'm concerned! I don't have time to spend deciding which sort of toothpaste I want to buy.

Tutor: Well, my view is that 50 kinds of different washing powder or 50 kinds of soap do not actually add to the quality of life, but in other areas – <u>such as CDs – then I might say yes, there are aspects of choice that do improve the quality of life.</u>

Pete: But what about things like choosing which mobile phone to get – that's a nightmare.

Tutor: Yes, there's definitely a problem when you're dealing with complex markets where there *appears* to be a large choice, but actually there isn't really – it's called <u>confusion marketing</u>. <u>With some mobile phone contracts, you need to be a trained mathematician</u> to work out which is the best deal!

Tom: Well, I think confusion marketing is one of the most irritating things I can think of. Each company offering a slightly different contract, so it's virtually impossible to compare prices. So how *do* people make a decision?

Tutor: Well, it seems to depend on what you're buying. There's a difference in decision-making between buying a loaf of bread and buying a house, for example. <u>When you buy a loaf of bread</u>, you generally use all the available information about it and then <u>choose the best option for you – probably based on price and taste.</u> However, psychologists say that, contrary to what you may think, <u>when you buy a house</u>, you make that decision in less than ten seconds – <u>that first impression counts most of all.</u> That's why people selling their houses are told to make some coffee so the house smells good, put fresh flowers out, make sure it's tidy, etc. First impressions matter a lot – it's the same when you buy a car or a holiday.

Pete: But what happens when there are two holidays and I want to choose between them? Is it better for me just to choose one immediately and save time, or put a lot of effort into finding out all I can about both holidays and making a rational choice?

Tutor: Well, generally, people use one of three basic strategies for dealing with choice. The first is simply to always <u>get what their parents have always bought in the past.</u>

Lucy: But I don't think many young people nowadays just follow what their parents did.

Tutor: Well, the second strategy is to <u>buy the latest thing – to be a trend setter.</u> More and more people seem to be doing this nowadays – you find people are throwing out perfectly OK TVs and other electrical equipment just because they're not totally up to date.

Pete: I know a lot of people who do that. Good for the economy though – keeping people in work making even more stuff.

Tutor: Well, I guess that's one way of looking at it. The third strategy is to <u>buy something which is unique, something few people buy – designer clothes</u>, for instance. Of course, if you have real problems choosing, then you can actually pay people to choose for you. They spend their time finding the best deal and then present you with the information.

Tom: You'll still have the problem of how to choose the best person to find out the information for you, of course!

9

Possible answers

1 Yes, I quite agree with this idea. What I mean is that when I go into a shop, I find it completely mind-boggling when I have a huge choice, and in the end, I tend to walk out without buying anything.

2 I had to choose whether to have tea or coffee, whether to have an apple or a fattening pastry and also whether to go to the cinema tonight with a friend or stay at home and do some coursework.

3 Not really, nothing very important. I suppose I'm quite lucky, in a way.

4 Well, first of all I weigh up all the evidence carefully. Then I go to bed. Let me put this another way: I think trying to sleep on a decision is probably the best way to come to a good conclusion.

Test folder 7

pages 90–91

Make sure you fully understand the notes and advice.

1 Read the description of the passage, and paragraph A. Then read the rubric and the example. Make sure you understand that 2 reflects *possible difficulties – such as resistance to their plans* in A. Now complete the task.

Answers (evidence from the passage is given, but this is not part of the answer)

1 E *It is an unstructured way of thinking, in which there is little criticism of ideas*

2 A (example)

3 D *It allows you to eliminate them, alter them, or prepare contingency plans to deal with problems that might arise ... make your plans 'tougher' and better able to survive difficulties ... spot fatal flaws and risks*

4 B *it has the benfit of blocking the confrontations that happen when people with different thinking styles discuss the same problem*

5 F *people chairing meetings ... may direct activity into Green Hat thinking ... they will ask for Black Hat thinking.*

6 B *As a result, your decisions and plans will be ambitious, creative and sensitive to the needs of others. They will be carried out effectively, and you will be prepared for the unexpected.*

7 C *analyse past trends, and try to work out from historical data what might happen in the future*

8 E *encourages you to think positively ... the optimistic viewpoint ... helps you to keep going when everything looks gloomy and difficult*

2

Answers (evidence from the passage is given, but this is not part of the answer)

1 C *they are not expected to do this all the time – when we meet them at parties or in the street, for instance.*

2 B *managers ... 'looking the part' by dressing differently from those below them in the company hierarchy*

3 D *Managers ... may feel under pressure to behave in an authoritarian manner, even if this conflicts with their personality and general approach to interaction with other people.*

4 A *one person may need to act as manager, husband, father, son, friend, and so on.*

5 E *once we know the relevant role of the other person, we assume that ... we, too, need to behave in certain ways.*

6 B *Clearly expectations are a product of a particular time and place*

Unit 14

14.1 pages 92–93

1 The photos are of:
- the iPod Mini in a variety of colours
- a Ferrari
- a child using a bottle of purple ketchup

Possible answer

I really like the colours used for the iPod Mini. I have a pink one and my sister has a silver one. I think the green one looks a bit strange and I personally don't really like the gold one.

Whenever I think of a Ferrari I usually think of a red one. I don't know why – I'm sure they make them in other colours, but red just seems to be the most appropriate colour for a Ferrari.

Purple ketchup? I'm not so sure about that. Maybe young children like the idea but I prefer my ketchup to be red.

2   Look at questions 1–4 and try to predict the answers. Then do the same for questions 5–8. For questions 5–8 you need to write the name of a colour in the spaces. For questions 9 and 10 you will need to draw lines showing the popularity of blue and green vehicles over the period 1987–2001.

Play the recording. Did you predict the right answers?

Answers

1 B   2 G   3 E   4 F   5 white   6 silver   7 blue   8 black

Questions 9 and 10

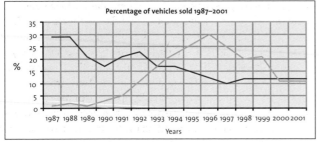

Percentage of vehicles sold 1987–2001

Recording script

Questions 1–4

Lecturer: Although the human eye can discern at least six million different colour shades, and theoretically there are an infinite number of colour possibilities, the colours which are popular at any given time will depend on a wide variety of factors – including technological advances, the economy and even politics. Colour fashions do not change abruptly, rather they are continually evolving, and one colour may be fashionable for up to ten or twelve years. Let's look now at some examples of colour trends.

When it comes to the world of work, most people are very traditional. Men go for suits, shirts and ties and, while there's a wide choice of colours for both shirts and ties – pink, purple and green proving popular recently – it would seem that blue, rather than black or grey, is generally the first choice for their main outfit. Apparently, it's a colour that appeals to people who are responsible, and is especially popular with bankers.

Now, offices always benefit from some colour. Even a small amount will improve mood and, although most offices these days are generally a rather boring white, by using a hint of colour – possibly with a green filing cabinet or red blinds at the windows – employers may find that their employees' stress levels are reduced and productivity is improved.

Turning to national flags, colour is of vital importance. The point made by one academic in the last century that 'national flags make use of only seven main colours: red, blue, green, and yellow, orange, black and white' remains true today. An analysis of the number of colours used on flags between 1917 and 1999 reveals that a combination of three colours is by far the most popular choice. The use of a single colour is negligible, but the use of four colours is increasing in popularity. Most countries go primarily for red, followed closely by white and then blue. Black, green and orange are among the least popular combinations.

The iPod Mini first appeared in January 2004. It came in a range of colours – blue, pink, green, silver and gold, which were supposed to appeal to different personality types. When it was first introduced, people were asked to vote on the Apple website for which colour they preferred, and the silver one stole a stunning 46 per cent of the vote, with none of the other colours coming near. Gold was particularly low in the polls, with blue, pink and green all a rather poor second.

Questions 5–8

Lecturer: Next, cars. Much like fashion, colour preferences follow trends and fall in and out of favour as the years pass. In 2004 global colour trend data showed that, interestingly, red and green were no longer popular, with less than 5% of vehicles manufactured using those colours, but silver, favoured often by first-time buyers, was far and away the leader, being the colour of 38% of vehicles produced. White, a favourite apparently with older, male drivers, had 19.6% of the market, followed by black at 13.9%. Interestingly, in North America, white cars had the lowest collision rates, while black had the most. The once trendy blue car is declining in popularity worldwide, and in 2004 made up only 9.3% of cars purchased, perhaps because it had been found that in the USA particularly, blue cars were the most popular with car thieves.

Questions 9 and 10

Lecturer: Let's look now at the rise and fall in popularity of blue and green cars in Canada.

Let's take blue cars first. Blue cars began at a high of 29% from 1987 to 88. They then began to falter, with a fall to 21% in 1989 and a further fall to 17% in 1990. Sales picked up in 1991, when they rose to 21% and reached a peak of 23% in 1992. There was then a gradual fall from 17% in 1993 and 94 to a low of 10% in 1997. Blue cars then remained more or less constant at 12% of the market until the end of 2001.

Turning now to green cars … from 1987 to 1990, sales of green cars were only very low – only 1%, with a high of 2% in 1988. There was an upturn in 1991, as sales hit 5%, growing to 20% in 1993. Sales continued to grow, reaching a peak of 30% in 1996. It was all downhill after 1996 though, with green car sales back to 20% in 1998. Sales then rose slightly in 1999 to 21%, but plummeted to 11% by 2000 and then levelled off.

3   You should be familiar by now with some of these words describing changes. Exercises 3 and 4 give practice in Task 1 of the Academic Writing Module.

Answers

to go down	to remain stable	to go up
to decline	to be steady	to grow
to weaken	to be consistent	to make progress
to plummet	to level off	to rise
to fall	to remain constant	to improve
	to remain unchanged	to pick up

4

5 Students often complain that they can't hear where one word ends and another begins. This exercise is to build awareness of what is happening when we are speaking in English.

6 This is a fun activity and should not be taken too seriously. You will probably need to have an English–English dictionary for unfamiliar words.

7 Try to use the phrases in the Useful language box. These are mainly phrases to do with generalising.

Possible answers

1 I haven't thought about it before but I guess, yes, it may be possible to tell someone's personality by looking at their clothes. For example, if you wear black all the time, it probably means that on the whole you're a gloomy type of person, very pessimistic, but also that you are probably very strong-willed.

2 In my country, people generally wear white for weddings and black for funerals. Red is used for danger.

3 I think that, as a rule, colour plays an enormous part in our lives. What would the world be like without colour? Very sad and grey. We need colour to help cheer us up, to calm us, to make us happy. For instance, I've heard that some prisons have been painted pink and green in order to put the prisoners in a better mood.

4 Colour has a large role in advertising. We associate different products with their colour. Often people can't be bothered to remember the name of the product, but they do remember the colour of the packet.

14.2 pages 94–95

1 You should be familiar with the concept of -ing forms and infinitives from Unit 10. In this unit, the grammar is extended to look at verbs which change their meaning, depending on whether they are followed by an -ing form or an infinitive. Play the recording. This first playing is for general understanding rather than anything more detailed.

Answers

Red and green: developed so humans could see red leaves or berries clearly in the forest.

Some birds and fish can see in colour, but mainly in blue and yellow.

Up to 8% of men are colour blind. More humans suffer from colour blindness than monkeys, so human beings may be losing their ability to distinguish between red and green.

Recording script

Student: Well, this morning I went to Dr Stanley's zoology seminar. It was quite interesting when I finally got there – on why man evolved the ability to see red and green colours. Apparently, it helped our ancestors to find food – you can see red leaves or berries more clearly among the green leaves in the jungle, or something like that anyway.

Well, I always like to get to his seminars on time, but this morning I was running late – I didn't remember to switch my alarm clock on last night. I remember getting into bed, but that's about all, I was so tired. Well, as I say, I arrived late, and although I tried to be as quiet as possible, Dr Stanley stopped talking and just looked at me. I was so embarrassed. I told him I hadn't meant to be late. Well, I got a seat, and he started explaining about which other animals could see in colour – apparently, fish and some birds do, but mainly only blue and yellow. It's only primates that can see red and green as well as blue–yellow. Interestingly, he went on to say that more humans suffer from colour blindness than monkeys, so we may be losing our ability to distinguish red from green. Apparently, in some groups of people, up to 8% of men have red–green colour blindness. Anyway, he then stopped to show us a video, which meant switching off all the lights. I tried everything to keep awake – eating mints, pinching myself – but it was no good.

2 Play the recording again. Try to answer using the same structure as in the recording. How is the meaning of *stop* affected by whether it is followed by *to do* or *stop doing*? (*stop to do something* = gives the reason why you stopped; *stop doing something* = cease/finish doing something, or not do it any longer)

There are a very few verbs which have no difference in meaning when they are followed by a different structure.

Answers

1 zoology
2 no
3 She didn't remember to switch on her alarm clock.
4 He stopped talking.
5 He went on to talk about colour blindness.
6 He stopped to show a video.
7 She tried eating mints and pinching herself.

3

> **Answers**
> 1 a She forgot to switch the alarm on before getting into bed.
>   b She got into bed and now remembers it.
> 2 a He didn't talk any more.
>   b He stopped what he was doing because he wanted to show a video.

4 This gives further practice. Try to give a paraphrase or synonym to explain the difference in meaning.

> **Answers**
> 1 a *tried* + infinitive = attempted
>   b *tried* + *-ing* form = experimented
> 2 a *went on* + *-ing* form = continued doing the same thing
>   b *went on* + infinitive = did something else in addition
> 3 no real difference in meaning
> 4 a *I like* + *-ing* form = this is something I generally enjoy doing
>   b *I like* + infinitive = this is an example of something I do regularly, often because I think it is a good thing to do

5

> **Possible answers**
> 1 When I couldn't wake up in time for school, I tried asking a friend to phone me.
> 2 When I realised I had forgotten my wallet, I tried to borrow some money for the ticket.
> 3 When I was young, I remember going to visit my grandparents on their farm.
> 4 I asked them to keep the noise level down, but they went on playing loud hip hop all night.
> 5 At the weekends, I like to go shopping / going shopping.
> 6 Next time, you must remember to take your keys with you or you'll be locked out.

6

> **Possible answers**
> 1 I first remember seeing the colour blue – it was a teddy bear that had a big, blue ribbon around its neck.
> 2 I often forget to take my diary with me to work.
> 3 I would try to make up with her as soon as possible.
> 4 I like to have a shower.

7 The words in this exercise are ones which are commonly confused by students.

> **Answers**
> 1 *lent* (you borrow something from someone)
> 2 *Remind* (someone reminds you, you remember yourself)
> 3 *receipt* (a *recipe* has the instructions for cooking)
> 4 *raised* (*rise* has no object – the sun rises)
> 5 *countryside* (*nature* is the general term for animals, plants, etc.)
> 6 *check* (*control* is to order or limit someone's actions)

> 7 *effect* (*affect* means 'to influence', 'to cause to change')
> 8 *economical* (*economic* relates to trade and industry)
> 9 *At the end* (*In the end* means 'finally', 'at the end of something')
> 10 *Standards* (*standard of living* is an expression meaning the amount of wealth or comfort people have in a particular society; *levels* refers to the height/amount/number of something)
> 11 *journey* (*travel* is more commonly used as an adjective not a noun, unless in *business travel / space travel*)
> 12 *discovery* (*invention* of something new; *discovery* of something that has always been there)

8 Read through the box on comment adverbs and look at the examples. Using a comment adverb correctly can lift your writing and speaking and make it seem more natural. This will help you to achieve higher marks in the exam.

> **Answers**
> 1 statistically 2 Personally 3 generously 4 logically
> 5 Interestingly 6 obviously 7 Disappointingly
> 8 Honestly 9 Surprisingly 10 wisely

9 Look carefully at the example and then write a short paragraph in a similar way, remembering to use as many comment adverbs as you can.

Writing folder 7
pages 96–97

1 The first aim of this Writing folder is to increase awareness of generalising and to encourage you not to make sweeping statements which you do not have the information to support. More marks are to be gained if a more tentative approach is taken.

> **Answer**
> B is more general and formal.

2 Refer to the Useful language box.

> **Possible answers**
> 1 It is widely believed that blue is / Blue is thought to be a cold colour and it is often said that it shouldn't be used to paint living rooms.
> 2 It has been claimed that the colour of the packaging influences customers' choice of products.
> 3 Green tends to be the colour of environmental awareness.
> 4 It is widely assumed that if you drive a red car, you like speeding.
> 5 Broadly speaking / On the whole, more women than men wear bright colours.
> 6 I think that red tends to be the best colour for a national flag. / Red is generally agreed to be the best colour for a national flag.

3 This exercise looks at ways of incorporating relevant examples into your writing. Make sure you try to use words and phrases from the Useful language box.

> **Possible answer**
> ... The following are examples of where there might be a problem: a career as a pilot, a police officer or a fire fighter may be impossible. For instance, it would be dangerous if a pilot couldn't tell the difference between red and green lights.

4

> **Possible answers**
> 1 For some types of animal, it is true to say that the male is more colourful than the female. Birds are the best illustration of this. There is a tendency for the male of each species to have very colourful plumage to attract the female. One clear example of this is the peacock, where the male bird is exceedingly beautiful and the female is very plain. Mammals such as bears, tigers and so on do not use colour as much as size and strength to attract the female.
> 2 Generally speaking, colour does help companies to sell their goods. If we look at packaging, for example, it would appear that certain colours help companies target particular consumers. Companies often favour bright, primary colours when they are targeting children and have a tendency to choose more sophisticated colours for young professionals. Another example of the way colour sells is in the use of yellow. It is widely believed that yellow, when placed on a supermarket shelf, will draw the eye more easily than any other colour.

5 Read through the paragraph first before attempting to do the exercise.

> **Answers**
> 1 B 2 A 3 C 4 B 5 A

6

> **Sample answer**
> How often do we think, I mean really think, about colour? Personally, I believe there is a tendency for us to take colour for granted, to not acknowledge its importance. However, I very strongly believe that the world would indeed be a poorer place without it.
>
> For a start, we would no longer be able to see the colours of nature. What would the world be like without a beautiful blue sky, a blood-red sunset or a rainbow after a rainstorm? It would literally be colourless – a word that not only means 'without colour' but also 'not exciting', and 'uninteresting'. Clearly, not everyone has the time to sit around admiring Mother Nature and her colours, but life would be much poorer without the possibility of a free artistic display to cheer our lives up.
>
> Another thing worth mentioning is the way we look. If there was a world without colour, we would all look the same. Ideally, this would be a good thing, with the result that there would be no discrimination on the basis of the colour of our skin. However, personally, I think that there would be a strong tendency to find something else to discriminate against – possibly a person's height.
>
> Colour is something that adds life and beauty to our world. You only have to look around you to see that. For example, when you look into a child's bright blue eyes, or catch a glimpse of a young girl's shiny red hair. To sum up, I really have to say that a world without colour would definitely be a much, much poorer place.
>
> (267 words)

Unit 15

15.1 pages 98–99

The pictures show people eating together in different circumstances. Think about the way the people in the pictures are relating to each other.

1 Think about how you would answer these questions. Remember to expand your answers.

> **Possible answers**
> • I generally enjoy meeting new people if there's a chance to get to know them, but I prefer meeting one or two new people at a time, rather than a lot.
> • I find it interesting to meet people from countries that I'd like to visit, because I can find out more about their country.
> • When friends come to my home, I usually offer them a cup of tea or coffee, and try to keep my younger brothers and sisters away from them.
> • When people invite guests to their home, it's usually for a meal in the evening. They might spend the whole evening sitting at the table and eating.

2 Think about possible problems and pleasures of staying with a family in another country.

Skim the passage and check if any of your ideas about problems and pleasures are mentioned. *Hospitality* means being friendly and welcoming to guests and visitors. Social anthropology is also called 'cultural anthropology' and is the study of different cultures and societies.

3 Read the first line of the summary, and lines 1–4 of the passage. Think about what other words from the box would more or less fit the meaning of **0** (*homes, host, people, resident, villages*), and why *household* is the only possibility. (The word needs to refer to something that can have members, and it must be singular.)

Read the rest of the summary, the words in the box, the relevant part of the passage (from the beginning) and complete the summary.

Answers (evidence from the passage is given, but this is not part of the answer)

1	customs	*everyday life (lines 2–3), how people managed their lives (line 4)*
2	guest	*an honoured guest (line 11)*
3	duties	*shopping, cooking or domestic chores (line 13)*
4	wine	*Wine had already been made, generally by the men, who were also responsible for pouring it. (lines 27–29)*
5	meals	*large amounts of food were prepared in advance, usually by the women. (lines 26–27)*
6	groceries	*it was not always easy to buy food. Grocery stores … (lines 32–33)*
7	markets	*people usually shopped in markets (lines 34–35), travelled to several locations (line 38), travelled across the city … to the central market (lines 16–17)*
8	bus	*travelled across the city on buses to the central market (lines 16–17), frequent trips to the market on … crowded buses (lines 36–37)*

Read questions 9–13 and find the answers in the passage.

Answers (evidence from the passage is given, but this is not part of the answer)

9 D *my Russian hosts seemed to feel that they could only succeed in their role as host if their guests … consumed far more than they would normally. (lines 44–49)*

10 B *an offer to help with the cooking may well be accepted (lines 71–72)*

C *guests are expected to eat as much, or as little, as they like (lines 77–78)*

E *Hosts usually don't feel that their food, cooking skills or hospitality are being criticised if a guest refuses second helpings (lines 81–85)*

F *a guest who offers to help with the washing up may be disappointed to find that their offer is accepted! (lines 85–88)*

4 Think of ways of talking about each part of the task. Remember that in the test what you say doesn't have to be true.

Give a short talk to a friend, or record yourself and listen to it afterwards.

15.2 pages 100–101

Think about what the pictures show.

Possible answers
- The first drawing shows a man and a woman shaking hands. Maybe they're friends.
- The second drawing shows people in a meeting. One person has arrived late, and the others seem annoyed.
- The last drawing shows two men having a conversation. The one on the left is leaning towards the other one, who seems uncomfortable and is backing away.

1 Think about what you could say on the topics.

Possible points to mention

Eye contact
When someone is talking to you, what would they think if you looked directly at them? And if you didn't look at them?

Shaking hands
Do you shake hands? If so, when, and who with? Do you use one hand or both? Do you grip the other person's hand firmly or weakly? While you're both gripping hands, do you move them up and down or not at all?

Punctuality
If you have arranged to meet someone at a certain time, how would you feel about keeping them waiting? And how would you feel if they arrived late?

Personal space
If you're standing talking to someone, what distance do you usually keep between you? How do you feel if they reduce or increase the distance?

2 Read the options A–C and the example. Check that you understand why the answer is C (*come straight out with it* = say it in a direct, straightforward way).

Read questions 1–8. Remember to write A, B or C for the answer. Play the recording.

Answers (relevant parts of the recording script are underlined; words in *italics* show answers to exercise 3)

1 B 2 C 3 A 4 A 5 B 6 A 7 C 8 C

Recording script

Tutor: Good morning, everyone. Now, as I told you last week, our topic this morning is cultural differences and some of the aspects of behaviour you'll need to be aware of when you go abroad on business. Helen and Bill, you've prepared a short presentation, haven't you?

Helen: That's right. We've concentrated on three areas: Japan, the Arab countries and the USA, because they're important business partners for Australia, now or in the future. I should say first of all that we've had to simplify by making generalisations, but of course people vary a lot within each culture. And what we've learnt from our research is that one way of doing things is usually no better or worse than another. *We just tend to be more comfortable with the way we're used to.* OK. Now Bill's going to start with communication.

Bill: Right. Thanks, Helen. Um, information, particularly something negative, is communicated in different ways around the world. <u>In the US, people tend to speak and write fairly explicitly and frankly, and many people pride themselves on saying what they mean. If they want to say 'no', they come straight out with it.</u> But in some societies, a great deal of information is transmitted *non*-verbally. The Japanese, for instance, usually don't want to displease others with a negative answer, so they may not *say* 'no' – but it's still clearly understood if you can read the non-verbal signs.

There can be a big difference in appropriate eye contact, too, from country to country. *In the United States, if you look someone in the eye when they're speaking to you, you're thought to be honest and reliable.* Looking away or at the floor indicates that you aren't paying attention or you're guilty. <u>But in Japan, an attempt to</u>

maintain eye contact isn't usually acceptable behaviour and may be taken as a sign of aggression. _Looking away is a sign of respect_, rather than of hiding something. On the other hand, in some Arab countries, such as in Saudi Arabia, eye contact is important and can help in communication. Helen …

Helen: Ways of shaking hands vary around the world, too. A weak grip, held for a relatively long time, is normal in Japan, and certainly doesn't mean the person is weak. In the United States, the way that someone shakes hands has long been taken as an indicator of their personality. _A firm grip is thought to show strength of character._

Attitudes towards time vary. If you make an appointment with an Arab business person, you may find that your meeting begins long past the appointed time, though it'll probably last as long as necessary to conduct the business in hand. _There, time is a servant_, not a master, and the idea that a person should be ruled by the clock is amusing. But in the United States, time is money. _If someone's kept waiting for a meeting half an hour beyond the time that was agreed, it's seen as a signal that they aren't important._ So Americans try to avoid this happening.

People are expected to arrive in good time for a meeting in Japan. Being late demonstrates that you can't be trusted to keep your word or manage your time. But in the Arab tradition, punctuality isn't regarded in the same way. People can show up hours late, or not at all, and it won't be taken as an insult. Of course a lot of Arabs, particularly business people, are aware that attitudes towards punctuality are different in other parts of the world.

In Japan, business meetings normally start with some casual conversation, because the Japanese are generally interested in getting to know the people involved. In America, though, meetings sometimes begin with phrases such as 'Let's get started'. Over to you, Bill.

Bill: OK, let's turn to personal space. When you're standing talking to someone, make sure you adopt the distance that's appropriate to the local culture. In the US and Britain, business people usually stand close enough to shake hands, about 75 to 90 cm apart. In the Arab world, it's less, maybe under 30 cm, and you sometimes see a British person backing away to maintain their preferred distance, while the Arab they're talking to keeps moving towards them, to maintain his or hers. The Japanese prefer a greater distance than either, perhaps 120 cm, and may see the British as getting too close. One reason for maintaining that distance in Japan is to have room to bow when they greet someone – a custom that to some extent corresponds to the American habit of nodding.

Helen: And finally, you need to get used to the fact that in much of Asia, people gravitate towards other people in public spaces. For example, if you're sitting in a movie theatre surrounded by empty seats and a local resident enters, he's likely to sit next to you – it's considered appropriate in many parts of the world, but an American, for instance, would feel they were sitting much too close. And that's as far as we've got.

Tutor: OK, thank you both. Now, are there any questions?

3 Complete the sentences as you listen. Play the recording: this is the same as the previous recording, but starts with _I should say first of all_ (in Helen's first speech) and ends at _So Americans try to avoid this happening_.

(Note that although completing sentences is an IELTS task, in the IELTS Test the recording is played only once, and each task follows on from the previous one, so you would never be asked to listen to a passage a second time.)

Answers (relevant parts of the recording script are in _italics_)
1 comfortable 2 frankly 3 honest and reliable 4 respect
5 strength of character 6 servant 7 important

---

4 As well as talking about facts, we often talk about possibilities, for example _I might invite some friends to lunch next week. I may ask them to help me cook._ Read the section in the tinted box. _Speculate_ means to guess possible answers to a question when you do not have enough information to be certain. This verb is often used in Part 3 of the Speaking Module.

Suggested answers
1 Customs may/might become more similar to those in other countries.
2 Shaking hands may/might not be so common in future.
3 People may/might copy the customs they see in foreign TV programmes.

Modal perfects (modal verb + _have_ + past participle) normally refer to the past. _May/might have done_ can be used to talk about the past when you do not have enough information to be certain. Read the introduction to questions 4–6, and rewrite the three sentences using _may_ or _might (not) have_.

Suggested answers
4 People may/might not have eaten much foreign food.
5 People may/might have been more hospitable.
6 People may/might not have spent much time enjoying themselves.

---

5 The picture is part of the original poster for the film _If it's Tuesday, this must be Belgium_. Read the paragraph below the picture. The deduction in the film title is about the present, and it is saying that something is true.

Read the task and find the right example for each explanation.

Answers
1 b 2 a 3 d 4 c

---

6 _Must_ is used to deduce that something is true, and _can't_ is used to say something is impossible. Remember that these are not the only meanings of _must_ and _can't_. For further information, refer to the Grammar folder on page 142.

Read the exercise and give some possible responses in each situation.

Possible answers
1 You must be tired. / You must have been out enjoying yourself.
2 He can't be a doctor – he told me he's a dentist.
3 You must be Sally Green.
4 Nur must have changed her email address.
5 No – he can't have received my message.

---

7 Read the information above exercise 7. Remember that *collocation* means words that are often used together, often for no obvious reason. The collocations in the three phrases are *large amounts, a great deal, a big difference*.

> **Answers**
> **A** large **B** great **C** big
> (In columns A and B, some words collocate with *big*, but others don't.)
> *Great* is not normally used with physical objects.

8 Complete the passage with words from columns A and B.

> **Suggested answers**
> 1 honour **2** extent **3** number **4** amount **5** sum
> 6 advantage **7** distance **8** success

Test folder 8

pages 102–103

Make sure you fully understand the notes and advice.

1 Read the task, and think of ways of suggesting that someone is a colleague, friend or relative, without using those words.

> **Possible answers**
> *Colleague*: we work for the same company; we're in the same office; he/she's my boss
> *Friend*: we spend a lot of time together; we were at college together
> *Relative*: he married my sister; he/she is a family member

Play the recording and complete the task. Remember to write C, F or R for each answer.

> **Answers** (relevant parts of the recording script are underlined)
> 1 R **2** C **3** F **4** C

Recording script

You will hear two friends discussing what to do at the weekend.
First you have some time to look at questions 1 to 4. (pause)
Now listen carefully and answer questions 1 to 4.

Woman: What do you fancy doing on Saturday?
Man: We could go and see Douglas – I don't think you know him, but <u>we met a few years ago</u>, at my brother's birthday party. <u>We've stayed in touch</u> and generally get together every few weeks. He's crazy about football.
Woman: Oh well, I'm not sure – if you're going to talk about football!
Man: Or there's Rachel, I'm sure you'd like her, she's very friendly and easy to get on with. <u>She's actually my cousin</u>, though we don't see each other all that often. I sometimes bump into her on the way to work – she's with a company that's quite near mine.
Woman: OK.

Man: In fact, if we go round to her place, we could go on to Suzanne's – <u>we work in the same department</u>. She's having a party Saturday evening, and she's invited everyone in the office, as well as lots of friends. I said I wasn't sure if I could go, but if you'd like to, I could give her a ring.
Woman: I think I'd prefer something quieter.
Man: Well, how about going to stay with Jack for the weekend – he lives in a beautiful part of the countryside.
Woman: Do I know him?
Man: I'm sure you do. Don't you remember? You met him at my firm's New Year's Eve party a couple of years ago. <u>His family lived next door to mine</u> when we were both children, so we've known each other for years. He works in the computer industry.
Woman: Oh yes, he was there with a friend of his, wasn't he? What was her name – Melanie, wasn't it?
Man: That's right.
Woman: So what was he doing at your office party?
Man: Well, <u>Melanie's our Finance Manager</u>. They've been friends for quite a long time.
Woman: OK, well, why not give him a call?

2

> **Answers** (relevant parts of the recording script are underlined)
> 1 B **2** A **3** C **4** C **5** A

Recording script

You will hear a student talking to her tutor about an assignment she is working on.
First you have some time to look at questions 1 to 5. (pause)
Now listen carefully and answer questions 1 to 5.

Tutor: Morning, Catherine. Have a seat.
Catherine: Thanks.
Tutor: Have you decided yet what aspects of Social Interaction to cover in your assignment?
Catherine: Not really. I've read so much that I find interesting, I'm having trouble choosing.
Tutor: OK, what have you read about?
Catherine: Well, there's interaction in <u>families</u>. That's fascinating.
Tutor: Mm.
Catherine: I think I'd like to write a whole assignment about it though, because there's so much to consider.
Tutor: Then <u>how about leaving it for now</u> and writing an assignment purely on that next semester?
Catherine: <u>That's a good idea. I'll do that.</u> Then there's how people interact in groups. I'd definitely like to write about that in this assignment.
Tutor: OK. It might be worth limiting it in some way, to <u>interaction in *social* groups</u>, for instance.
Catherine: <u>Right. Yes, I'll put that on the list.</u> But work teams are also very interesting. I'd be sorry not to include them.
Tutor: Maybe we should see what else you've thought about, and <u>come back to the question of work teams later</u>.
Catherine: Fine. Well, I read a good article about the sort of interaction we have with acquaintances – mostly about the people we recognise but don't necessarily know by name. It really opened my eyes to everyday behaviour, so I'd quite like to write about that. On the other hand, there are other things that I wouldn't want to leave out.

Tutor: I think you should consider how long the assignment is going to be, and how these different topics relate to each other.

Catherine: That's a point. Then I'd better put off deciding about acquaintances for the moment, until I've managed to plan this in more detail. But I think friendship networks are an important aspect of interaction, so that's something I definitely want to include.

Tutor: Right. Now have you considered …

3 Read the task, in particular noticing the three options A–C, then skim the passage. Read the example and the underlined part of the passage. Then complete the task.

> **Answers** (evidence from the passage is given, but this is not part of the answer)
>
> 1 A *Most people also engaged in handicraft production in the home, the family being paid by a company to work* (paragraph 4); *home and workplace were physically separated* (paragraph 6)
>
> 2 C *their contributions to the family income were likely to make the difference between starvation and survival* (paragraph 2); *the already bad economic situation of families worsened* (paragraph 7)
>
> 3 A *Children worked from an early age, girls helping their mothers, and boys their fathers* (paragraph 3); *Few children now worked with their parents at home* (paragraph 7)
>
> 4 B *virtually all family members were engaged in agricultural work in one form or another, usually growing food for their own consumption* (paragraph 1); *Most people also engaged in handicraft production in the home* (paragraph 4); *Men, women and children were employed as individuals for a wage, often by different employers … husbands, wives and children were also physically separated for a good part of their time* (paragraph 6)
>
> 5 A *School was an occasional or irrelevant factor in their lives* (paragraph 3) Note that although this may also have been true of the industrial period, this is not stated in the passage.
>
> 6 C *his wife and children, too, had an economic value as their contributions to the family income …* (paragraph 2); *Men, women and children were employed as individuals for a wage* (paragraph 6); *children … had generally become greater economic assets than before* (paragraph 7)
>
> 7 B *children's working hours were limited and their employment prohibited* (paragraph 7) There is no reference to restrictions in connection with the pre-industrial period.
>
> 8 A *The majority of English families of the pre-industrial age … lived in a rural location* (paragraph 1); *… numerous factories in many towns and cities. These in turn encouraged migration from the countryside* (paragraph 5)
>
> 9 C *the husband, the undisputed master of the household* (paragraph 2); *men were still regarded as the head of the household* (paragraph 6)

Unit 16

16.1 pages 104–105

1 Think what you could say about the signs, using the Useful language as far as possible.

> **Possible answers**
> - *Descriptions and meanings of the signs*
> 1 This is a road sign. It's white with a red circle round the outside. It shows a car and a motorbike. The red circle means that something is prohibited – no motor vehicles are allowed to enter the street.
> 2 This is a thick black line forming a particular pattern, and it means *and*. The symbol is called an 'ampersand'.
> 3 This is another road sign. It's a triangle with the apex at the top, surrounded by a thick red line. It shows a man with a spade and a pile of something that might be earth, sand or stones. It means that there are road works going on, so it's a warning to drivers to be careful.
> 4 This sign shows a dog on a white background, surrounded by a red circle, and with a red diagonal line across it. It means dogs are banned from this place, which might be a park or beach. *(It's a Canadian sign.)*
> 5 This is a square sign, with a white object against a dark background. The meaning isn't very clear, because the white object in the sign could symbolise a castle or a pair of binoculars. *(In fact it's binoculars, and the sign means this is a good place for watching wildlife. It's an American sign.)*
> 6 This is a square sign, with a white pattern on it that I think represents a snowflake. I'm not sure, but it might mean that this is a good area for winter sports. *(It is. Again, it's an American sign.)*
> 7 This is an international sign, consisting of two horizontal lines of equal length, one above the other. It means *equals*, and is used in maths.
> 8 This is another road sign, and it's triangular, which means it's a warning. The black exclamation mark probably means that you're going to have a surprise, so you should be careful. It's a warning of danger.
>
> - *Do you need to understand a particular language to understand them?*
>   All these signs are intended to be easy to understand, whatever language you speak. So '&' means the same in all languages, whatever the word for *and* is. Most of the signs represent sentences, for example 4 'You mustn't bring a dog here' or 5 'This is a good place for watching wildlife', but the sentences could be in any language.
>
> - *How easily can they be understood by someone seeing them for the first time?*
>   It isn't obvious that red circles mean that something is banned, or that triangles are warning signs. Some of the things that are shown are clear, like the dog, but the binoculars are more difficult to interpret.
>
> - *Can you think of ways in which they could be interpreted wrongly?*
>   You might think that 1 means you *can* drive here. Some people think 3 shows a man having trouble with an umbrella, so it could mean it's very windy. You might interpret the binoculars as showing the gate to a castle.

2 Skim the passage and decide if the signs (as a group) are more like Egyptian hieroglyphs, Chinese characters or letters of an alphabet.

3 Although there are usually three options in a classification task in IELTS, it's possible to have four.

Answers (evidence from the passage is given, but this is not part of the answer)

1 C *Chinese … Like many Egyptian hieroglyphs, the signs were originally pictures, and gradually became more abstract.* (lines 31–34)
2 B *Chinese characters are used … in the unrelated languages of Japanese, Korean and, until the 20th century, Vietnamese.* (lines 36–39)
3 A *others indicate sounds* (lines 14–15)
4 B *The writing system consists of characters representing words, sections of words …* (lines 34–35)
5 D
6 A *the third group are used to distinguish between two words that are otherwise identical:* carve *and* retreat *are represented by the same hieroglyph, but a knife symbol is added to show when the former meaning is intended, and a pair of legs to indicate the latter* (lines 15–20)

7 TRUE *A totally new development in writing appeared in the Middle East about 3,700 years ago, when Egyptian hieroglyphs were well established. This was the North Semitic alphabet* (lines 48–51)
8 FALSE *This was the North Semitic alphabet, which evolved in Palestine and Syria. The Phoenicians … adapted it to form their own alphabet.* (lines 50–54)
9 TRUE *This in turn spread into northern Africa to become the writing system of the Arabs, and north-west to Greece.* (lines 54–56)
10 NOT GIVEN *The Greek letters were further modified to become the Cyrillic alphabets of Russia* (lines 57–58) This does not mean the languages are related, even though the alphabets are.
11 NOT GIVEN Lines 68–73 refer to the number of letters in various alphabets, but do not relate them to the number of words.
12 FALSE *there is rarely great consistency between spelling and pronunciation* (lines 77–79)
13 TRUE *the writing system has not kept pace with changes in pronunciation over the centuries.* (lines 81–83)

16.2 pages 106–107

1 Think about how you could answer the questions.

2 Some college courses include writing book reviews, and the ability to assess books is likely to be essential in most courses.

Answers (relevant parts of the recording script are underlined)
1 *The Human Mind* 2 popular science 3 non-specialists
4 theories 5 function 6 personality 7 medical
8 stories 9 word list 10 goal

Recording script

Rachel: Oh, hello, can you spare me a few minutes, please?
Tutor: Yes, of course, Rachel. What can I do for you?
Rachel: It's about the book review you've asked us to write as part of the Academic Writing course. You said we should ask if we didn't know how to set about it.
Tutor: OK. Well, sit down, and let's talk about it. I presume you've chosen the book you want to write about.
Rachel: Yes.
Tutor: Good. Then have a look at this outline. If we talk it through and you make notes on it, it'll help you to structure your review. Right, first of all, what's the name of the book?
Rachel: *The Human Mind.*
Tutor: Ah yes, by Robert Winston. It was tied in with a very good television series, wasn't it? So you should start your review with the title and author. The next question is, what category would you put it in? For example, fiction, history, math …
Rachel: Well, I suppose it's science.
Tutor: Can you limit the field a little?
Rachel: How about popular science?
Tutor: Yes, I think that's more helpful.
Rachel: Then I suppose the subject area is the brain.
Tutor: OK. And it's important to mention the intended readership, because you can't judge how effective a book is without considering who it's meant for.
Rachel: Well, it doesn't assume you know a lot about the subject, so I'd say it's for non-specialists. It was promoted in general bookshops.
Tutor: Right. Now the overview. What would you say Winston is trying to do?
Rachel: Er … it's very informative, but I think he's also telling us how to make the most of our brains.
Tutor: Then you should briefly discuss the main topics. I'd recommend mentioning the ones that *you* found the most significant and interesting.
Rachel: Mm-hm. Well, it starts by looking back at the last few thousand years, and looks briefly at some of the theories that have been developed about the brain, and about its importance. It wasn't always considered as important as we now believe.
Tutor: True. And the next topic?
Rachel: I think it should be the structure and activities of the brain that make it function. I found that chapter very interesting, but it was probably the hardest to understand.
Tutor: Mm, I'd probably agree with you. Any more topics you want to mention?
Rachel: Oh, it covers so much, like the emotions, memory … but I think the role of the brain in creating personality should be mentioned, because I think that's an important aspect of the book. And then there's the advice on how we can use our brains to boost our intelligence. I've already started acting on some of the suggestions!
Tutor: Good luck! Now let's look at the next section of your review, where you should analyse and evaluate the book. This is the main

section where you give your own opinions. This first point is really a question of whether we should take the writer seriously. A musician may be qualified to write about music, but not necessarily to write about the brain, for instance.

Rachel: Mm. Winston is a professor at the University of London, and <u>he's done a lot of research in various medical fields</u>. So he's very well qualified to write about this subject.

Tutor: What would you say are the strengths of the book?

Rachel: Mm … it's a complex subject, but he makes it as accessible as it can be for the general reader. That's partly because <u>he illustrates his points with a lot of stories</u>, both about well-known people, like Einstein, and from his own life.

Tutor: OK. Are there any other strengths you want to add?

Rachel: <u>I was glad he included a word list</u> to explain the meanings of medical terms. And I didn't find any weaknesses.

Tutor: Mm. Right. Then that brings us to the conclusion. How would you sum up your overall response to the book?

Rachel: Well, I found it fascinating. I think Winston is quite <u>ambitious in the goal he's set himself, but he's succeeded in reaching it.</u>

Tutor: Well, there you are – you've got the skeleton of your review. Keep that in front of you while you're writing it up, and it should be fine.

Rachel: Thank you very much.

Tutor: You're welcome.

3 Spend one minute preparing a short talk. Write down only key words or other brief notes. Remember that you can invent the book, or the influence it had on you. After a minute, talk about the topic to a friend, or record yourself, for one to one and a half minutes.

4 Read the information in the tinted box. Work out the correct versions of the two rules, and decide which one refers to example **A** and which one to **B** in the box.

> **Answers**
> 1 an active (example **A**)   2 a passive (example **B**)

5 Remember to be careful with the spelling when the verb ends in *-e*.

> **Answers**
> 1 concerning (active: could be paraphrased *some queries which concern the use*)
> 2 dated (passive: *your letter is dated 18 February*)
> 3 introduced (passive: *which were introduced*)
> 4 Attended (passive: *The conference, which was attended*)
> 5 Attending (active: *While she was attending*)

6 Before you do exercise 6, read the pairs of sentences **C–I**. The sentences in each pair are paraphrases of each other, and the parts in italics are non-finite clauses. Note that *having* + past participle is required in **F** and **H** to make it clear that they refer to a time before the time of the main clause. In **G,** *after* serves the same function.

Notice the position of *not* in **E**: negative non-finite clauses normally have *not* preceding the verb. For example, the negative version of the non-finite clause in **F** is *Not having grown up in Korea*.

> **Answers**
> 1 facing learners of a foreign language
> 2 Having lived in Japan for many years,
> 3 required for your essay.
> 4 After being / Having been very variable for hundreds of years,
> 5 while travelling by plane or train.

7 While some languages don't have consonants following vowels in the same syllable, in English this is very common. Speakers can easily be misunderstood if they don't pronounce these final consonants clearly.

Play the recording and repeat each sentence immediately after hearing it. Then read each pair of sentences aloud.

Writing folder 8
pages 108–109

1 Students often fail to read the question carefully, especially under exam conditions. The result is that they often write quite a good essay, but it does not answer the question and they lose marks. It is important to keep the title of the essay constantly at the front of your mind and not wander off the point.

> **Answers**
> The key words are:
>
> With the <u>increase in use</u> of the Internet, <u>books will no longer be needed</u>.
> To what extent <u>do you agree</u> or <u>disagree</u> with this statement?
>
> Give <u>reasons</u> for your answer and include any <u>relevant examples from your own knowledge or experience</u>.

> **Suggested answer**
> It has been suggested that in the future the Internet will totally take over the role that has always been taken by books. Personally, I believe that this will, in fact, happen sooner than people think.
>
> It is often said that books are useful, but if we are talking about communicating news to the public, then in this case books are not so useful. ~~I don't often read books, even though I know they might help me. I find them boring, because most novels are really silly love stories.~~
>
> Personally, I think the Internet is very useful and I use it all the time both at college and at home. ~~I have had a computer for ten years and the one I have at the moment is an Apple Mac. It is particularly useful for finding information quickly and for keeping in touch with friends via email. I also use it to talk to people in chat rooms. People in chat rooms are really interesting and I have met many friends there. They give me a chance to practise my English which I find really interesting.~~ All the information I need I can find on the Internet. Some people say that it is hard to read from a screen, but I don't have this problem.
>
> So in conclusion, ~~I think the Internet is a good thing~~.
> (226 words)

Commentary

There is very little on books in this essay – most information, and it is very lightweight and not very well developed, is on the Internet. The examples from own experience and knowledge are sketchy.

The first paragraph introduces the topic, but needs to be expanded, as the other paragraphs do not continue with this theme. The second paragraph seems to be comparing the Internet and newspapers rather than books, and the reference to novels is irrelevant. There needs to be a paragraph on the disadvantages and advantages of books with some comparison of the Internet and books included. There is also repetition of vocabulary, which shows the candidate has only a limited vocabulary range and will lose marks. However, the candidate has used pronouns, which do help in reducing the repetition of nouns.

This essay is really an answer to a question asking why you personally prefer the Internet to books, but even then the information is very limited. The examination task is also asking a general question which isn't answered – all the information we receive is about why the writer prefers the Internet. The conclusion is very poor and the essay is too short.

2 Look at the checklist in the book. Work through the questions, thinking of what you would say.

3/4/5 Check that you are familiar with the suggested alternative adjectives.

Suggested answers

3 **Adjectives** (see numbers in answer below)
   1 *fascinating, absorbing, worthwhile, valuable, informative*
   2 *Not adjectives used in 1: helpful, effective*
   3 *tedious, predictable, uninspiring*
   4 *helpful, valuable*
   5 *helpful, valuable, efficient*
   6 *friendly, sociable, helpful*
   7 *absorbing, beneficial, helpful, worthwhile, effective*

4 **Linkers**
   but, and, so are repeated (see Writing folder 6 for alternatives)

5 **Pronouns** (see letters in answer below)
   a *this* = the fact that the Internet will take over from books
   b *they* = books
   c *them* = books
   d *it* = the Internet
   e *the one* = the computer
   f *It* = the computer / my Apple Mac
   g *it* = the Apple Mac / computer
   h *there* = in chat rooms
   i *They* = chat rooms

   underline (= adjectives, exercise 3); **bold** (= linkers, exercise 4); *italics* (= pronouns, exercise 5)

   It has been suggested that in the future the Internet will totally take over the role that has always been taken by books. Personally, I believe that (a) *this* will, in fact, happen sooner than people think.

It is often said that books are (1) useful, **but** if we are talking about communicating news to the public, then in this case books are not so (2) useful. I don't often read books, even though I know (b) *they* might help me. I find (c) *them* (3) boring, because most novels are really silly love stories.

Personally, I think the Internet is very (4) useful **and so** I use (d) *it* all the time both at college and at home. I have had a computer for ten years **and** (e) *the one* I have at the moment is an Apple Mac. (f) *It* is particularly (5) useful for finding information quickly **and** for keeping in touch with friends via email. I also use (g) *it* to talk to people in chat rooms. People in chat rooms are really (6) interesting **and** I have met many friends (h) *there*. (i) *They* give me a chance to practise my English which I find really (7) interesting. All the information I need I can find on the Internet. Some people say that it is hard to read from a screen **but** I don't have this problem.

So in conclusion, I think the Internet is a good thing.

6

Sample answer

Although it is true to say that the Internet is expanding at an amazing rate, and much faster than anyone could have predicted, my feeling is that books will never disappear completely. I may be proved wrong, but I believe there will always be a place for books in the world.

Why do I think this? Well, I think first of all we need to look at the reasons we have books. They give us information, and the type of information they give us is perhaps the key to why they will always be with us. We are not talking here about news or weather. That can be obtained from the Internet or the TV and radio. We are also not talking about facts – we obtain those also from the Internet. So, what do we use books for? Well, personally, I read books for relaxation and for pleasure. You might say that I could read a book on the Internet instead, but I do not feel it would be quite the same thing.

The Internet has many uses, but I think it is very hard to imagine lying curled up on the sofa reading a computer screen for pleasure. Books are also easy to transport, generally light to carry, inexpensive and can be read anywhere. The same cannot be said about computers, although there may come a time when an easily portable computer with an easy-to-read screen becomes available.

Until that time, I firmly believe that books will not be replaced by the Internet.

(254 words)

Units 13–16 Revision

pages 110–111

The aim of this revision unit is to focus on the language covered in Units 13–16.
Exercises 2–5 can be done as a test.

1 Give your own answers.

2

> **Answers**
> 1 to grow   2 getting   3 being   4 worrying   5 to choose
> 6 to buy   7 to say   8 to be   9 to make   10 complaining

3

> **Answers**
> 1 catches   2 would/'d have been   3 pay
> 4 don't/won't mind   5 was/were (could be is also possible)
> 6 are/'re   7 don't have   8 would be   9 had been
> 10 keeps

4   The photo shows someone wearing clothing dyed with cochineal.

> **Answers**
> 1 used   2 Obtained   3 sucking   4 indicating
> 5 lighting   6 building   7 Realising   8 dyed

5   In this exercise you need to use the language that's appropriate to Task 1 in the Academic Writing Module. The description is a little longer than is required in the test.

> **Answers**
> 1 slide   2 picked up   3 levelled off   4 declining
> 5 was fairly steady   6 rose   7 fell
> 8 made steady progress   9 declined

Unit 17

17.1 pages 112–113

1   This unit deals with the effect working at night has on the body.

> **Possible answers**
> - If I could choose, I'd get up about 10.30.
> - It depends – sometimes I'm really chatty and other times I can be terribly grumpy.
> - I usually get up about 7.30 in the week, but at weekends it varies – it depends on what I need to do that day. I go to bed about 10 in the week and often at weekends too. I can never get enough sleep.
> - I never go shopping late at night – what a waste of time!
> - Yes, I think my country is so keen on shopping that people want to do it any time of the day or night. But you could argue that for some people it's really necessary, so why not?

2   The passage is about 650 words long and should take about two and a half minutes to read through. Larks and owls are species of birds.

> **Answers**
> 1   to regulate our waking and sleeping
> 2   Larks are alert in the morning; owls are alert in the evening.

3   The questions are in the order of the text.

> **Answers**
> 1   NOT GIVEN   Paragraph 1 tells us what types of places are open at night, but there is no mention of demand.
> 2   NOT GIVEN   Paragraph 2 tells us that people maintain a natural rhythm if they are kept in isolation, but there is no mention of reacting to day or night – in fact, if people are in isolation, they don't know whether it is day or night.
> 3   FALSE   *is likely to cause ourselves both physical and psychological damage (lines 18–19)*
> 4   TRUE   *Our prehistoric ancestors would have needed their biological clock to get them out hunting during the day and probably in bed around nightfall (lines 32–34)*
> 5   FALSE   *owls may pay a price for this in terms of health problems (lines 47–48)*
> 6   D   *needed their biological clock to get them out hunting during the day (lines 32–33)*
> 7   B   *Larks are 'morning people' – communicative from the time their eyes open (lines 44–45)*
> 8   E   *The fatigue … is similar to that of jet lag (lines 54–56)*

4   There are many collocations with *time* in English and students often confuse them.

> **Answers**
> 1 run out of   2 waste/spend   3 give   4 Take
> 5 spent/wasted   6 passed   7 find   8 took
> 9 killed   10 run out of

5   Try to expand your answers and not just answer *Yes* or *No*. Some collocations are very similar, and the difference between them may depend on the structure, e.g. *pass the time*, but *kill time*. Both have the idea of having to do something to make the time go faster / to fill the time.

> **Possible answers**
> 1   I usually pass the time reading.
> 2   I think watching TV, especially football, is a complete waste of time. Also, playing snooker and knitting.
> 3   Yes, I usually set aside an hour or two every evening for my homework. That usually gives me enough time.
> 4   Yes, I read a newspaper every day – I usually spend about twenty minutes reading it at lunchtime.
> 5   Very often. I think most people run out of time because they spend too much time on the first exercise and don't give themselves enough time to do the last one.
> 6   I would spend my time travelling the world.

17.2 pages 114–115

1 The pictures are of people who often have to work at night: a security guard, a pilot, a fisherman, and a doctor.

> **Possible answers**
>
> I wouldn't mind doing the nightshift if it was for a long period – for example, for a month. What I wouldn't like is to work two nights, then work three days, as I would find that very disorientating.
>
> *Advantages of working the nightshift*
> Being paid more
> Fewer problems travelling to work
> Quieter at work
> Fewer interruptions
>
> *Disadvantages of working the nightshift*
> No social life
> Hard to get a proper sleep pattern
> A feeling of being sidelined – not being at the centre of things
> Hard to go shopping, have your hair cut, etc.

2 There are three different tasks here: questions 1 and 2 are multiple choice; 3–5 require a short answer and 6–8 also require a short answer. Play the first part of the recording and answer questions 1–5 as you listen. Then play the second part and answer questions 6–8.

> **Answers** (relevant parts of the recording script are underlined)
> **1** A **2** B **3** wear/wearing dark glasses **4** take a bath
> **5** unplug the telephone
>
> **6** 20 minutes
> **7** operate machinery **8** 4 a.m.

Recording script

Questions 1–5

Speaker: Do you work at times other than the usual 'nine to five' business day? If so, you are not alone – there are millions of nightshift workers across the world who don't have to travel to work in the rush hour. Nightshift workers perform critical functions in hospitals, on police forces and as emergency personnel, and in the transportation and manufacturing industries. In addition, they're meeting the demand for 'round-the-clock' service in an age of global interaction. In the USA, for example, more than 22 million people work nightshifts, and that number is growing by 3% each year.

However, nightshift workers still need to get a reasonable amount of sleep. When shifts fall during the night (11 p.m. – 7 a.m.), the worker is fighting the natural wake–sleep pattern. It will be hard for them to stay alert at night and harder for them to get to sleep and stay asleep during the day than it is for daytime workers. Night workers get less sleep than daytime workers do, and the sleep is less restful. Sleep is more than just 'beauty rest' for the body; it helps restore and rejuvenate the brain and organ systems so that they function properly. Chronic lack of sleep harms a person's health, on-the-job safety, task performance, memory and mood.

For humans, the desire to sleep is strongest between midnight and six a.m. Many people are alert in the morning, with a natural dip in the mid-afternoon. It's not surprising that 10–20% of nightshift workers report falling asleep on the job, usually during the second half of the shift. That's why people who work all night may find it difficult to sleep for part of the day, even though they're tired.

If you're a night worker, there are several steps you can take to help you fall asleep and stay asleep. First of all, wear dark glasses. If you put these on just before leaving work, it can help enormously. They'll get the eyes gradually used to the dark and make it easier to fall asleep when you get into bed. In addition, take a bath just before getting into bed. This will soothe and relax you, preparing your body for sleep. Last but not least, unplug the telephone – there's nothing worse than having your much-needed sleep interrupted by a casual caller.

Questions 6–8

Speaker: Nightshift workers face special problems in trying to maintain family relationships and social and community ties because they have to work anti-social hours. It becomes difficult to balance work, sleep and personal time. The need to sleep during the day could mean nightshift workers have to miss out on family activities. But this doesn't have to be the case – with a bit of effort, it should be possible to reschedule some of them.

But nightshift workers must try to have a regular sleep schedule, even on weekends. However, if they can't get enough sleep or feel drowsy, naps can also be helpful. Twenty minutes is about right. Naps shorter than that – perhaps five minutes – are not really long enough. Some people feel groggy or sleepier after a nap. These feelings usually go away within 10 minutes, while the benefits of the nap may last for many hours.

Nightshift workers should try to have someone to work with – someone they can chat to while they're working. This work-buddy can help to keep them alert. Whatever they do, they mustn't operate machinery when feeling sleepy. To help guard against this, they should exercise during breaks and eat three normal meals. Finally, most nightshift workers find that the worst time is the period around 4 a.m. This is a natural low for all humans, and workers especially should be aware of it.

If you want to know more about how to handle working on the nightshift, then take a …

3 For this exercise some knowledge of modals for obligation is assumed. You should be familiar with the form and basic use of *must* and *have to*.

> **Answers**
> **1** c **2** e **3** f **4** a **5** b **6** d

4 The aim of this exercise is to establish the difference between *have to* and *must*. Both *must* and *have to* are used in British English to talk about obligation. In the US *have to* is more common.

Answers

1 That's what the rules say; someone else has the authority – strong obligation coming from outside, from laws, regulations and other people's orders. We also say *have got to*.
2 Obligation coming from the speaker.
3 It is unnecessary.
4 It is not allowed.

5

Answers

1 You mustn't smoke in the factory.
2 You don't have to leave home early to beat the rush hour now.
3 We have to begin work at 9.30.
4 All workers have to wear a hard hat on site.
5 'You mustn't make personal calls,' said the manager to the staff.
6 I don't have to get up tomorrow.
7 When I work nights, I have to do my shopping on the Internet.
8 I don't have to go to the bank in the daytime as I can ring them at any time now.

6

Sample answer

(This is slightly longer than required. You are not penalised for a slightly longer answer, only for too short an answer.)

There is no doubt that today people are becoming accustomed to being able to access services like banks and shops at all hours of the day and night. Personally, I am not sure that we can say categorically that this has a negative effect on society. I believe that there are definite advantages to living in a 24-hour society.

In the past in my country, most people worked from nine to five, from Monday to Friday, and had the weekend free for leisure. Sunday was a total day of rest, and all the shops and businesses were closed. However, today we have a situation where every day is the same. This change has come about because of the need for greater production in industry and also from consumer demand.

One of the main arguments in favour of 24-hour opening is that people today work hard and want to play hard. They have no time to shop when they are at work and need to be able to buy clothes, have their hair cut and so on when they are free. The labour market is also more flexible today than in the past, and there are more people willing to work unsocial hours. In addition, the Internet has enabled people to shop and bank when businesses are normally closed. I often shop online after midnight when I have difficulty sleeping, and I do not think I am unusual in this.

To conclude, I believe that times have changed and that we have to accept that life goes on 24 hours a day, not just 12. This does not necessarily mean that we become less productive – in fact, I believe it means we can become more productive and we have more control over both our working and social lives.

(297 words)

Test folder 9

pages 116–117

Make sure you fully understand the advice.

1 Before you do exercise 1, read the information about Part 1.

Answers

1 C   2 A   3 F   4 E   5 B

Recording script

1

Examiner: Do you work or are you studying?

Candidate: I work in a restaurant. Um, I used to work in an office, but when I came to this country, it was easier to get a job in a restaurant. I enjoy it quite a lot, although you have to work long hours and the pay isn't very good. Now I'm thinking about going into restaurant management as a career.

2

Examiner: How do you spend your free time?

Candidate: Swimming.

3

Examiner: How long have you been studying English?

Candidate: Most people in my country start learning English quite early at school, when they are six or seven.

4

Examiner: Why do foreign tourists visit your country?

Candidate: I don't really know, but maybe some are interested in culture, and others come to go shopping.

5

Examiner: What is your favourite type of food?

Candidate: *(long pause)* I like pizzas, but I prefer traditional food from my own country.

2

Possible answers

1 I come from Beijing, which is the capital. It's in the north-east of the country.
2 There are plenty of opportunities for certain types of work, for instance in the construction industry.
3 Luckily I've never needed to work at night, but just before exams I sometimes study until midnight, or even later.
4 Often night work is well paid, and that attracts people who need the money. Others work at night to fit in with family commitments.
5 I think I'd get very sleepy about two or three o'clock in the morning. I wouldn't like to try working at night.

3 Before you do exercise 3, read the information about Part 2.

Possible answer

It is a good answer, because it focuses on the topic, uses a range of grammatical structures and vocabulary, there is a brief introduction, the mistakes don't make it difficult to understand, and the speaker varies the intonation, speed and volume to make it sound interesting.

Recording script

Examiner: I'd like you to describe an occasion when you did something that you don't normally do.

Candidate: Yeah, let me tell you an experience I will never forget. Two years ago, when I went back to see my parents in China, and, you know um – in the Chinese culture we shake hands, we say hello, but we never, er, kiss each other, or even hug each other – even between parents and children. But because I have been living in this country for so long, and get used to the way people, you know, show their affection and friendliness to each other. And I haven't seen my mum for a long time, so, um, when I saw my mother, she was greeting me from the door, I went over and gave her a big hug, and she was kind of very … nervous and … and a bit embarrassed, you know, she just … she behaved somewhat differently than normal and she didn't know what to say. But I know at that moment she would feel very warm, you know, from a daughter, a hug from the daughter. And, um, so that is something that I wouldn't normally do, or I have never … I had never done before then.

Examiner: Have you done it again since then?

Candidate: Yes, I did, when my mother came to visit me this summer.

Examiner: Do you think other people should have a similar experience?

Candidate: I think they should. I think the Chinese and the British should learn from each other for the good things they do.

4 Read the card and spend about one minute planning a talk. Only write key words or brief notes. Then give the talk to a friend, or record yourself.

Think of short answers to the two 'rounding-off' questions.

> **Possible answers**
> - I prefer surprises, because if you know what's going to happen, you may be disappointed.
> - It's best if people only have three or four special occasions a year. Otherwise they stop being special.

5 Before you do exercise 5, read the information about Part 3.

Recording script

Examiner: Could you describe how society can benefit from people working at night?

Candidate: Yes, I think talking about working at night, I can think of policemen, as a necessity for security for the society, and also as, er, cab drivers for people to transport, er, travel from one place to another, and all these are necessary because without them, life would be more difficult.

Examiner: Can you compare going to the cinema or other entertainments at night with going to the same entertainments by day?

Candidate: I think it's the atmosphere that is different, saying if you are going to a concert or a cinema at night, and then the lights, the atmosphere, you know, sometimes you have the music. It just make you feel, well brilliant, you know. After a long days' work it's relaxing, it's entertaining, it's fun!

Examiner: What would you recommend people to do if they have to work at night?

Candidate: Can you repeat that question, please? Sorry, I didn't quite catch …

Examiner: What would you recommend people to do if they have to work at night?

Candidate: First, I would recommend that they get enough sleep, so that they can maintain a high level of energy at night, to achieve the best performance when they do what they do.

Examiner: Thank you.

Think about the answers to questions 4–8.

> **Possible answers**
> 4 Nowadays most people accept that night work is essential, because we want all sorts of things to be available at night – from hospitals to supermarkets.
> 5 Some parents work at different times so one of them is available to look after the children. It's difficult for them to do things together as a family.
> 6 In a 24/7 society, buses and trains need to operate all night. Otherwise, it would be very difficult for people to get to work, to provide the services we demand.
> 7 It's difficult to tell, but on the whole I think we're more likely to move back towards working during daylight hours, except for emergency services.
> 8 People could be offered higher salaries for working at night, or could work fewer hours for the same salary.

Unit 18

18.1 pages 118–119

1 The photos are of backpackers, a cruise ship off a tropical beach, Bondi beach in Sydney, tourists in Old Town Square, Prague, tourists buying souvenirs in Guatemala and the rubbish left by visitors to Mount Everest.

> **Possible answers**
> - I think there are many advantages to getting away from the daily routine. You see new people and places, and this helps to put life into some sort of perspective.
> - Workers in my country usually get about four weeks' holiday a year.
> - A good tourist is someone who leaves nothing behind them – no litter especially.

2 The recording is similar to a Part 4 Listening in the test. First, study the summary, then play the first part of the recording and answer questions 1–5 as you listen. Then study the table, play the second part of the recording and answer questions 6–10.

> **Answers** (relevant parts of the recording script are underlined)
> 1 technology   2 wealth   3 developed   4 skiing
> 5 art galleries
> 6 (the) railway   7 (the) Internet
> 8 literature/writers   9 garlic   10 drama (festival)

Recording script

Questions 1–5

Lecturer: Travel and tourism is the largest industry in the world, but calculating its economic impact is quite difficult. The one thing everybody can agree on, though, is that it's huge. There are two things which have influenced the growth of tourism. These are firstly – social factors, and secondly – technology and the way it's developed. Let's consider the social factors first of all. Demand for tourism is determined mainly by the amount of wealth a country has, which is why countries such as Japan, Australia, the USA and western European countries have contributed most in terms of tourist numbers in the past. However, growing wealth in developing countries will mean that demand for holidays abroad will take off there in the near future, boosting tourism enormously.

That said, the majority of tourists are still from what are called the developed nations. However, studies show that their numbers will not rise much further in the next few decades because their populations are fairly stable. As a result there'll be a growth in the number of retired people who'll have more time on their hands. This will influence the kind of tourism wanted: fewer skiing holidays will be required, but there'll be an increase in the number of people wanting to visit art galleries.

Questions 6–10

Lecturer: Let's turn now to the second factor in the growth of tourism. The technology that sustains mass tourism today is the jet plane. Air travel has opened up the world. In 1970, scheduled planes carried 307 million passengers. Today there are four times as many. In fact, cheaper and more efficient transport has been behind the development of mass tourism from its beginnings in Britain in the nineteenth century. The first package tours were arranged in 1841 by Thomas Cook, an entrepreneur whose company subsequently became one of the world's largest tour operators. In his day, it was the railway that allowed his business to flourish.

Today, technology is proving very important in other ways as well as in transportation. In the past people went to a travel agent to find and book their holiday. Now many of these people are bypassing the High Street travel agent and booking their holidays themselves on the Internet. Airlines have been keen to encourage this direct approach as it keeps down their costs, and increasingly High Street travel agents are finding their business is disappearing.

These days there may be more tourists to go round, but there is also more competition among destinations, as cities, countries and continents all compete for tourist revenue. But becoming a tourist destination is not quite as straightforward as it might seem. For example, Ireland used to sell itself as a place to go to and enjoy the beautiful countryside. However it soon discovered that it was attracting young student backpackers without any money. So how did Ireland set about increasing revenue from tourism? Well, the Irish Tourist Board came up with the idea of promoting the country's literature, using the names of writers such as Oscar Wilde and James Joyce to appeal to older, richer tourists who would spend their money in the hotels and restaurants of the country.

However, there are other ways of appealing to tourists. The US is dotted with places that claim to be the capital of something or other – sometimes things which may seem rather strange: Crystal City, for example, is the world capital of the vegetable broccoli, and then there's Gilroy – famous for its garlic. These towns are trading on a single gimmick to attract the tourists.

Festivals are another way to bring them in – literary, food, art – they're all staged for one reason only: to attract tourist revenue. Many a town has sought to copy the success of Stratford, Ontario, which was transformed from a small run-down blue-collar town to a bustling cultural centre by the efforts of Tom Patterson, who managed to persuade a British director to stage their first drama festival in 1953.

But then boosting a city through tourism is nothing new. In 18th century England, Bath Spa became fashionable after the owners of the hot baths employed Beau Nash, the trend-setter of his day, to promote the city. I want to end the lecture there for today. Now, next week …

3 Play the extract and notice the lack of stress on the pronoun. Then play each phrase and repeat after each one.

4

> **Possible answers**
> 1 You don't need a coat inside – take it off.
> 2 Those trees are rotten – cut them down.
> 3 The girl's fainted – bring her round.
> 4 The bill's very high – I'll use a calculator to work it out.
> 5 The baby's on the floor – you'd better pick him up.
> 6 It's an emergency – let me through.
> 7 Look at all these forms – I'll have to fill them in.
> 8 I hope those boys ask us out.

5

> **Answers**
> 1 long-haul 2 sightseeing 3 tour 4 student
> 5 travel 6 far

6 Point out that the figures give the average amount of money spent by a British household on their holidays in one year (2002).

> **Sample answer**
> Although all age groups spent much more on holidays abroad than on holidays at home, some age groups spent up to five times as much on overseas trips as they did on holidays in the UK. The biggest spenders on holidays abroad were the 50 to 64 age group. They spent nearly £800 per household, compared with almost £700 for the next age group (30- to 49-year-olds) and around £600 for the 65- to 74-year olds. The lowest spending group on overseas holidays were the elderly, at less than £250 a year.
>
> When it came to holidays within the UK, the age group who spent the most were the 65- to 74-year-olds, followed by the 30 to 64 age group. In contrast, the under-30s group spent the least on UK holidays – only around £80 a year.
>
> In conclusion, it would appear from the graph that spending on overseas holidays rose with age to reach a peak between the ages of 50 and 64, whereas for holidays in the UK, a peak was reached later, between the ages of 65 to 74.
>
> (180 words)

18.2 pages 120–121

1 Although you may be familiar with phrasal verbs as vocabulary items, you may not realise that phrasal verbs have their own grammar rules. Look at the tinted box with the explanation and then work through exercise 1.

> **Answers**
> 1 came up with
> 2 take off – intransitive, no object here
> 3 keeps down

2

> **Answers**
> 1 made up her face (= used cosmetics; object)
> 2 passed out (= lost consciousness; no object)
> 3 make out her handwriting (= understand; object)
> 4 checked in (= registered; no object)

3 Read through the explanations in the tinted boxes carefully before you do the exercise.

> **Answers**
> 1 It was hard to make the cruise ship out through the fog.
>   It was hard to make it out through the fog.
> 2 A rival took the student travel company over when it went bankrupt.
>   A rival took it over when it went bankrupt.
> 3 Can I put forward Maria as a suitable replacement for Lisa?
>   Can I put her forward? / Can I put her name forward?
> 4 My father set the holiday company up in 1967.
>   My father set it up in 1967.
> 5 We'll have to take extra staff on when it's high season.
>   We'll have to take them on when it's high season.
> 6 Josh was asked to give out free tickets to the guests.
>   Josh was asked to give them out to the guests.

4 Some examples of three-part phrasal verbs are:
go down with
fall back on
get along with
catch up with
come up against
back out of

> **Answers**
> 0 f are looking forward to   4 c woke up to
> 1 e came up against   5 g put up with
> 2 d went down with   6 b face up to
> 3 a make up for

5

> **Answers**
> 1 which 2 due/still 3 since 4 before 5 who
> 6 already 7 for 8 if

6 If possible, record yourself speaking so that you can analyse your mistakes. A memorable trip can be about anything – a business trip, a holiday or a trip to see an exhibition. What matters is that all the points are mentioned and that you say why it was memorable.

Writing folder 9

pages 122–123

The introduction gives examples of how the various cause and result connectors are used. Look at Unit 3 for further exercises on cause and result.

1 There are no correct answers to this exercise. You will need to use your imagination.

> **Possible answers**
> 1 The hotel has used so much water to keep the golf course green that this has led to a water shortage on the island.
> 2 A new airport has been built, and as a consequence people have found jobs there and now have more money to spend.
> 3 As a result of global warming, skiing centres are having to close early in the season because of lack of snow.
> 4 The badly trained staff and dirty kitchen have resulted in the hotel guests being ill.
> 5 We tipped the museum guide really well because he was so knowledgeable and helpful.
> 6 The art gallery is only opening in the morning as a consequence of staff shortages.

2

> **Suggested answers**
> 1 There has been a rise in hotel construction over the past decade, which / and this has led to increased traffic congestion and water pollution.
>   A rise in hotel construction over the past decade has led to increased traffic congestion and water pollution.
> 2 An increase in housing development has resulted in a reduction in agricultural land.
> 3 Because of the rapid urbanisation in some Mediterranean islands, local culture has suffered.
>   Local culture has suffered because of the rapid urbanisation in some Mediterranean islands.
> 4 Growth in air transport connected to tourism has resulted in an increase in acid rain, global warming and local pollution.
> 5 The development of marinas has caused changes in sea currents and coastal erosion.
> 6 As a result of a large increase in tourists attracted to the area, the local people can find jobs more easily.
> 7 The hotel can't get enough staff. As a consequence, it can only open for a short season.
> 8 The visitors have complained about poor service. As a result, the management have decided to give the staff extra training.

3   Read through the text carefully before attempting the exercise. Only one answer is correct for each. The exercise tests a range of linking words.

Answers
1 B   2 A   3 C   4 A   5 A   6 B   7 C   8 A   9 A   10 B

4   This sample has been done in the form of a case history.

Sample answer
There is no denying that tourism today is big business. However, people are beginning to question whether tourism is, in fact, a good thing for a country or not. Does it cause more problems than it solves or is it the solution to all problems? I'm going to answer this question by looking at a place that I know well – Cornwall.

Cornwall is situated in the south-west of the United Kingdom. Its main industries for many years were tin mining and china-clay extraction, but both of these industries declined in the early twentieth century. As a result, there has been unemployment and hardship. There is still some sea fishing, but less and less as time goes on.

Cornwall is an area of outstanding natural beauty and so attracts tourists in very large numbers. The council does everything it can to bring in the tourists in order to boost the economy. As a result, in the summer, the narrow roads are jammed with tourists, and the small towns are full of cafés and souvenir shops. Many people have also bought holiday homes in the county.

However, in the winter, the area takes on a different look. The towns are empty, and it is difficult for locals to buy ordinary goods, as most of the shops have been turned into souvenir shops. Many villages are ghost villages as the holiday cottages are empty. Consequently, community services such as schools and post offices close, and local people move out.

In conclusion, I think it is important for an area or country to think long and hard about tourism. Yes, it can be a force for good, but it needs to be managed. Without good management, tourism can cause serious problems.

(287 words)

Unit 19

19.1 pages 124–125

Look of the methods of transport in the photographs. The first shows a stretch limo (limousine) in New York, the second – a subway (underground) train in Washington DC, USA, and the third – people cycling to work in Ho Chi Minh City, Vietnam.

1   Think about possible answers to the two questions.

Possible answers
I'd rather travel by train than bus or plane, because you can see the countryside and you can walk around.

I cycle in fine weather, for short distances, but for longer distances, or if the weather is bad, I go by car.

2

Possible answers
Cars are far more convenient than buses, because you can go from your home to your destination without changing.

Trains have a very good safety record – far better than cars.

It's much cheaper to travel by bus than by car, if you consider all the costs of driving.

Planes are very harmful for the environment, because of the gases they emit – ships do much less damage.

3   Make sure you understand *congested* (blocked or crowded and causing difficulties).

Possible answers
Banning non-essential traffic would greatly reduce the number of vehicles, but would make it very difficult for people to get to where they need to go.

Making driving very expensive would encourage people to find cheaper alternatives, like public transport. On the other hand, it would be much more difficult for people living in rural areas, and people without much money.

Improving public transport would reduce the number of private cars being used, but would need a lot of investment by the government, and people would probably object to paying higher taxes.

Encouraging people to live near their work would make life less stressful for people who commute to work every day. However, people won't want to move home every time they change jobs, if their new job is in a different area.

4   This exercise will help you to understand the listening passage. The words in each set are *similar* in meaning, rather than being exact synonyms. Use an English–English dictionary for words you don't know.

Answers
1   crash, collision
2   elevation, levitation, suspension
3   disruption, disturbance, interruption

5   Think what you know about monorails. Look at the picture and identify the features of a monorail.

Possible answers
The vehicle travels on a single rail. The one in the picture, in Las Vegas, USA, is on top of the rail, but they can also be suspended from the track. They're often above ground level. The vehicles are quite short – more like a bus than a train

6 Read questions 1–4 and think about what information you need to listen for. Then play the relevant part of the recording and answer questions 1–4 as you listen. Then do the same for questions 5–9. Note that *Disadvantage* suggests that the previous notes are all advantages.

> **Information you need to listen for**
> 1 a description of the tracks, e.g. *expensive, concrete*
> 2 things that can be transported, e.g. *goods, animals*
> 3 a year, probably in the twentieth century
> 4 a number, to give a speed – probably about 200–300
> 5 something bad, e.g. *a crash*
> 6 something that affects the environment negatively, e.g. *damage, emission of greenhouse gases*
> 7 examples of busy places, e.g. *town centres*
> 8 a good quality, e.g. *cheap, good value*
> 9 a possible disadvantage, e.g. *a track, a driver*

> **Answers** (relevant parts of the recording script are underlined)
> **1** elevated **2** passengers/people **3** 1901 **4** 430
> **5** (a) collision **6** pollution
> **7** shopping centres/centers (*shopping malls* is acceptable as it has the same meaning, but you should always try to write the exact words you hear)
> **8** reliable **9** fixed route

Recording script

Questions 1–4

Tutor: OK, let's begin. First, Hannah is going to give a short introduction to monorails, then Stuart will talk about some of their advantages. Finally Sharon will describe a particular type of monorail. Right, Hannah, over to you.

Student: Thanks. Well, monorails are a bit like railways, but there's just one rail, which is wider than each of the rails of a railway. Actually, 'mono' means 'one', which is how it got the name. <u>Some monorails are at ground level or in subway tunnels, though in most cases the track is elevated</u>. The vehicles are always wider than the track. In some types of monorail the vehicles run *on the* track, like a normal train, and in other types they're suspended from it.

  <u>Some monorails are used to transport freight, but the majority carry passengers.</u> A lot of them take visitors around amusement parks – there are plenty of these all round the world – and some form part of an urban transport system. Most of these are in Japan.

  Monorails were first constructed in the 19th century, though <u>the one that's been in operation for longest dates from 1901</u>. It's in the town of Wuppertal, in Germany. The vehicles are electrically operated, but a different kind of technology is used by one fairly new monorail. This went into service in 2004, between the city of Shanghai, in China, and its airport. Here too, the energy source is electricity, but it's used to create a magnetic field which propels the train forwards. And while they're travelling, the trains are levitated, which means they're suspended about one centimetre above the track. This technology is called 'maglev', short for 'magnetic levitation'. Though the trains are capable of going at over 500 kilometres an hour, <u>they regularly travel at up to 430</u>. Right, that's a short introduction to monorails, and now it's Stuart's turn.

Questions 5–9

Stuart: Thanks, Hannah. I'm going to say something about the advantages of monorails.

  The most important point is, of course, safety, and here monorails score very highly. Unlike trains, the design of monorails means that derailment is virtually impossible. And as they're normally quite separate from pedestrians and road traffic, <u>there isn't any danger of a collision</u>.

  Nowadays we're far more concerned about the environment than we used to be, and monorails have advantages over many other forms of transport. They're electrically operated, so <u>they don't cause the pollution that cars and buses do</u>, though admittedly some pollution is produced by the electricity generating stations.

  The vehicles move much more quietly than trains, because they normally use rubber tyres. <u>This allows stations to be situated in busy areas like shopping centres</u>, without creating disturbance.

  From an economic point of view, monorails have a lot going for them. For one thing, construction of all the elements takes place off-site, so installation can be very fast, and cause very little disruption. Once they're up and running, they've very cost-effective to operate. <u>And as they're not held up by traffic jams or accidents, they're far more reliable than trams and especially buses</u>.

  On the other hand, monorails have the same disadvantage as other railways, that <u>they operate over a fixed route</u>: the vehicles can't transfer to the road. So routes can't be changed without constructing a new monorail, and people have to get to and from the stations, so they may not be as convenient as buses or, in particular, private cars.

  So those are some of the disadvantages, and now I'll hand over to Sharon.

Read the instructions before questions 10–14, then look at the diagram of a monorail, and notice what each number refers to. Try to label the diagram with words from the box, using an English–English dictionary to help you.

Read the instructions by the headphones symbol, then play the third part of the recording, check your answers, and write the actual words you hear when they are different.

> **Answers** (Relevant parts of the recording script are underlined. When the words used in the recording are different from those in the box, they are given in brackets.)
> **10** pillar (*columns*)
> **11** beam
> **12** walkway (*for people to walk along it*)
> **13** vehicle (*car*)
> **14** operating unit (*operating units called bogies*)

Recording script

Questions 10–14

Sharon: OK. Most monorail systems consist of a single track, with the vehicles moving either on top of the track, or suspended from it, as Hannah said. One advantage is that the track is narrow, so it's particularly suitable for towns and other built-up areas. But it may mean that two tracks have to be constructed, one for travel in each direction.

An alternative is a single track which can be used for travel in both directions, and this diagram shows a monorail of this type.

In this particular example, the track is elevated, so <u>it's supported on a series of columns</u>, made of concrete reinforced with steel. They stand about five metres above ground level, and are generally positioned about 40 metres apart.

<u>The track itself consists of a series of horizontal concrete beams</u>, each 25 metres long, and joined end to end. They're 2 metres wide, and almost as high. They're hollow, to reduce their overall weight, so part of the internal space can be used for data cabling. <u>There's enough room on the top of the track for people to walk along it</u> in an emergency, and handrails can rise to provide support for people using it.

As this is a two-way system, <u>each side of the track supports a car</u>. The cars are a bit like balconies on the side of a building: they're cantilevered from the side of the track, and because their weight is balanced, they can't fall. But unlike balconies, of course, they can move.

<u>The car is connected with the track by several operating units</u> called bogies. These are what make the car travel, and each one contains a range of equipment, including an electrically powered motor, a braking unit, and three sets of wheels, which engage the car with the track.

So with this system there's one track, and the big advantage is that it can have cars travelling along it in both directions at the same time.

Tutor: Right, thank you, all of you. Now let's open it up to questions.

7 In English, stressed syllables tend to come at fairly regular intervals, regardless of how many unstressed syllables come in between. (In the first example there is one unstressed syllable, *a*, between the stressed syllables, and in the second example there are three: *it, in, my*.) This is not the case in all languages.

Read the information, then play the recording and repeat each sentence immediately after hearing it. Try to say each sentence without gaps, making the unstressed syllables weak. Keep the time interval between stressed syllables roughly the same.

19.2 pages 126–127

1 Write some possible answers to the questions.

> **Possible answers**
> We travel far more often than in the past, and far greater distances. For instance, many people go on holiday or business to other continents.
>
> People's lives may have been less stressed when travel was slower, because they had to work close to their homes.

2 Think about what the picture shows – you'll find out by reading the passage. Skim the passage and think of a one-sentence summary.

> **Possible answer**
> The picture shows a clock on the main railway station in Bristol, in the west of England, showing national time, 5.50, and Bristol time, 11 minutes behind it.
>
> Possible summary: Developments in transport in the 19th century brought about the standardisation of time in Britain.

3

> **Answers** (evidence from the passage is given, but this is not part of the answer)
> 1 unreliable *All these devices were unreliable.* (line 15)
> 2 watches and clocks *Until late into the 18th century, very few people could afford watches and clocks* (lines 16–17)
> 3 coaches *The guards on these coaches carried timepieces* (lines 32–33)
> 4 London time *In November 1840, the Great Western Railway ordered that London time should be used in all its timetables and at all its stations … It was usually referred to as 'railway time'.* (lines 66–72)
> 5 standard time *it was not until 1880 that Parliament introduced a standard time* (lines 92–94)
> 6 conference *the International Meridian Conference in 1884* (lines 104–105)

Questions 7–12. Read the task and complete the sentences. Remember that the sentences must be grammatical, must make sense, and must reflect the meaning of the passage.

> **Answers** (evidence from the passage is given, but this is not part of the answer)
> 7 F *Across Britain there is a difference in time of approximately half an hour from the eastern to the western extremities.* (lines 23–25)
> 8 C *When travel and communications were slow, these local time differences were of little importance* (lines 26–28)
> 9 H *These timepieces were adjusted to gain about 15 minutes in every 24 hours when travelling from west to east, to compensate for the local time differences. And they were adjusted to lose 15 minutes in 24 hours when returning.* (lines 35–40)
> 10 D *A baby born in London early on Saturday morning might officially be a day younger than a baby born a few minutes later in Dublin – where it was still Friday evening.* (lines 48–53)
> 11 B *the railways, the telegraph companies and the Post Office – and it was the first of these that started the process of standardising time in Britain.* (lines 58–61)
> 12 G *The last major resistance to standardisation came from the legal profession, which operated by local time for many years.* (lines 84–87)

4 The 'unreal present' refers to things that aren't true, for example, *If we had wheels instead of feet, we wouldn't need bicycles* – this means we *don't* have wheels, and so *do* need bicycles. The 'unreal future' means things that probably won't come true.

When checking your answers, don't read the recording script, as you'll need to listen again for exercise 5.

> **Answers**
> 1 No 2 No 3 Yes 4 Yes

5

> **Answers** (relevant parts of the recording script are underlined)
> 1 had 2 was 3 came 4 weren't; didn't stop
> 5 didn't need

Recording script

Mr Smith and his car

Mr and Mrs Smith have got two cars. Mr Smith loves his car. Virtually every time he leaves his home, he goes by car, even for fairly short distances. His car is quite old, but if he had plenty of money, he'd buy the car of his dreams, a black sports car.

Every day, during the rush hour, Mr Smith drives to work and back, and Mrs Smith drives to her work and back, in a different direction. They drive at the same time as thousands of other people. This of course creates traffic jams, which have got much worse in the last few years. Mr Smith thinks it's high time the problem was solved, before there's complete gridlock on the roads. He hopes that the government will build some new roads, to reduce congestion. However, he doesn't think motorists should pay for road-building: he would rather the money came out of general taxation.

In fact, Mr Smith can't see any alternative to greater investment in roads. He finds driving so much more convenient than public transport. He sometimes travels by train, but he wishes they weren't so crowded and didn't stop at so many stations. Mr Smith really enjoys driving. He often says to himself, 'If only I didn't need to earn a living, and could spend much more time in my car.'

6

> **Answer**
> past

7 Read the information about *wish + would*.

Read the example. Another wish in the same situation might be *I wish people didn't use their cars so much.* Think of one or two wishes for the two situations.

> **Possible answers**
> 1 I wish Ann would phone me when she says she will.
> 2 I wish John would return the book I lent him a year ago.

8

> **Possible answer**
> You live a long way from your college or work: *I wish I lived nearer my college/work.*

Test folder 10

pages 128–129

Make sure you fully understand the notes and the advice on listening. Note that in the test there is no significant difference between diagrams, maps and plans: they are all graphic.

1 Study the plan and orientate yourself. The plan shows the arrivals section of an airport terminal. You should start at 'from baggage claim'.

> **Answers** (relevant parts of the recording script are underlined)
> 1 E 2 I 3 J 4 F 5 L 6 C

Recording script

You will hear a telephone conversation between two friends about meeting in an airport terminal.
First you have some time to look at questions 1 to 6. (pause)
Now listen carefully and answer questions 1 to 6.

Jean: Jean Clark speaking.
Tom: Hello, Jean, it's Tom.
Jean: Hello, Tom. Nice to hear from you. I'm looking forward to your visit.
Tom: Me too. In fact, that's what I'm calling about. I've booked my flight, so I can give you my arrival time now.
Jean: Good.
Tom: I'm due to land at 15.20 on June 7th. But I expect you'll be at work, so don't worry about meeting me.
Jean: Well, I can get to the airport a couple of hours later, so if you don't mind waiting, it won't be for very long.
Tom: OK, that's fine.
Jean: You won't want to carry your suitcase around, so you might like to put it in a locker. When you come out of the baggage claim area, you'll see a big clock just ahead of you. Turn right into Lobby East, and you'll come to a sign to the car park on your left. There are some lockers just after that passageway.
Tom: Good. I don't suppose there's much to do at the airport, but a cup of coffee would be nice.
Jean: Well, if you go from the clock into Lobby West, you'll see various shops and things on both sides. The first two on the left are both cafés. The second one is more popular, but I prefer The Coffee House – the staff are much friendlier, and they serve better coffee. It's the first one you come to.
Tom: OK. I've made a note of that.
Jean: But you'll need some local currency. Will you be bringing any with you?
Tom: I thought I'd draw some out when I arrive. I presume I can get some money at the airport.
Jean: Mm, let me think … er yes, there are several cash machines close together. Imagine you're going from the clock into Lobby East, and they're immediately to the right, before the hotel.
Tom: Right.
Jean: You might like to go to the exhibition space. It's only small, but there are usually some interesting paintings by local artists. It's at the end of Lobby West. You can see the entrance facing you as you walk along.
Tom: That sounds as though it's worth a visit. I'd also like to buy some CDs. Do you know if there's a store in the terminal?

Jean: Yes, there are a couple. There's one more or less opposite the exit from the baggage claim, on the corner of Lobby West …

Tom: Do they stock classical CDs?

Jean: Oh, no, I don't think they do. But there's another store that does. From the clock, go along Lobby East, then turn right just after the hotel. You'll see the store – it's opposite the side of the hotel. It's very small, but there's a reasonable selection.

Tom: That's great. I'm sure I can fill in the time before you arrive. Where shall we meet?

Jean: There's a quiet lounge – no mobile phones allowed! Would that be OK with you?

Tom: Perfect.

Jean: It's beside the main exit, in Lobby East. I'll see you in there about 5.30 on the 7th.

Tom: Great. Look forward to seeing you, Jean. Bye.

Jean: Bye, Tom.

2   Make sure you fully understand the advice on reading before you complete the task.

> **Answers** (evidence from the passage is given, but this is not part of the answer)
> | | | |
> |---|---|---|
> | 1 | lighting | *The lighting is at the top of the tunnel, virtually at its highest point (paragraph 2)* |
> | 2 | concrete lining | *The wall is made up of four main elements … on the inside of the tunnel, a concrete lining. (paragraph 2)* |
> | 3 | base slab | *The road surface lies on the base slab (paragraph 3)* |
> | 4 | mains drainage | *Mains drainage, just below the road surface on one side (paragraph 3)* |
> | 5 | fire main | *The fire main is at the side of the tunnel, at the level of the road surface. (paragraph 3)* |

Unit 20

20.1 pages 130–131

Look at the picture. It shows immigrants arriving by ship in New York in the late nineteenth century.

1   Think of possible answers to the questions.

> **Possible answers**
> - to join friends or family; to get a better job; to increase their income; to learn a foreign language; to gain religious or political freedom; to study
> - They work, and the taxes they pay contribute to national income; they provide skills that may be in short supply; they help to make the country more cosmopolitan, e.g. by adding to the variety of food and festivals.
> - People might move because of conflicts in their own country; as countries like India and China become richer, they may attract immigrants from poorer countries.

2

> **Answers**
> 1 b   2 c (one aspect of migration)
> 3 e (another aspect of migration)   4 a   5 d

3   This reading passage, with 13 questions on it, is like one section of the Academic Reading Module, so try to deal with it in 20 minutes, as practice for the test. Remember to skim through the passage first, and to read the rubrics carefully.

> **Answers** (evidence from the passage is given, but this is not part of the answer)
> | | | |
> |---|---|---|
> | 1 | B | *While some theories about migration emphasise individual choice, and others focus on the influence of governments and business, it is more realistic to understand migration in terms of a complex interaction among all these elements. (lines 21–25)* |
> | 2 | F | *People begin to see their life as being based in the new country. This is particularly true of migrants' children: once they go to school in the new country, learn the language and make friends, it becomes more and more difficult for the parents to return to their homelands. (lines 57–62)* |
> | 3 | C | *While some theories about migration emphasise individual choice, and others focus on the influence of governments and business, it is more realistic to understand migration in terms of a complex interaction among all these elements. (lines 21–25)* |
> | 4 | I | *migrants may find it hard to save as much as they require, and stay on in the hope of succeeding eventually. (lines 81–83)* |
> | 5 | E | *Social networks based on family or a common place of origin help to provide housing, work, assistance in coping with bureaucratic procedures and support in personal difficulties. (lines 44–48)* |
> | 6 | D | *Large-scale institutional factors, such as international relations (line 26), For instance, migration from some North and West African countries to France is linked to earlier French colonisation (lines 34–36)* |
> | 7 | B | *It is hardly ever a simple individual action, in which a person decides to move in search of a better life, leaves the home country and quickly becomes assimilated in the new country. (lines 11–15)* |
> | 8 | H | *They want to save enough in a higher-wage economy to improve conditions at home, to buy land, build a house, set up a business, or pay for education. (lines 72–75)* |
>
> (The model referred to in questions 9–13 is described in paragraph J)
> | | | |
> |---|---|---|
> | 9 | earnings | *First, young workers move in order to work abroad temporarily, and send money home. (lines 89–90)* |
> | 10 | friendships | *Secondly, the stay is lengthened, and social networks are developed (lines 91–92)* |
> | 11 | Reunion | *Thirdly, the original migrants' families join them (line 93)* |
> | 12 | belonging | *There is an increasing orientation towards the new country (lines 94–95)* |
> | 13 | residence | *And finally settlement becomes permanent. (line 97)* |

20.2 pages 132–133

1

> **Answers**
> **1** Ottawa   **2** Toronto   **3** English and French
> **4** Pacific (west), Arctic (north), Atlantic (east)   **5** maple

2   Look at the pictures of the two people you are going to hear about, Azim Lila and Tatyana Litvinova.

First, study the notes and the words in the box, then play the first part of the recording and answer questions 1–5 as you listen. Then read questions 6–12, play the second part of the recording and answer the questions as you listen.

> **Answers** (relevant parts of the recording script are underlined)
> **1** coast   **2** education   **3** challenges   **4** jobs
> **5** talents
> **6** chemistry   **7** research   **8** (twin) sister
> **9** (their) homework   **10** speeches   **11** countryside
> **12** kindness

Recording script

Questions 1–5

Presenter 1: Azim Lila spent his childhood in East Africa, in a remote part of Tanzania. <u>He lived at the end of a dirt road by the sea</u>, far from the capital and other big towns, just as his great-grandparents had done. His life was hard, but now he feels that overcoming the difficulties he faced was the most valuable experience in his life and made him stronger.

When he was growing up, <u>his parents</u> gave him love, support and encouragement. Above all, they <u>taught him something very important: you need to learn</u>, if you want to achieve your dreams. When Azim was nine, <u>his family left Tanzania and settled in Canada, which they found demanding. They needed to adjust to life in a new cultural context, and develop their understanding of other people and cultures. They had to find employment and speak a different language.</u> Most importantly, Azim believes, they had to develop a positive attitude.

At the same time, Canada presented unparalleled opportunities, but Azim's family weren't affluent. All the same, <u>he was able to attend York University, thanks to scholarships and part-time work, which meant that he could complete his studies without disruption.</u> He won several awards, and he was also selected to represent Canada in the Far East, as a member of a trade mission to China.

In Azim's opinion, Canada has changed his life. <u>He sees Canada as a country that takes pride in encouraging everyone to discover their skills and capabilities.</u> He describes this as a distinguishing feature of the country, a country that believes in diversity, self-expression and pluralism.

Questions 6–12

Presenter 2: Tatyana Litvinova is Russian, and now lives in Canada, where she's currently an Assistant Professor at the University of Alberta. <u>She studied at one of the top universities in Moscow, and is a graduate in chemistry.</u> She and her husband and their two sons moved to Canada in 1998, mainly because <u>she thought there would be better opportunities to get funding for research.</u> She was appointed to a position in a science laboratory.

Of course, <u>she missed her family, especially her twin sister.</u> They'd never been separated before, and Tatyana found it very difficult not to be able to speak to her every day. At that time it was quite expensive to make international calls.

At first, her greatest problem was her lack of English. Not being able to understand or express herself fully made it difficult for her to register <u>her children</u> in school, and <u>she couldn't give them the support they needed with their homework.</u> All that soon changed, however.

<u>She learned to speak English in quite an unusual way, by joining a Toastmasters' Club and paying close attention to the speeches that people made.</u> She found it a very enjoyable experience.

Tatyana has always felt welcome in Canada, and that's what makes it a very special place for her. While she enjoys living in big cities, <u>she loves the wonderful countryside</u>, and the similarities between Canada and Russia: both are very big countries, and the people living in them come from all over the world.

Tatyana says that she still loves Russia, but she loves Canada too, in a different way. She's never felt she was a second-class citizen. <u>She feels great affection and respect for Canadians, above all for the kindness they've invariably shown her.</u> Whenever she had a problem, there was always someone willing to help her. Because of that, she believes that anyone who truly wants to settle in Canada will find a way.

3   Think about possible answers to the questions.

> **Possible answers**
> Becoming part of the community makes it easier for immigrants to get a wider circle of friends and to be involved in all aspects of life in the country. On the other hand, they may not feel fully part of the community, and if they have to use a foreign language they may find it frustrating.
>
> Feeling part of the country immigrants have come from maintains their emotional links with family, friends, culture and language. On the other hand, it may make them feel homesick if they spend many years in the new country.

4   There are no extra phrasal verbs in the box, so when you do the exercise, try to work out the meanings of any you aren't familiar with.

> **Answers** (definitions in brackets)
> **1** lived up to (was as good as previously expected)
> **2** turned out (was in the end)
> **3** deal with (do something about)
> **4** look forward to (wait for something with pleasure)
> **5** put up with (tolerate)
> **6** hold on to (keep, retain)
> **7** work at (make efforts to do something)

5   There are three positions for adverbs: at the beginning of the sentence (*Recently I went to Canada ...*), with the verb (*I recently went to Canada*) and at the end (*I went to Canada recently*). *Recently* can occur in all three positions. However, some adverbs normally occur with the verb.

Answers
1 c (first example: *were both*)
2 b (second example: *soon found*)
3 a (third example: *had never been*)

6

Answers (Relevant rules 1–3 are given in brackets)
1 Tatyana Litvinova **is currently working** at the University of Alberta. (*rule 3*)
2 Before emigrating to Canada, Tatyana **had never been separated** from her sister. (*rule 3*)
3 Years after moving to Canada, she **still loves** Russia. (*rule 2*)
4 However, she **is still** happy with her life in Canada. (*rule 1*)
5 Some people **have hardly ever left** their home before deciding to emigrate. (*rule 3*)
6 Because of my new job, I **almost changed** my mind about emigrating. (*rule 2*)
7 Since moving inland, I **no longer go** to the beach every day. (*rule 2*)

7

Answers (Relevant rules 1–3 are given in brackets)
1 We **can also see** from the chart that the number of immigrants rose sharply. (*rule 3*)
2 An immigrant who **already has** work experience will find it easier to get a job. (*rule 2*)
3 People who are living in a foreign country **can still find** happiness in their lives. (*rule 3*)
4 *correct*
5 I **particularly like** meeting people. (*rule 2*)
6 Immigrants **will sometimes miss** people and things from their old home. (*rule 3*)
7 It **will still be** very cold next month. (*rule 3*)
8 The number of immigrants to Canada **has also been affected** by economic conditions in other parts of the world. (*rule 3*)

8 If you don't know some of the answers, you might like to do research, for instance on the Internet.

Answers (background information in brackets)
1 **A**: New Zealand   **B**: USA   **C**: Australia ($\frac{1}{2}$ *mark if 2 are correct, no mark if only 1 is correct*)
2 a musical instrument (a long wooden wind instrument played by Australian Aborigines to produce a long deep sound)
3 Canberra (Sydney is sometimes wrongly thought to be the capital, because it is the largest city.)
4 koala (It lives in trees and looks like a small bear with grey fur.)
5 North Island and South Island
6 the kiwi (It is a flightless bird; the people of New Zealand are nicknamed 'kiwis'.)
7 sheep (There are roughly 12 times as many sheep as people. Kangaroos are native to Australia, not New Zealand.)
8 Spanish
9 a type of music (a type of folk music from the southern USA, typically played on banjos and guitars)
10 eight years (Presidents are elected for a four-year term and can be elected for a maximum of two terms.)

Writing folder 10

pages 134–135

Read through the Advice box carefully and check you understand each point.

1

Answers
1 I ~~am~~ agree that people should be allowed to travel to find work.
2 If people have **a lot of / a great deal of** experience I think they can become citizens quite **easily**.
3 Young people **who** are new to a country have to learn many things about it.
4 There are many **places**, for example ~~in~~ factories, ~~in~~ where they can work.
5 In some countries people ~~they~~ can ~~be~~ stay ~~there~~ as long as they want (to).
6 ~~The~~ Families are not as close as they **used to be / once were, due to / because of** widespread emigration.
7 It is known that **problems come / every problem comes** from poor communication.
8 You need **a large amount / a great deal of / a large sum of** money for taxes, for clothes, for food, for everything in a new country.

2

Answers
1 growing   2 children   3 First of all   4 such as
5 and so on   6 educational systems   7 Children
8 receive   9 Secondly   10 enrich   11 Admittedly
12 a considerable amount   13 fees   14 accommodation
15 a great deal   16 In addition   17 suffer from loneliness
18 However,   19 for educational purposes   20 study
21 fluently   22 problem   23 an appropriate
24 Money permitting   25 most suitable   26 At this time
27 independently   28 more effectively

Task 1

Sample answer
The charts show us the changes in both the numbers of immigrants to the United States in the late nineteenth and early twentieth centuries, together with changes in the country of origin of those immigrants.

Apart from a slight fall of approximately half a million in the 1860s, there was a steady rise in the number of people emigrating to the USA from the 1850s to the 1880s. Numbers fell sharply from the 1880s to the 1890s, by almost one and a half million, but then climbed dramatically to a peak of nearly nine million in the period from 1900 to 1910. This was followed by a steady decline in immigrants until the 1930s.

In 1882, the majority of immigrants were European, with large numbers arriving from Germany, Britain and Ireland. However, by 1907, a large proportion of immigrants were from Russia, Italy and Austria-Hungary – about a quarter of the total number of immigrants were from each of those countries. Also, there was a smaller proportion of non-European immigrants in 1907 than in 1882.

(172 words)

Task 2

Sample answer

Although it is true to say that people are crossing borders in search of work, I am not sure that it is true to say that it is at a greater rate than ever before, or that there will come a time when there are no borders.

The decision to emigrate is not an easy one, and people who emigrated in the past did not take that decision lightly. They were driven to emigrate because of persecution or famine or lack of work. People are still having to take that decision and, proportionally, probably in fewer numbers than in the past, when large numbers of people emigrated to the United States.

Today, we have a situation in most of Europe where people are moving from country to country, with few, if any, restrictions, as a consequence of the European Union. The Union is being expanded rapidly, and more and more countries are being invited to join. This has resulted in an exchange of ideas and experience, which can only be a good thing.

However, I am not sure that this will happen worldwide. Many countries guard their borders jealously, and some live in fear of what they see as an invasion of people from another country or culture. I, personally, think that this way of thinking will take many years to overcome and that we will not see the removal of all borders at any time soon. In fact, I think that it is possible that more and more restrictions will be put in place to prevent people moving freely. This may be very pessimistic, but I think it is very difficult to know what will happen in the future.

(280 words)

Units 17–20 Revision

pages 136–137

The aim of this revision unit is to focus on the language covered in Units 17–20.
Exercises 2–7 can be done as a test.

1 Give your own answers.

2

Answers
1 taken over 2 deal with 3 put forward 4 set up
5 take on 6 keep; down

3

Answers
1 forward to 2 up against 3 up to 4 up with
5 up with 6 away with 7 up to 8 up for

4

Answers
1 deal with it 2 *correct* 3 came across it
4 give them out 5 work at it 6 *correct* 7 make it out
8 went down with it

5

Answers
1 monorails are hardly ever involved in accidents
2 I nearly always travel by public transport
3 are rarely able to sleep well during the day
4 The passengers were all asleep
5 It has often been said
6 We can only hope
7 the special offer on tickets is no longer available
8 I almost missed the plane.

6

Answers
1 don't have to 2 must 3 must (*have to* is also
possible, but less likely, as this is described as a rule)
4 must (as for 3) 5 mustn't 6 must / has to
7 doesn't have to 8 have to

7

Answers
(Other verbs might also be possible, but they should all be
in the past simple tense.)
1 had 2 made 3 came / travelled 4 didn't live
5 were 6 went 7 didn't make 8 bought / had

Acknowledgements

The authors would like to thank Alyson Maskell for her painstaking editing, encouragement and unflappable support.

Thanks also go to Annabel Marriott at Cambridge University Press for her constant diligence and support, and to Stephanie White at Kamae for her creative design solutions.

The authors and publishers would like to thank the teachers and consultants who commented on the material:

Australia: Stephen Heap; Brunei: Caroline Brandt; Spain: Chris Turner; Taiwan: Daniel Sansoni; United Arab Emirates: Paul Rawcliffe; UK: Jan Farndale, Roger Scott, Rob Shaw, Clare West

The author and publishers are grateful to the following for permission to reproduce copyright material. It has not always been possible to identify the sources of all the material used or to contact the copyright holders and in such cases the publishers would welcome information **from the copyright owners**. Apologies are expressed for any omissions.

p. 8: *The Times* for the adapted article, 'Where are the locals?' by David Sharnock, 4 December 2003 and p. 86: for the adapted article, 'We're Spoilt for Choice' by Anjana Ahuja, 25 March 2004, © NI Syndication; pp. 12–13: David Crystal for the adapted material from 'The Functions of Language', Cambridge Encyclopaedia of the English Language, September 2003, © Cambridge University Press, reprinted with permission of the publisher and author. p. 14: PageWise for the adapted text from www.essortment.com, 'What is the history of rice?', © 2005 by PageWise, Inc, Used with permission; p.14: Bento.com for the adapted text about the Shin-Yohama Ramen Museum; p. 47: Toby Young for the adapted article 'Sex, greed and humour; that's what we always say', from *The Guardian*, 1 April 2002. There is a copy of the viral at www.tobyyoung.co.uk. © Toby Young; p. 61: National Geographic for the adapted text from ' Warming to cause catastrophic rise in sea level', 26 April 2004, Stefan Lovgren/National Geographic Image Collection; p. 70: 'Television: the Public's View 2000, ITC. Source adapted from Fact File, Carel Press, www.carel.org.uk; p. 76–77: *The Guardian*, for the adapted text 'More than meats the eye' by Laura Spinney, 17 March 2005, p. 90–91: Mind Tools Ltd, for adapted text from 'Six Thinking Hats. Looking at a decision from all points of view' from www.mindtools.com, © Mind Tools Ltd, 1995-2005, All Rights Reserved; p. 91: Roger Bennett for adapted material from 'Personal effectiveness roles'; p. 103: Adapted extract from 'Social Emotions, Communications and Feelings about other people' from *Human Relationships*' by Steve Duck, reproduced by permission of Sage Publications, Thousand Oaks, London and New Delhi, © Steve Duck, 1986; p 112: Luisa Dillner for the adapted article, 'Wide awake club', from *The Observer*, 2 July 2000, © Luisa Dillner; p. 126: Peter E. Davies for adapted text from 'Railway Time', www.carnforth-station.co.uk; p. 132: The Dominion Institute for the images and adapted texts from www.passagestocanada.com; p. 135: Idea Works for the graph showing the number of immigrants to the USA per decade, 1820–1890.

CD ROM

Section 1 Listening: *The Daily Telegraph* for the adapted material, 'Speaking with forked tongue', from *The Daily Telegraph*, 19 April 2003, © Telegraph Group Limited; Section 5 Listening: Cathedral Communications for the adapted extract reproduced from *The Building Conservation Directory*, with kind permission of Cathedral Communications Limited, Wiltshire, England; Section 6 Listening: BBC News for the extracts adapted from http://news.bbc.co.uk/sportacademy: Section 3 Reading: David Attenborough Productions Limited for the adapted text from *Life on Earth*, Fontana, 1981.

The publishers are grateful to the following for permission to include photographs, logos and other illustrative material:

Key: l = left, r = right, c = centre, t = top, b = bottom, u = upper, l = lower

Alamy/© S.T. Yiap p 22 (r); © Brian & Cherry Alexander Photography p 123; © Apple p 92 (l); BUZZ Pictures/©Neale Haynes p 78 (cr, tr), / © Mark Potts p 78 (l); © John Cleare Mountain Camera p 118 (bl); CORBIS/© Araldo de Luca p 37 (tr), /© Mark Cooper p 37 (br), /Chuck Savage p 52 (b), /© Paul A. Souders p 58, /© Bryn Colton/Assignments Photographers p 66 (b), /© Pawel Libera p 69 (b), /© Najlah Feanny p 89 (b), /© Martyn Goddard p 92 (c); CORBIS SYGMA/©PITCHAL FREDERIC p 32 (b); © Deep Sea World www.deepseaworld.co.uk p 20 (b); ©Dynamic Earth www.dynamicearth.co.uk pp 20 (c), 21; EMPICS/PA/TOBY MELVILLE p 69 (t); Getty Images/AFP/PAUL RICHARDS p 41, /AFP/SVEN NACKSTRAND p 32 (t), /AFP/DASSKI p 78 (tc), /Michael Buckner p 42, /China Photos pp 22 (bl), 78 (br), /Marti Coale/BIPs p 46 (l), /Heinz p 92 (r), /The Image Bank/Barry Rosenthal p 28, /The Image Bank/Yann Layma p 34 (tr), /The Image Bank/David Sacks p 57, /The Image Bank/Steve Satushek p 72 (cr), /The Image Bank/Jeff Hunter p 76, /The Image Bank/Kaz Chiba p 90, /The Image Bank/MJ Cardenas Photography p 98 (l), /The Image Bank/Yann Layma p 98 (r), /The Image Bank/Jen Petreshock p 106, /The Image Bank/Ghislain & Marie David de Lossy p 108, /The Image Bank/Steve Dunwell p 111, /The Image Bank/Richard Kolker p 112 (r), /The Image Bank/Sean Justice p 114 (br), /The Image Bank/Jurgen Vogt p 124 (tc), /Bryn Lennon p 82, /Photographer's Choice/ Lisa J Goodman p 77, /Stone/Mark A Leman p 20 (lc), Getty Images/Stone/©Robert Mort p22 (tl), /Stone/Sylvain Grandadam p 34 (bl), /Stone/Nick Daly p 52 (tc), /Stone/Rene Sheret p 66 (t), /Stone/Darren Robb p 105, /Stone/Doug Armand p 118 (tc), /Stone/GDT p 114 (tl), /Stone/Sean Justice p 122, /Stone/Paul Chesley p 124 (tr), /Jenna Bodnar p 124 (b), /Stone/Ryan McVay p 132 (b), /Taxi/B&M Productions p 24, /Taxi/Walter Bibikow p 34 (tl), /Taxi/Vega p 34 (br), /Taxi/Chris Ryan p 40 (t), /Taxi/Tobias Prasse p 40 (b), /Taxi/David Fleetham p 54 (l), /Taxi/David Kjaer p 72 (cl), /Taxi/Dick Luria p 89 (t), /Taxi/Ty Allison p 98 (c), /Taxi/Adastra p 114 (tr); ©Paul Irish/Toronto Star p 132 (t); The Kobal Collection/United Artists p 101; Reproduced with Permission from Motorola, Inc. ©2005, Motorola, Inc. p 10; ©naturalvisions.co.uk p 73; ©NASA p 65; Patronato de Turismo de La Gomera www.gomera-island.com p 8; Photographers Direct/©Karl Lang p 118 (c), /©Ian Butterfield p 126; Rex Features/©Mark Brewer p 20 (t), /©Alistair Linford p 20 (uc), /©Times Newspapers p 25, /©Sipa Press p 26 (r), /©Paul Cooper p 46 (r), /©Patrick Rideaux p 46 (c), /©Guy Cali p 52 (tr), /©20th Century Fox/Everett p 60, /©Alisdair Macdonald p 68, /©Rick Colls p 118 (tl), /©Tess Peni p 118 (tr), /©Per Lindgren p 124 (tl), /©Roger-Viollet p 130; Ronald Sheridan@Ancient Art & Architecture Collection Ltd p 80; Superstock/age fotostock pp 33, 37 (l), 54 (c), 72 (l), 97, 114 (bl), 118 (br), /Mauritius pp 52 (tl), 72 (r), /StockImage p 53; Topfoto/©Don Boroughs/The Image Works p 38, /©Ellen Senisi/The Image Works p 54 (r).

The following pictures were taken for Cambridge University Press on Commission:

Gareth Boden pp 26 (1), 86, 116. The publishers would like to thank Mayhem Designs UK (Sidney Street, Cambridge) for the use of their premises for the photo on p 86.

Freelance picture research by Hilary Fletcher

The publishers are grateful to the following illustrators:

Kathy Baxendale: pp. 19, 63 (b); Mark Draisey: pp. 13, 15, 16, 27, 55, 63 (t), 74, 80, 93, 94, 95, 112, 127, 136; Kamae Design: pp. 14, 17, 18, 61, 104, 125, 128, 129, 133; Mark McLaughlin: pp. 49, 84, 121; Valeryia Steadman: pp. 8, 88, 100

The publishers are grateful to the following contributors:

Alyson Maskell: editorial work
Hilary Fletcher: photographic direction, picture research
James Richardson: audio recordings